M

SHORT TERM
LOAN

FI

PROMISED THE
MOON

PROMISED THE
MOON

THE UNTOLD STORY OF THE FIRST WOMEN IN THE SPACE RACE

STEPHANIE NOLEN

FOUR WALLS EIGHT WINDOWS
NEW YORK/LONDON

Library of Congress Cataloging-in-Publication Data:

Nolen, Stephanie.
    Promised the moon : the untold story of the first women in the space race / by Stephanie Nolen.
        p. cm.
    Includes bibliographical references and index.
    ISBN 1-56858-275-7 (hc.)
        1. Women astronauts--United States--Biography. 2. Women in astronautics--Political
aspects. 3. Feminism. 4. United States. National Aeronautics and Space
Administration--History. 5. Space race. 6. Sex discrimination against women. I. Title.

TL789.85.A1N65 2003
629.45'0082'0973--dc21   2003052770

Printed in Canada

10 9 8 7 6 5 4 3 2 1

For my grandmother,
Helen G. Amy Webb,
with love

We're very grateful, because now we have a future.
—The Fellow Lady Astronaut Trainees to
Lt. Col. Eileen Collins, shortly before
she became the first woman to pilot
the space shuttle on February 3, 1995

I'm very grateful, because now I have a past.
—Lt. Col. Collins to the FLATs

CONTENTS

INTRODUCTION

*Jerri Sloan in her pink flying suit with her pink
plane, as the Most Active Woman in America, 1964.*

This is the story I heard.

Jerrie Cobb was in the heart of the Amazon jungle. It was
a summer night and the air was thick and dense and hot. She
lay in a rough woven hammock strung between a wingtip and
a door of her twin-engine Islander. She looked up and tried,
as she had a thousand times before, to count the stars. Then
there was a crackle on the radio. She scrambled into the

cockpit and fiddled with the tiny dials, trying to bring in the voice. It was a priest at a missionary station a couple of hundred miles away, calling with news he thought Jerrie would want to hear. It was July 20, 1969. A few hours earlier, two American men, Neil Armstrong and Buzz Aldrin, had walked on the moon.

Jerrie leaned out of the cockpit and pulled herself up onto the wing. Arms in the air, she did a little dance of joy, from the tip of one wing to the end of the other.

"Vaya con Dios," she whispered, looking at the night sky.

And then she looked down at the ground around her, and she spoke again.

"It should have been me."

That story made me shiver. Jerrie Cobb was a pilot, a world-record-setting pilot, when she was recruited to take the astronaut tests at the dawn of the space race. The United States was losing to the Soviets, who were clearly much closer to the goal of putting a person in space. The Americans had smaller rockets than the Russians, and they couldn't launch a man. Then engineers at the National Aeronautics and Space Administration began to think women—smaller, lighter women—might be the answer to their problems. They tested Jerrie, and she excelled. So they recruited more female pilots, and found a dozen who were prime astronaut material. Those women were all set for space when NASA abandoned them. Dumped them, sent them home, and they never knew why.

It was a gripping story. But as I would come to learn, it wasn't quite a true story.

I first heard it from an author I interviewed in my work as a reporter for the *Globe and Mail.* She mentioned, in passing, "those first female astronauts in the early sixties." I was startled. Female astronauts before Sally Ride? I know women's stories frequently don't make the history books, but how could I possibly have missed the first female astronauts?

I looked for a book. There wasn't one. I looked for magazine articles, newspaper interviews. The files were painfully slim. If America once had secret female astronauts, they were still unknown.

But I couldn't get their story out of my head. Over and over I heard Jerrie Cobb's voice. *It should have been me.*

So I went hunting. I tracked down Jerrie, and she agreed to tell me her story—but Jerrie, as I would come to learn, still keeps secrets of her own. One by one I found the other women. Feeling a little awkward, and very young, I told them I was a Canadian newspaper reporter curious about an event that happened almost half a century before. I wanted to hear their story—and I wanted to tell it.

What unfolded in the months that followed was not one story, but many. There were more versions of the events than there were would-be astronauts. And by the time I had knit the various threads together I realized that even the women themselves did not know what really happened in 1961. In the end, they learned that from me.

The story I first heard wasn't quite true, but the real events are every bit as dramatic: a bitter clash of personalities between powerful women; masterful public performances by American heroes with an agenda of their own; a hush-hush experiment by a pioneering scientist who trammeled social conventions to satisfy a curious mind; and a vicious emotional outburst at the highest level of government.

In telling this story, it is important to summon the shape of American society in the 1960s—a landscape so different from the one in which we now live that is hard to believe it existed only forty years ago. Talking to the Fellow Lady Astronaut Trainees (as they once were known), I was continuously amazed. For someone who grew up in the era when a space shuttle launch barely made the evening news, the women's stories of the early space race were intoxicating. They described the way they watched each rocket launch, holding their breath and willing it to fly, willing their country to pull this off. To survive: because that's what the space race was about then, the very survival of the country. I came to see that their story was a fascinating example of the subtle interplay between technological achievement and political propaganda.

It was only forty years ago, and yet the world these women described was almost impossible for a woman my age to imagine. Needing your husband's signature to buy a car. (Needing a husband.) Having the boss chase you round the desk each afternoon. Being turned down, job after job, because it wouldn't "look right to have a girl" in the manager's office or at the front desk. And no discrimination laws to turn to.

When we look back at the pictures of women in the fifties and sixties, it all looks a bit quaint—the beehive hairdos and the sweater sets. And it is tempting to see the story of these "first women astronauts" as a curious historical footnote: as *The Right Stuff* very nearly cast with female players. But above all else, the story of these extraordinary women, who ignored traditional roles, defied convention and broke through barriers, is a tale of the painful, destructive experience of being caught on the cusp of social change.

These women were able to see the future but could not, despite their ambition, their passion and their talent, make it present.

Jerrie Cobb is still in the jungle. I don't know if it should have been she who stepped out on the moon that July night—but I now know she never got the chance to prove it.

Stephanie Nolen
Toronto, June 2002

UNLIMITED VISIBILITY

*Jerrie Cobb prepares to pilot
a TF-102 "Delta Dagger" in 1959.*

There were no clouds. Just empty sky, still brushed pink by the sunrise. She scanned the horizon absently, the way a pilot always checks the sky: no ceiling. Unlimited visibility. She had plenty of flying to do today. It would be fine.

It was early September 1959, and Geraldyn—Jerrie—Cobb was walking on the beach in Miami. She would have liked to have this quiet hour to herself, to walk just above the water's edge and have the waves lick her bare feet. She was happiest by herself. But she had company that morning—the beach stroll was the suggestion of her boss, Tom Harris. They were attending the annual convention of the Air Force Association, and they had plans to make.

At twenty-eight, Jerrie was a pilot and manager for Aero Design and Engineering Company in Oklahoma City, one of the largest aircraft manufacturers in the United States. That made her one of just two or three women in the country with a senior job at an aeronautic company—a distinction of which she was acutely aware at gatherings such as this. There weren't many women around, and those there were tended to be wives brought along for the trip, or secretaries, or sales assistants, at best. There would be some raised eyebrows when Jerrie pulled herself up into the cockpit of her twin-engine Aero Commander later. But she had long since stopped noticing those.

By that September morning, Jerrie had logged more than seven thousand hours in the air. She had set three world records—for altitude, distance and speed—in the Commander. Just that summer, she was awarded the Gold Wings of Achievement of the Fédération Aéronautique Internationale in Paris, one of aviation's highest honors.

Flying at conventions like this was a regular part of her job, attracting publicity for the company and showing off the Commander to potential buyers—she would fly with one engine deliberately cut out, then come in low, just fifty feet above the ground. And make it all look easy, so easy a girl with a ponytail could do it.

Her boss, Tom Harris, had plenty of admiration for Jerrie's flying. But he also liked the way the record holder with the freckles and the spectator pumps sold his airplanes. He told her the plan for the day: where she would be flying, who was interested in the plane and what the customers wanted to see.

Just as they turned back toward their hotel, they passed two men emerging from the surf, flushed from an early morning swim. Harris knew the pair, and he introduced Jerrie to them: Donald Flickinger and Randy Lovelace.

Every pilot in the country in 1959 probably knew those names—these were two of the most important men in aerospace medicine. Jerrie certainly knew them. She knew Lovelace ran a research clinic in New Mexico and held a top post at NASA: he had helped select the Mercury 7, the United States' first astronauts. And she knew Flickinger was an air force brigadier general, a pioneer in aviation medicine who had led the tests that told the National Aeronautics and Space Administration that a human might survive spaceflight.

The two men didn't know Jerrie Cobb.

But Jerrie and Tom joined them as they strolled along the shore. Lovelace and Flickinger had just flown in from Moscow where they had attended a conference of space scientists. They told Harris how it had buzzed with rumors that the Soviets were trying to put a man into space. They were musing about developments in Soviet aeronautics when Jerrie quietly commented on the problems that a particular plane caused Russian pilots. Lovelace and Flickinger turned to look at her in surprise.

"Are you a pilot?" Lovelace asked.

At that moment, Jerrie says, "I met destiny in one tiny question."

Oh yes, she told them. "I've been flying for sixteen years."

Flickinger was startled. "Sixteen years! You don't look old enough to have a license."

Jerrie began to blush and stuttered about how she'd started flying at twelve.

Harris jumped in to brag a little, telling them about the records Jerrie had set for Aero, and her Gold Wings. "She's got more than seven thousand hours in her logbook," he told them.

Flickinger said he was always interested in what women were doing in aviation and mentioned that the air force had just designed a pressure suit for the French aviatrix Jacqueline Auriol to use for her jet record attempts.

"You better make one of those pressure suits for Jerrie," Harris replied with a laugh. "She's liable to try for a record in space next!"

But Lovelace didn't laugh.

"As a matter of fact," he said, suddenly quite serious, "we had indications at the Moscow meeting that the Russians are planning to put women on spaceflights."

There was, Jerrie recalls, a pause in the conversation. "The two scientists were obviously mulling something over." They asked Jerrie if she could meet with them again later in the day.

And so that afternoon, Jerrie joined Flickinger and Lovelace in an ornate room off the lobby of the Fontainebleau Hotel. Lovelace asked her about the other female commercial pilots in the United States: could she estimate their average age? What kind of physical shape were they in?

Then he explained why he was asking: "Medical and psychological investigations have long shown that women are better than men at withstanding pain, heat, cold, loneliness and monotony," he began, and all those were sure to be factors in spaceflight. But there was no research on how women held up in space stress tests. Jerrie was startled to hear it. The space race was consuming America, and the nation knew all about the elaborate tests used to select the Mercury 7 and to see how they might fare in the challenges of this new environment. But nobody had looked at women?

Lovelace told her the last testing of female pilots was done on the Women Airforce Service Pilots in World War II, a corps of eleven hundred female ferry pilots. Research on their flying hours showed they were better able to tolerate isolation and extremes of temperature than male pilots. But there had been no further study in the past fifteen years. Flickinger and Lovelace had decided it was high time someone got back to the question. The general envisioned a "girl astronaut" program for the Air Research and Development Command, the experimental wing of the air force trying to get America into space. Lovelace, who was Flickinger's mentor in the emerging field of bioastronautics, had been pushing a program for women. And so they had a question for Jerrie: "Would you be willing to be a test subject for the first research on women as astronauts?"

It was a fateful invitation.

Donald Flickinger was a risk taker (best known for parachuting into cannibal-populated islands in the South Pacific to treat victims of plane crashes) consumed by the desire to put an American in space. Randy Lovelace was a pioneering research scientist, a man who loved a puzzle. When they asked Jerrie to volunteer, they had big plans.

They made their offer to a woman who had been flying since she was twelve, flying at the cost of all else, flying faster and higher, pushing planes so far up into the darkening blue that her hands froze to the controls. Would she volunteer for astronaut testing? Oh, yes.

On October 4, 1957, the United States heard the crack of the starter's gun in the race for space. "Soviets Fire Earth Satellite Into Space . . . Sphere Tracked in 4 Crossings Over U.S.," said a banner headline on the front page of the normally circumspect *New York Times.*

The story seemed too fantastic to be true, like something out of one of those creepy science fiction movies playing at the drive-in. A Soviet rocket had taken a little machine and put it into orbit around the earth. The newspapers called it a "Red Moon." It was up there, impossibly high—so high it was *in space*—but you could see it going overhead. In the late evening or early morning, when the sun was near enough to the horizon to reflect off its polished surface, you could see Sputnik making its steady, unfathomably fast trek across the sky.

The Soviets had been promising they would launch an earth satellite for some time. In fact, they had even invited U.S.

scientists to include measurement equipment on the craft. But the Americans dismissed their talk as empty bragging. Everyone knew the Russians were backward peasants who could not match American technical innovation. The U.S. science establishment was so sure that it would be first with a human-made object in space that the Americans did not even have the equipment to monitor Sputnik, and could not pick up its radio signal until the third ninety-six-minute orbit.

In 1946 military engineers had told U.S. president Harry Truman that the first rockets could possibly be modified to carry a small payload—basic communications equipment, for example—into orbit, but he saw no value in the plan. His successor, Dwight Eisenhower, understood that an earth satellite would give a country access to the airspace of its enemies, but he proved as deaf to the political value of the satellite as Truman was to its strategic value.

Eisenhower approved a plan to launch a satellite sometime in the International Geophysical Year, an innovative international collaboration to study the upper atmosphere that began on July 1, 1957. Eisenhower was told that Russians were also working on a satellite, but he wasn't bothered by the idea that the Soviet Union might be first—that, the president felt, would establish an international "open skies" policy, allowing monitoring of enemy countries from the reaches of space. If the United States did it first, on the other hand, the Soviets could make angry charges about American spying; Eisenhower pictured the Russians getting a twisted public relations advantage from an American satellite.

The man behind the Soviet space program, however, saw the U.S. plans for the IGY as a challenge. Sergei Korolev, the rocket scientist whom the Soviets identified only as the Chief Designer, was determined to launch a satellite before the confident Americans.

The idea of the race was not new: it had been building since the end of World War II. But until Sputnik, the contest had centered on weapons. In 1945, the United States was supplying the ill-equipped Russians with technology and hardware in their joint war with Germany. Just four years later, the two nations were in a competition of their own over arsenals. By the early 1950s, both countries had ten-megaton thermonuclear weapons—bombs so big that planes could not carry them. Now the race moved to ballistic missiles: bombs carried farther and faster by rockets.

At the turn of the twentieth century, a Russian school teacher named Konstantin Tsiliovsky had devised an equation to launch a rocket past the pull of earth's gravity, and he suggested the liquid fuel mix of liquid oxygen and hydrogen that is the basis for modern rocketry. But it was an American physicist named Robert Goddard who was the first to make it work. In 1926, he fired a small rocket 184 feet into the air—this first shot in the American bid for space landed ignominiously in a cabbage patch.

While Goddard was making his homemade rockets, a German engineer had arrived at the same technological breakthrough. Wernher von Braun was a brilliant and charismatic aristocrat. As a teenager, he became convinced that liquid-fueled rockets could be made big enough to carry people into space, and he developed a crude rocket. His talents were soon enlisted by the military because the Treaty of Versailles, which strictly curbed German military expansion, did not ban rockets. The Nazi general Walter Dornberger set up von Braun in a rocket research center on the Baltic peninsula of Peenemünde, and by October 1943 he had produced a guideable rocket. Hitler ordered mass production of this new weapon, the V2, by concentration camp labor. The V2 could carry more than a ton of explosives 150 miles in less than five minutes, and the Nazis' "vengeance rocket" wreaked havoc on Britain and Western Europe in the last years of the war, killing seven thousand people. That legacy of destruction was to shape the American space program.

In January 1945, von Braun realized Germany was losing the war and decided to take his pioneering technology to the

Americans. Most of his team and much of their huge trove of engineering documents were brought to the United States in a secret project called Operation Paperclip. The German engineers were installed on a base in Fort Bliss, Texas. Their first assignments were mostly low priority, such as upper-atmosphere probes. But in 1949, after the Soviets exploded a nuclear bomb, the Germans in Texas were given orders to upgrade the V2 into a tactical nuclear missile for the army. The next year, the Americans brought them to a newly established army base in Huntsville, Alabama, and put the Germans to work on what would become the Redstone rocket. But it was some time before von Braun got to show what he thought rockets should be doing.

When it became obvious in the mid-1950s that the launch of a satellite could be part of the International Geophysical Year, Eisenhower gave responsibility for the project to the Pentagon. The military chiefs in turn chose the navy, which proposed to upgrade its small Viking research rocket. Wernher von Braun had heard the Soviets talk about the satellites, and he ground his teeth in frustration: he knew his rocket was capable of launching a small satellite, that with his rocket America could be first, yet the grapevine told him the navy was months or years away from being able to do it. Von Braun, famous in the United States for writing about the imminent settlement of Mars, began to develop Project Orbiter, a plan to launch a satellite on his rocket.

But von Braun's rocket was military, a direct descendant of the V2 that had terrorized Britain, and Eisenhower was determined to keep the optics peaceful. In truth, the president had put a high priority on space spying, and the Defense Department was secretly at work on satellites that would give the U.S. military a way to look behind the iron curtain. But the Viking rocket had no military history, and the navy project would look, as much as possible, like a civilian research effort. Von Braun was told to keep working on missiles, but Orbiter was scrapped. Nonetheless, von Braun and his team quietly continued work on the follow-up to the Redstone, a four-stage rocket called Jupiter C, which he was sure could launch a satellite.

Then came Sputnik—properly called *Iskustvennyi Sputnik Zemlyi*, Russian for "traveling companion of the world." It is difficult today to understand the fear Sputnik created in 1957. Through the lens of history, the satellite looks like a shiny steel beach ball. All it could do was take temperature readings and emit a regular, monotone radio signal, which reached earth as a chirp somewhere between newly hatched chick and alarm clock. The technology of the first satellite was less sophisticated than that found in a typical blender today. But Americans were stunned, humiliated and, most of all, frightened. If the Communists could send something racing over the backyard, then surely it was a matter of weeks until they were, in Senator Lyndon Johnson's phrase, "dropping bombs on us like kids dropping rocks onto cars from freeway overpasses." The Senate majority leader, already an unannounced candidate for the 1960 presidential race, proclaimed Sputnik a national emergency that required a full mobilization of U.S. resources. Opinion polls showed most people thought Sputnik was a serious blow to American prestige, that the country was lagging behind the Soviets—not just in missiles, but also in education and overall development of science and technology. Editorials savaged America as fat, lazy and complacent, a nation more interested in suburban patios and tail fins on cars than in the discipline and hard work required of a world leader.

And here Eisenhower totally misread the public. Presidential historians say he sincerely believed the political and psychological impact of Sputnik would be limited. Two days after the launch, the president said he didn't know what all the fuss was about: "The Russians have only put one small ball in the air . . . that does not raise my apprehensions one iota." He refused to concede that there was a race with the Soviets, saying the United States would proceed in space at its own pace. In his memoirs,

Eisenhower said he thought Sputnik had kicked off a public relations war, not a space race, and he was seeking to "relieve the
current wave of near hysteria." The historians give the position
some credit: had he acknowledged that the Soviets had just
clearly shown they had long-range missile technology,
Eisenhower might well have driven the level of national anxiety
even higher. But the president did not understand how important the contest in space would be in the next few years.

The American humiliation didn't stop. A month later the
Soviets launched Sputnik II, and this satellite carried a female
dog, Laika, who lived for six days in orbit, the first living creature in space. Two more satellites followed in quick succession.
The nuclear threat was at its height by then: most communities
had a fallout shelter, and plenty of people had built their own in
the backyard. Children had practice drills in school for nuclear
war, climbing beneath their desks with their heads covered.
Clearly the Soviets had access to American air space, and now the
threat of destruction seemed that much closer.

Sputnik brought Wernher von Braun in from the cold. He
read the news of the Soviet launch and fumed, knowing—and
telling anyone in Washington who would listen—that he could
have beaten them. The Pentagon authorized him to resume work
on his satellite project. Meanwhile, the navy tried its Vanguard
launch on December 6, 1957. Unlike the Soviet launch, which
had been shrouded in secrecy, Americans could watch this one
on their little black-and-white television screens. For the first
time, the country heard an announcer in Cocoa Beach, Florida,
count down "ten . . . nine . . . eight . . ." and at zero there was a
mighty burst of flame. The rocket rose into the air for a moment,
stopped, wobbled, fell sideways, then exploded. The tiny satellite
at its tip was thrown off, rolled into the grass and lay there,
chirping obediently.

The Soviets had plenty of failures too, but they were veiled by
the iron curtain, and American scientists would not learn about

them until decades later. As it was, the Soviets seemed to succeed effortlessly in every launch they attempted. American failure, though, was terribly public. It fell to the former Nazi rocket engineer to salvage American pride. The United States finally launched a satellite on January 31, 1958: *Explorer I,* a thirty-one-pound bullet-shaped satellite carrying a Geiger counter to detect radiation belts in space. The satellite was carried into orbit on von Braun's Jupiter C rocket. It was something—the Soviets had been answered—but it did little to quiet the sense of American unease.

An attempted Vanguard launch went wrong in early February, when the rocket's control system failed halfway to orbit. A Jupiter C launched a month later fell back to earth when its fourth-stage rockets failed to ignite. Finally, the navy got Vanguard to work, and a three-pound satellite was launched March 17. Von Braun got *Explorer III* into orbit on March 26. Then in April another Vanguard malfunctioned before it hit orbit. And just to rub it in, the Soviet's Sputnik III reached orbit on May 15 and began to return a wealth of data from its instruments. Two weeks later, another Vanguard went awry at third stage and dumped its satellite in the Atlantic Ocean. On June 26, a Vanguard lost power at second stage and crashed into the sea. While the Soviets racked up what appeared to be an effortless string of space successes, the American disasters were front page news. "How do kids in Cocoa Beach learn to count?" ran a popular if slightly bitter joke. "Four! Three! Two! Damn!"

Then came reports the Soviets intended to launch a man. Eisenhower, battered in the press, asked for proposals on a human space flight to match the Soviets. And he got a half dozen: the army suggested, for example, Project Man In Space Soonest (MISS), a plan that would replace the nuclear warhead on a missile with a man in a little capsule. The air force favored the X-20, a plane to be launched on a rocket and shot through gravity. (It would fly too fast to bring it in to land, so the pilot would have to eject at about ten thousand feet and let the million-dollar aircraft smash into the desert.) The flurry of proposals was enough to convince Eisenhower that America needed a centralized space program. That led to a new problem: who would run it? The Department of Defense was the front-runner, but the Atomic Energy Commission, working with nuclear warheads and propulsion, had supporters in Congress, and so did the National Advisory Committee for Aeronautics (NACA), the world's most advanced aeronautical research organization. There was a split, in fact: players such as the National Sciences Academy (which also had backers in the Senate) said space exploration was about scientific advancement and national prestige. The armed forces, however, thought it was perfectly clear that space was about missile delivery, access to air space and defense.

Finally, someone (often said to be Vice President Richard Nixon) suggested a political solution: create a new civilian agency with responsibility for science missions and any other peaceful aspect of spaceflight, and let the military do its own defense-related research. The compromise had political support. So Eisenhower gave the job to NACA—an organization with close ties to the military but a history of peaceful civilian application of technology. The agency was founded in 1915 to provide federal supervision for aviation research in the United States, which was then lagging behind progress in other countries. During World War I, NACA quadrupled in size and forged close ties with the military. After the war it continued its key role in research as the focus shifted to jet and then supersonic flight. By the mid-1950s, the agency had state-of-the-art research facilities, and as the space race heated up, NACA was drawn into the military rocketry projects.

In July 1958, Eisenhower signed into law the National Aeronautics and Space Act, turning NACA into the space administration. The new space agency was given a $100 million budget; three research centers; sections of Edwards Air Force Base in California designated for high-speed atmospheric flight; a rocket-sounding facility in Virginia; eight thousand employees, and instant responsibility for a host of space-related projects (including Vanguard and *Explorer*). Keith Glennan, former commissioner of the Atomic Energy Commission, was named chairman, and NACA's director Hugh Dryden was his deputy.

NACA had a rocket division, under the direction of a brilliant engineer called Robert Gilruth. He had been with the agency since 1937 and had quickly risen through the NACA ranks, doing innovative research first in flight-testing, and later in rocketry. In the spring of 1958, while Congress was still debating the form of this new civilian space agency, Dryden asked Gilruth to put together a plan. He gathered his best designers, and by April they were drafting the blueprint for a blunt-ended capsule that could carry one man and be launched on the top of an air force Atlas rocket.

The National Aeronautics and Space Administration officially came into being in October 1958. And a week later, Glennan created the Space Task Group. He and Gilruth decided that their first project would be called Mercury, after the winged messenger of the Greek gods. They already had the plans for a capsule to hold a man. Now they needed men to fly it.

AVIATRIX

*Record-setting pilot Ruth Rowland Nichols
in the early 1920s.*

In 1959, pilots were broad-shouldered, square-jawed, keen-eyed types: in a word, men. Jerrie Cobb, with bare feet, a blond pony-tail and freckles across her nose, didn't look like a pilot when the doctor and the general met her on the beach. She certainly didn't look like a record-breaking pilot with the Fédération Aeronautique Internationale's Gold Wings. She was used to the shock—"*You're* the pilot?" She could count on two hands the number of women in the United States, who, like her, made a living from flying, and they were all used to that question.

From the time Thérèse Peltier first lifted off a runway in France in 1908, women who wanted to fly had to fight to do it. Flying was dangerous, noisy, dirty—it wasn't *ladylike*. It required great personal courage and a knowledge of engines: men's work, clearly. Peltier, a French sculptor, was among the huge crowds that turned out when the Wright brothers showed off the first fragile airplanes in Europe. Plenty of women wanted to watch the incredible invention, and a few wanted to fly it. Peltier took a five-hundred-foot flight as a passenger in Turin, Italy, in July 1908, and a few weeks later, flew solo in a Voisin biplane. She was the first in a long line of independent women who would fall in love with the freedom of flying. An Englishwoman named Gertrude Bacon flew in Paris a year later and wrote of her flight, "The ground was very rough and hard, and as we tore along at an increasing pace that was greater than any motor I had yet been in, I expected to be jerked and jolted. But the motion was wonderfully smooth—smoother yet—and then! Suddenly there had come into it a new, indescribable quality—a lift—a lightness—a life!"

Europe embraced it first, but the Wrights' invention soon caught on at home. The first American woman in the air was Blanche Scott, the tomboy daughter of a wealthy society couple in Rochester, New York. Enamored of airplanes from the moment she heard about them, she went to the flying school in Long Island set up by aviation pioneer Glenn Curtiss. He allowed her to drive planes back and forth but did not believe that women should fly. He had blocked off the throttle so that Scott could only rattle along the grass runway. One day in September 1910, she spotted the wood block on the throttle, removed it and took a brief journey off the ground. Curtiss was furious, sure she would smash up his plane. (And if a woman were to die, it would be disastrous for his new business.) But

Scott landed beautifully, and she was hooked. She persuaded Curtiss of her ability, joined his famed aerial performance troupe and toured the country. "I was the first skirt to fly a plane—and that happened when there were only seventy-five men pilots in the United States," she recalled sixty years later.

In 1911, a thirty-five-year-old Michigan journalist named Harriet Quimby attended her first air show and decided that she must learn how to fly one of the fragile biplanes that swooped above the spectators. The Wright brothers' flying school wouldn't admit women, but Harriet had a friend with a brother who could fly, and he taught her. Harriet earned her license from the FAI (then aviation's governing body), the thirty-seventh ever issued, and the first to an American woman, and weeks later flew in an air meet where she made the first ever night flight by a woman. She joined a troupe of performing pilots, did loops and rolls above Mexico City to mark the inauguration of a president and was a fixture in magazine photographs in the elegant satin flying suits, with split skirts, that she designed herself. The newspapers called her the "Dresden China Aviatrix," but Harriet was serious: she wrote about the future of aviation, predicting multipassenger aircraft with scheduled routes, mail carried by planes around the world and aerial photography for mapping. Then she conceived a bold plan: she would be the first woman to fly the English Channel, which no one had yet done. A year later Harriet did it, in a fifty-nine-minute flight through dense fog, and returned to the United States a national hero. She was performing with a male pilot three months later, in a two-seater monoplane above Boston, when the plane rolled and they were tossed to their deaths in the harbor. Their plane glided to a landing with little damage.

The women who flew in the next decade were, like Harriet, determined, independent—and aberrations. Katherine Stinson was a pianist from Alabama who took up aviation in 1912 to pay for music lessons and then never returned to her piano. The fourth woman to earn her license, at the age of twenty-one, she began exhibition flights a year later. Crowds flocked to see her fly—just to see a woman take up an airplane—but Stinson was determined to impress; she did increasingly difficult stunts, was the first woman to skywrite, and then to skywrite at night with flares tied on the ends of her wings. She was the first woman to deliver airmail, in 1913; she flew exhibitions in Japan and China (where the president declared her the Granddaughter of Heaven) and was the first woman to fly in Asia. In 1912, her sister Marjorie, then sixteen, became the youngest U.S. woman to earn a license. When the United States entered World War I, Marjorie and Katherine tried to enlist as military pilots, but the air corps would not have them. Instead the sisters opened a flying school and taught dozens of army fliers, including much of the Canadian Aviation Corps.

The Stinson sisters were remarkable, but Bessie Coleman was extraordinary. One of thirteen children born to a Cherokee father and an African-American mother, she was working as a manicurist in Chicago at age fifteen when she decided she wanted to fly. Few flying schools would teach a woman, but none would teach a black woman. So Bessie taught herself French, moved to France, and earned her pilot's license in 1921, making her the only licensed black pilot in the world. "I decided blacks should not have to experience the difficulties I had faced so I decided to open a flying school and teach other black women to fly," she told a reporter a few years later. "I needed money for this so I began giving flying exhibitions and lecturing on aviation. The color of my skin, at first a drawback, now drew large crowds wherever I went. At first I was a curiosity, but soon the public discovered I could really fly. Then they came to see 'Brave Bessie,' as they called me."

She was killed when her plane locked into a dive at an exhibition in 1926. These were profoundly dangerous years to be flying. The planes were rickety and unstable, their engines were erratic, and pilots would not wear parachutes regularly for another ten years. Yet at the same time, audiences wanted stunts that were more and more daring.

The price of airplanes dropped sharply after the World War I, with surplus planes sold off even as factories with war capacity built new ones. But there were few jobs in aviation—and a glut of ex-war pilots. Unless they were extremely well off, women (and most men) had only one route into the field: barnstorming. They would fly around the country performing stunts and offering rides (the name comes from the habit of the early exhibition pilots who would fly into rural towns, buzz the barns and set down in plowed fields). This was a decidedly nontraditional activity, but audiences would pay to see women do stunts, and a few women were willing to sacrifice reputation for adventure. Women began as wing walkers and parachute jumpers: Lillian Boyer would change planes in midair, and Gladys Roy danced the Charleston on the wing of her plane. It was a way to raise money for a real aviation business, such as flying deliveries or taking passengers on thrill rides.

And it was a way to fly. There was still something magical about flying then—the thrill of being in the air and doing something a little miraculous. The planes in which these women first flew had no altimeter, no fuel gauge, no starter. Just a stick and rudder pedals and, if the pilots were lucky, a compass. They used a dangling key chain to tell them if they were flying level, and they came in low enough to read the signs on the train stations to tell where they were. This flying was an entirely different undertaking from the big commercial flights of today. In a small single-engine plane, there is only the thinnest of skins between the pilot and the sky. It is a feeling of being small and powerless, and simultaneously of immense control. Modern jumbo jet passengers are lulled into detachment—but a pilot in a little Taylorcraft or a Staggerwing is intensely aware of how much space there is between her and the ground, of how quickly she is moving and how removed she is from the confines of rooms and walls and roads.

Flying was liberating for everybody, but for women it offered something extra: certainly social norms had loosened in the 1920s, but women were still valued for looks and domestic skills and still steered toward passive accomplishments. But in the air, at the controls of their own planes, they had freedom and total independence. And with huge crowds gathered to watch below, female pilots had respect. The aviatrix became something of an icon: competent, serious, a little rebellious, very much a woman of the Roaring Twenties. At the same time, however, the feeling endured that flying was no activity for a lady: it was noisy and dirty. Female pilots had to know about wires and spark plugs. They wore jodhpurs and boots and, as often as not, bandages and casts.

At the start of the 1920s, aviation became less of a fad and more of an emblem of progress; its backers advanced the still questionable idea that air transport, of goods and people, would one day play a crucial economic role. Now the focus shifted to setting records: for speed and altitude, distance and endurance. Aircraft manufacturers would give women the planes in which to try for new records, knowing the publicity of a woman lasting fifteen hours in a plane, or flying Boston to Los Angeles, would be even greater than that for a man who achieved the same stunt. And it all served the purpose of convincing the public about the safety of planes.

The competition for records held more than just a challenge for women: it was a way to prove they could fly as well or better than men. Elinor Smith, "the Flying Flapper of Freeport," set a world altitude record of 11,663 feet in 1929. For her next stunt she flew under the four East River bridges in New York, for which the authorities ordered her grounded for fifteen days. All through that spring, Elinor and two pilots named Louise Thaden and Bobbi Trout competed for endurance records, lasting eight, then fourteen, then seventeen, then twenty-two hours aloft alone at the controls of their planes. They landed sore, dirty, faces worn raw by the wind—and jubilant. One would accept the flowers and the trophies, and then, two weeks later, another of the bobbed-hair women who had become household names would snatch the record away.

Records were being broken every week when a tall, serious young woman named Amelia Earhart went to a California air meet with her father. Born in 1897 in Atchison, Kansas, the young Amelia was unlike any other little girl in her neighborhood: she played football and hunted rats and rode her toboggan off the roof. Her father was a railroad attorney—but he was also an alcoholic, and there was considerable grief behind the closed doors of an outwardly prosperous family. In 1920, Amelia took her first ride in a plane at a fair—ten minutes in a helmet and goggles—and when she landed told her parents she had to learn to fly herself, "knowing full well I'd die if I didn't." She found a teacher, an equally boyish and determined young aviatrix named Netta Snook, and did odd jobs to pay for the classes. Amelia soloed in 1920, and earned her license two years later. Her mother, Amy, and sister Muriel helped her buy her first plane, a Kinner Airster that she named *The Canary.* By October 1922, she had joined the record-breaking craze, and set her first, a women's altitude record of fourteen thousand feet. (It was broken a few weeks later by another flapper pilot, Ruth Nichols.) The attention amused Amelia, but she also wanted a career, and aviation didn't seem serious. She moved back East, to Boston, and began a job as a social worker. She kept flying on weekends, and she was the subject of considerable media attention: female pilots were still rare.

In 1927, Charles Lindbergh made an astounding solo flight across the Atlantic and became the world's biggest celebrity. Immediately a race was on among the aviatrixes to be the first woman to cross the ocean that then seemed to lie at the center of the world. In the year following Lindbergh's flight, fifty-five adventurers in eighteen planes attempted to fly the Atlantic;

three succeeded and nineteen died, five of whom were women. Ruth Nichols tried it, but crashed near Saint John, New Brunswick, smashing her spine in five places in the process. In 1928, a wealthy society matron named Amy Guest purchased a three-engine Fokker and decided to get the transatlantic record herself, but her family was horrified, and so instead Guest directed her attorneys to find a suitable woman to make the trip in her plane. Publisher George Putnam sensed a potential coup in having the story of the first woman to make the trip. He had read about the boyishly glamorous flying social worker in Boston and suggested Amelia Earhart. Guest's team made the offer. The proposal appealed not only to Amelia's sense of adventure but also to her desire to prove that aviation was safe. In June, she flew with pilots Wilmur Stultz and Louis Gordon from Trepassey, Newfoundland, to Burry Port, Wales, in twenty hours and forty minutes.

Earhart landed to instant fame. She never touched the controls in that first flight—she did not have a multiengine or instrument rating and most of the journey was through fog—and so the acclaim embarrassed her; she said she had been "as useful as a sack of potatoes." But the fans didn't care: she was feted in France and England, addressed Parliament at Westminster and returned home to rapturous crowds who jammed airfields to see "America's Sweetheart of the Air." Stultz and Gordon were more or less forgotten, but Putnam had a bestseller with *20 hrs. 40 mins.,* Amelia's account of the journey. Amelia and her publisher spent considerable time together, and in 1931 George divorced his wife and he and Amelia were married (after she first made him sign a pledge that he would not hold her to any old-fashioned ideas about fidelity). Earhart was aloof and enigmatic, but she put her celebrity to work: she wrote for magazines, gave public lectures, advised the government on aviation, launched her own line of luggage and endorsed Camel cigarettes.

In 1929, organizers announced that for the first time a woman's race would be part of the National Air Races and

Aeronautical Exposition. They had a single, practical motive: in the words of the race's marketing director, Frank Copeland, "If the feminine is considered the weaker sex and this weaker sex accomplishes the art of flying, it is positive proof of the simplicity and universal practicality of individual flying. It is the greatest sales argument that can be presented to that public upon which this industry depends for its existence." The race was set to run from Santa Monica, California, to Cleveland, Ohio; the winner on the tough course would get a real reward, for eight thousand dollars in prize money was put up. But then various men on the race committee and some male members of the National Aeronautic Association began to have second thoughts, picturing the headlines if a female pilot were killed. They proposed that every woman carry a male navigator with her and that the race start somewhere east of the Rockies so that no women would crack up in the mountains.

Amelia led the angry outcry: "I for one and some of the other women fliers . . . think it is ridiculous to advertise this as an important race and then set us down at Omaha for a level flight to Cleveland," she told *The New York Times* on July 12, 1929. "As for suggesting that we carry a man to navigate our own course through the Rockies, I, for one, won't enter. None of us will enter unless it is going to be a real sporting contest. How is a fellow going to earn spurs without at least trying to ride?" The proposed changes were dropped, and the women were given the same eligibility requirements as men. Delighted, Amelia called the race "a chance to play the game as men play it, by rules established for them as flyers, not as women." Will Rogers dubbed the race a "Powder Puff Derby" and reporters seized on the nickname, but that didn't change the fact that female pilots, in a thrilling race, were on the front pages of all America's newspapers.

An astonishing collection of women idled their planes at the start line in California. There were twenty of them altogether, some in white coveralls or jodhpurs, others in drop-waist flapper frocks and cloche hats. There was a glamorous, long-lashed star of silent movies named Ruth Elder, who had made an attempt at an Atlantic crossing and had to ditch midocean (she was rescued by a Dutch oil tanker). And Phoebe Omlie, the first woman to have her own flying circus—she was walking with a cane, recovering from two broken legs in a recent crack-up. Twenty women started out in California and sixteen reached Cleveland nine days later. There was a horrible accident on the second day, when Alaskan bush pilot Marvel Crossan succumbed to carbon monoxide poisoning caused by a faulty engine exhaust in her new plane. She crashed in a mesquite forest in Arizona and did not survive. The other women were devastated by Marvel's death but decided that the best way to honor her memory would be to continue the race. There were more near disasters—the wires holding on one pilot's wings snapped, while other women had clogged fuel lines and engine failures. But fifteen women crossed the finish line, and as Amelia pointed out to reporters, that was the highest percentage in any cross-country race, men or women. Louise Thaden, her face burned brown by the sun and her bobbed hair in tangles, was the first to cross the line in Cleveland, and she was enveloped by a delirious crowd.

The race was the first time many of the women had the occasion to spend time in the company of other female pilots, and along the route they decided they should organize to promote the cause of women in aviation. In October, invitations went out to each of the 117 licensed women in the country, inviting them to a meeting at Curtiss Field in November. Twenty-six women flew themselves in and gathered in a noisy room above a hangar. They served tea and biscuits on a toolbox and resolved to work for jobs for women in aviation. There was a debate about what their new organization should be called. The "Noisy Birdwomen" was one suggestion. Eventually, Amelia Earhart spoke up from the back of the room, suggesting they take their name from the number of members they wound up with. When all the registration forms were returned, they counted ninety-nine, and so "The 99s" they became. Today the 99s is an international federation of female pilots with seven thousand members in thirty-five countries. Louise Thaden was appointed secretary and began to organize them; by 1931, the group was formalized, and Louise suggested Amelia as president, as her fame would attract certain publicity.

The next year, on May 22, 1932, Amelia became the first person to have twice flown the Atlantic. But this time she was at the controls of her red-and-gold Lockheed Vega, making the first solo flight of a woman across the ocean. She kept herself awake with smelling salts and brought only a Thermos of soup and a tin of tomato juice with her. The thirteen hours and thirty minutes in the air cemented her fame; she single-mindedly used her enormous public profile to convince people that aviation was a safe and viable means of transportation. Three months later, she made the first solo transcontinental flight by a woman, from Los Angeles to Newark. In 1935, she made the first solo trip from Hawaii to the U.S. mainland by a man or woman, and the first nonstop flight from Mexico City to Newark.

That same year Amelia led a campaign on behalf of her friend Helen Richey, who was hired by Central Airlines as the country's first female airline pilot. It fast became clear that Central had hired Helen only as a publicity stunt; under pressure from male pilots, the company would not let her fly. The Commerce Department (then aviation's ruling body) was also determined to keep Helen grounded; it issued a directive to Central that they not let Helen fly in bad weather. Amelia fought that successfully, but Helen quit in frustration after three months.

In June 1937, Amelia set out on what she said would be her last record-setting flight, a journey around the world. The trip went flawlessly through Africa and Asia. Then, on a 2,566-mile journey over the Pacific, Amelia and her navigator, Fred Noonan, disappeared. Headlines blared the news, and an anxious country sat by the radio, listening to bulletins until a huge search by the United States Navy was finally abandoned, having turned up no sign of the Electra or its crew.

Wing walkers, barnstormers and Amelia Earhart: that's what a girl who grew up in the 1930s knew about airplanes.

Geraldyn Cobb was born in Norman, Oklahoma, just as the Great Depression took a firm hold on the country. She was the second daughter of Harvey and Helena Cobb. Her sister, Carolyn, born in 1929, was very much a little girl: she played house, threw tea parties for her Shirley Temple doll and had plenty of little girl friends. But when Geraldyn arrived in March 1931, she was something very different. She ran before she walked, climbed trees and crawled on her belly holding an imaginary rifle, imitating her father's friends from the National Guard.

She was "Jerrie" from the time she was tiny. She was born with a speech impediment, an extra membrane that kept her tongue literally tied and twisted her words. She lisped and slurred; big sister Carolyn was "Taro." Jerrie's family understood her peculiar speech just fine, but she had trouble communicating with anyone else. Her first day of kindergarten brought humiliation: the teacher asked the students to stand, one by one, and say their names. Jerrie repeated hers three times, but the teacher still could not understand her. The rest of the class tittered while Jerrie held back tears. When she told her parents what had happened, they made arrangements for a long-postponed trip to the doctor. Three times, on three separate visits, he tried to snip the membrane below her tongue with a shiny silver instrument; the first time, Jerrie wriggled free and fled the office. The next time she kept her mouth clamped shut and could not be persuaded to open it, and the next, she simply screamed in terror. Finally, the doctor anesthetized her and made the snip.

After the operation and "talking lessons," her speech improved. But at six, Jerrie had already learned another lesson: "School is no good. Talking can be distressing. Sometimes the best fun is to be alone." She didn't need to talk to do the things she loved best. With horses, she didn't feel strange, and she didn't have any trouble making herself understood. On her sixth birthday, her father took her to Will Rogers Park and agreed that instead of the usual poky pony, she could ride a proper horse this time. She took off up the bridle path before her startled father even had his horse saddled.

In 1938, the family moved to Texas: with war looming in Europe, Harvey's National Guard unit was put on active duty. When the United States entered the war in 1941, he was deemed too old to be sent overseas, so he requested a transfer to the air corps. Here, too, he was classed too old for pilot training—unless he already had a commercial license. Harvey quietly set about getting one.

His daughter, meanwhile, was distracted: she had planted a Victory Garden, intent on raising the twenty dollars she needed to purchase a horse of her own, an old farm nag called Snowball. The garden suffered under benign neglect until her mother took over the weeding and watering: Jerrie was out at the stables, learning the finer points of hoof cleaning and currycombing. She spent all her free time riding bareback on the scrubby flatland around Abilene. "There were no fences, and you could ride as long and as fast as you wanted."

Harvey came home at lunch one day in 1940 with an envelope and a gleam in his eye. He made his wife and daughters try to guess what was in it. Helena was sure it was military orders and they were moving again; the girls thought maybe photographs or a war bond. Harvey chuckled. "Nothing very important," he said, elaborately casual. "Just my license as a private pilot!" And he had another surprise: tired of waiting for access to a plane on the airfield, he had bought one of his own, a tiny

Taylorcraft. His daughters could not wait another moment to see it: they skipped school that afternoon, and Harvey drove his family out to the airfield. He took Carolyn up for a ride first, and then it was Jerrie's turn.

"Even before the old Taylorcraft had reached 300 feet, I recognized the sky would be my home," she wrote later. "For a child who distrusted ordinary everyday speech . . . for an adolescent who yearned for the freedom of the fields and the winds . . . for a girl who had learned to be alone—the sky was the answer. I tumbled out of the airplane with stars in my eyes."

In that first flight, Jerrie found the same wonderful freedom that came with horseback riding. "In the sky there are no fences. In a field there are no roads, no paths, no limits on you and your horse. You move as you wish . . . in either case you are *moving*—deciding which way to move, and controlling the movement. And whether you control the power of one horse or the harnessed power of 1000 horses is only a matter of degree."

Jerrie's mother watched her giddy daughters with some trepidation; as the afternoon's third passenger, she was less than excited about climbing into the fragile little plane. Harvey tried to thrill her with some banks and dives, but the engine failed and he had to "dead stick" (making a powerless landing) into a field, where Helena vowed never to get back in the plane. Eventually she let Harvey fly her back to the girls, but she was sure this flying business was foolish—and dangerous.

Harvey was working toward a commercial license and needed to fly bigger planes, so he soon traded in the little Taylorcraft for a heavier, open-cockpit Waco biplane. He was, by then, the target of an unrelenting campaign: daily requests from his younger daughter for flying lessons. It went on for years. He tried "no" and "you're too young" and "it wouldn't even be legal" before retreating behind that paternal standard, "ask your mother." Helena, of course, said, "No, absolutely not." But that did nothing to dissuade Jerrie: every day she appealed again, asking, but *why?* until her mother snapped, "Because your grades are so poor, that's why."

That was a response that allowed for some negotiating. Jerrie, at twelve, was still quiet and intensely shy. She didn't have much to say to kids her own age; horses and planes were all that interested her. She wore her mother down and placated her with at least the show of attention to homework, until finally Helena allowed the flying lessons. Jerrie wasn't old enough to ride a full-size bike to the airfield for her first lesson, and her father had to put several pillows in the cockpit so she could reach the controls.

The Waco was a fragile craft with thin fabric over its wings and fuselage and a maximum speed of ninety-two miles per hour, but it felt like a rocket for Jerrie. "In few planes today can you be so permeated by the sensation of flight," she wrote twenty years later. "The propwash from the Waco's sturdy little wooden propeller was a rushing, gushing stream of wind; once aloft, you also felt every gust on your cheeks, and the sun was hot and near." In that flight, she says, she felt truly free for the first time.

After that, she met her father out at the airfield every day when he got off work. The plane would be waxed and gassed and ready to go when he arrived—"so we didn't waste any time on the ground." Pigtails poking out beneath her helmet, Jerrie spent hours in the air with her father, working the controls in the seat behind him.

The lessons went well until Harvey's unit was abruptly transferred to Denver, and he had to sell the Waco. Jerrie also had to sell Snowball. Her parents tried to ease the transition by letting her buy a new horse (which led to a part-time job at the local pony farm), but she was miserable at her new high school. In fact, she rarely went to class. When her father found her truant in a park one afternoon, her plans poured out.

"I just don't like sitting in classes when there's so much going on outside. I can't seem to get interested in most of the stuff in school." Instead, she told him hesitantly, she had been talking to the pony farm about a full-time job. (It was, after all, wartime and help was scarce, even help in the form of horse-mad fourteen-year-old girls.)

Her father spoke to her gently, agreeing she had learned important skills at the farm, but asking if taking care of horses was really what she wanted to do for the rest of her life. "I wish you could see the cockpits of some of the new planes at the base, Jerrie. Hundreds of gauges, switches, controls, dials. The pilots and engineers practically have to be mathematicians. People can't just fly by the seat of their pants these days." He told her how he ran away from school himself, how his days in the navy taught him what a mistake that was, and how he came back to the university much older than his classmates. They talked for hours, Jerrie says, and in the end she heard the truth in his words. She agreed to go back to school, and work as hard at it as she did with the ponies. But she didn't expect to *like* it any better.

In Denver she joined the Civil Air Patrol—the corps of volunteer pilots founded in 1941 to fly sentry missions along the borders or search for downed aircraft above forests and deserts. The CAP admitted women from the first, and they made up a fifth of its membership by the end of the war. As a cadet, Jerrie got to spend time in the air, but only occasionally was she allowed to follow along at the controls. By then, she had plenty of flying hours with her dad, but they didn't count as legal instruction hours. In her junior year, however, a kind biology teacher who was also a private pilot gave Jerrie her first formal flight lessons in his two-seater Aeronca Champion. One day in March 1947, they landed and were taxiing toward his barn when the teacher jumped out and told her, "Take her—she's all yours."

The Aeronca had an enclosed cockpit but the noisy engine made a rumble that surrounded its pilot. Jerrie pointed the plane down the runway, remembered not to yank the controls and gently pulled back, feeling the surge of sixty-five horsepower. "I was in a wonderful state of silent aloneness, floating high and free on a small kite I could control." After a brief flight and three textbook-perfect landings, she was on the road to her private pilot's license.

For that, of course, she needed solo hours. All through high school, she haunted the little local airport. She washed and gassed planes, occasionally trading her labor for a few minutes of flying time. If she waxed an all-metal Cessna, she got a whole hour in the air—and the waxing only took her three days. "I thought I had a good deal," she says. Flying time cost money, so she picked peaches and berries, worked as a cashier at the movie house, made drugstore deliveries and drove a scooter around town ferrying parts for the local garage.

And she waited: student pilots had to be sixteen to get a license. By March 5, 1947, her battered little logbook listed two hundred hours, accumulated since she was twelve. That day, her sixteenth birthday, she flew and passed the exam. Jerrie Cobb was a licensed pilot.

JACKIE'S GIRLS

Jean Hixson, right, and two of her fellow WASPs at Avenger Field in Sweetwater, Texas, 1944.

In those heady days when Jerrie was newly licensed, finally able to fly alone, she quickly got used to being the only girl at the airfield. She didn't know any other female pilots—and there was just one in the newspapers.

But that pilot was extraordinary: Jackie Cochran made headlines every week. She won races and set records and even flew a bomber in the war. She ran a huge company; she was a self-made millionaire married to an even richer man. She was said to have told her secretary to take a message from President Roosevelt because she was washing her hair. She won the great Bendix Air Race in 1938, when she was the only woman entered. And these days, she was souping up a sleek P-51 Mustang she had bought to win the next Bendix, the first to be flown since the war.

To a sixteen-year-old picking berries to pay for flight time in a small town in Oklahoma, Jackie Cochran seemed rich and glamorous and more than a little unreal. Jerrie never imagined meeting her—and she certainly never imagined that she and Jackie would one day square off in a pitched battle over the chance to fly in space.

Jackie was wealthy and powerful by 1947, but she had not begun her life that way. She always said she was an orphan, raised in a foster family of sawmill workers in northern Florida, and sometimes gave her birth name as Bessie Lee Pittman. She said she grew up miserably poor. "Until I was eight years old, I had no shoes. My bed was usually a pallet on the floor and sometimes just the floor," she wrote in her autobiography. "Food at best consisted of the barest essentials—sometimes nothing except what I foraged for myself in the woods. . . . I remember eating a lot of mullet and beans, with an occasional bit of sowbelly added when we were in clover. . . . No butter. No sugar. My dresses were made from cast-off flour sacks." Jackie said she went to school for only two years, during which a kind teacher gave her a first store-bought dress and taught her to read. She went to work at seven, first minding other people's children and fetching water, then working for six cents an hour, twelve hours a night, in a cotton mill. At age nine, as boss of a crew of children, she would tell them how she was going to grow up to be rich, have her own automobile and endless great adventures.

At ten, Jackie said, she persuaded the woman who ran the local beauty parlor to take her on as maid of all work, and she learned to mix the dyes and set the permanents that then took fourteen hours. She made some money, bought the fine clothes and the Model T she dreamed of, but a benefactor encouraged her to go to nursing school. She finished the three years of training, she said, but skipped the certification exam because she knew that with her second-grade handwriting and arithmetic skills that she'd fail. Instead, she went to work assisting a doctor who treated mill workers just like the family she grew up in—but that was too bitterly familiar, so she went back to the beauty business. "I could give them hope along with a new hairdo," she wrote. She picked the name Cochran out of a phone book, seeking, she said, distance from her foster family. She would later say the privation formed her. "I could never have so little that I hadn't had less. It took away my fear."

Florida was no place for a young woman to make her fortune. In 1929, Jackie set out for New York and talked her way into a job at Antoine's, the city's most fashionable salon. At a cocktail party thrown by friends in 1932, she was seated next to a quiet, blond fellow. She knew he was in business, but he kept her talking the whole night, saying he was always interested in the stories of working women. She confided her ambitions to open her own cosmetics company, putting her hard-won knowledge of the beauty business to work. Jackie learned later that her unassuming dinner companion was the tycoon Floyd Odlum. Floyd was the son of a Methodist minister who worked his way through law school, became something of an investing whiz and founded the Atlas Corporation in 1923. He liquidated all his assets—into the then astronomical sum of $14 million—months before the stock market crash of 1929, then grew even richer picking up shares in utilities and railroads when the market floundered. Through the thirties, he held stakes in everything from Paramount Pictures to Bonwit Teller to the New York Plaza. He was a confidant of Herbert Hoover, Franklin Roosevelt and Harry Truman; the Eisenhowers spent Christmas at his California ranch.

Floyd was fourteen years older than Jackie and married with two children when they met, but they were soon dating discreetly: they shared a ferocious drive and a certain steely fearlessness. Floyd divorced his first wife in 1935 and married Jackie in secret in 1936. When the news got out, there was, of course, considerable gossip, as there will be when orphaned hairdressers marry millionaires—but those who knew Jackie and Floyd say you only had to be in the room with them to see how intensely they loved each other.

But about that question of being an orphan: a family now scattered across California and the South tells a different story. They say their aunt Jackie was never orphaned but raised by her own loving parents. Bessie Lee Pittman, as she was then, was born near Mobile, Alabama, in 1903; she was indeed the daughter of a mill worker, and he moved his family to Florida when she was young. They were poor. They didn't have shoes, but none of the other kids did either, and everyone in town wore dresses made from flour sacks. But, say her surviving nieces and nephews, there was always food on the table, she never ate pig slop or had to forage, and Bessie Lee, the youngest child, got the best of whatever there was. Her father died when she was young and her mother, Molly, scrabbled to keep the family together.

Bessie, they say, married at fourteen or fifteen (as did her sisters)—Bessie to Robert Cochran, a young aircraft mechanic from the nearby naval base at Pensacola, where she first saw airplanes. They had a child, Robert Junior, who died in a fire at the age of five while playing with matches behind the house. His father disappeared not long after—some people said he was killed in a car accident, others that he left Jackie a "grass widow." Whatever happened, young Bessie set out for the East Coast. She took a new name and, it seems, created a new story about her childhood. "When she got to Boston she was running with some real high society people, and she concocted the story that she was an orphan, because it was easier to say that her foster parents were poor mill people than to say her parents were— maybe her parents were somebody," explains her niece, Norma Denny. "I don't suppose she expected to have to live with it all her life. But it grew and stuck with her and she got more famous, and there was no way she could get rid of that story." Her nephew Jerry Hydle says he was at the Cochran-Odlum ranch once when his angry mother, Mamie, cornered Jackie about the orphan story. "She said, 'Hell, Mamie, people want to hear something, so I just told them something.'"

Jackie told the story of her orphaned childhood to hundreds of reporters and audiences over the years; she said the privation formed her "backbone." She said she never minded her murky background herself, but when she married, she thought her husband should "know as much about me as anyone could." She said she went south and "got letters from the two people still living who might have more facts than I had" and gave them to Floyd, sealed. The outside of the envelope read, in Jackie's appalling handwriting, "This is For you Floyd. I have never Read the contents. You can Burn it or Read as you wish. I Love you very much. Jackie." Floyd opted not to open it, she said, and the letters were burned after her death.

But if there ever were such letters in an envelope, Floyd didn't need to open them to learn the truth about her childhood: he was supporting her family. Bessie Lee Pittman used Floyd's money to move her family out to California from Florida right around the time they were married. He settled them on farms on the fringes of the sprawling Indio ranch. Jerry Hydle lived there as a child and learned that the terms of contact were dictated entirely by Jackie. She sent gifts and checks at Christmas, flew his mother to the Lovelace Clinic when she needed an operation and used her money to put some of her nieces and nephews through college. But she did not introduce them to the powerful guests at the ranch, nor did they ever meet Floyd's family.

The local paper in Indio once interviewed Jackie's mother, Molly, and suggested that the orphan aviatrix story was less than accurate, but otherwise the family stayed hidden as Jackie wanted. Denny has letters Jackie wrote her branch of the family over the years—sometimes declining to send more money and on one occasion telling Denny she could not come to visit her own mother, who was dying, because she was going to the Paris air show. ("She did send some flowers," Denny says.) But no correspondence with the family survives in the collection of her papers willed to a museum archive, and those who were close to her, including Chuck Yeager, the famed air force pilot who would years later help her break the sound barrier, reject the idea that she made up the tale of her childhood. "Jackie was straight up," Yeager says firmly.

In Jackie, Floyd seems to have found a way to live vicariously, taking risks closed to him by both his conservative nature and the early onset of crippling arthritis. He indulged Jackie's fantasies (such as arranging for her to ride an elephant into Madison Square Garden, a leftover dream from a childhood visit to the circus) and pushed her adventures. She amused and intrigued him. "My wife is the most interesting person I ever met," he told a reporter. He also opened doors for her, for there was no one in business or politics in the thirties and forties who would not take a call from Floyd Odlum.

And then there was the flying. It was Floyd, so the story goes, who encouraged Jackie to get a pilot's license. When they met in 1932 and she told him about her dreams of a cosmetics company, he immediately said she would need to fly in order to cover enough territory to make money in the depression years. Floyd was already fascinated by this brash creature, and over dinner he bet Jackie the $495 the nearest flying school was charging for twenty hours of lessons that she could not get her license in six weeks. She countered that she would do it in three, since she had plans for the rest of her vacation. In 1932, $495 was a fair bit of money: admission to a movie cost twenty cents and ten dollars bought a ton of coal.

Jackie Cochran took her first flight on an ordinary August day in 1932 in upstate New York. When she came back to earth, after just half an hour, everything had changed. "Why have I waited so long?" she wondered, as the little biwing Fleet trainer settled back on the tarmac. "I can't believe that I have put this off—a reason for living—for so long." She had never even seen a plane up close before that first lesson. The engine quit on her first solo flight, forcing her to make a dead-stick landing. But Jackie had her future figured out: she said, almost casually, "I wanted to be the world's greatest pilot. . . . I decided there was a real place for women like myself in aviation and I'd take it up as a profession. I'd make it pay and I'd learn everything I could possibly learn about flying."

Floyd lost the bet: Jackie soloed after fewer than forty-eight hours of lessons, and she had her license in three weeks. She quit her job at the salon, headed to California and earned a commercial and instructor ratings. She was one of the few women in the air. There were six hundred licensed female pilots in 1933 and just three hundred a year later: few women could afford to keep up their flying time through the Depression.

Now Jackie's days were spent in grease-spotted coveralls, her hair tangled by the wind, but it did nothing to dampen her obsession with her personal appearance. She was stunning when fully turned out: shiny golden curls, gold-flecked brown eyes and skin described by a friend as "like the loveliest whipped cream." (Women who fell out with her also noted "pipe fitter's hands" and a boxy torso.) Jackie was a fanatic about fashionable clothes, smart shoes and cosmetics. Many of the early reporters who wrote about her contrasted her with Amelia Earhart, so rakish in her bomber jacket and jodhpurs; Jackie didn't "look like a pilot."

In 1934, when she had been flying for just two years, Jackie decided to enter the MacRobertson London-to-Australia Race.

The prize was the huge sum of $75,000, but more than that, Jackie knew that winning the race (it doesn't seem to have occurred to her she might not win) would give her an entrée into the world of aviation that was, in the 1930s, still largely the territory of the wealthy and the privileged. The race covered 11,300 miles over mountains, rain forest, desert and vast stretches of water. Jackie entered a few small races for practice and tried to scrape together a plane and sponsors. In the end, she wound up in a notoriously unreliable Gee Bee, and she was forced down over Romania. But there had already been headlines about the lone female American entrant.

And Jackie had a redoubled determination to race and to win. The next year, she entered the Bendix Air Race, sponsored by manufacturer Vincent Bendix. She and Amelia had to lobby organizers to let women fly it—the men were nervous about bad publicity, after a female pilot crashed and died in a California race. Jackie was flying an untrustworthy Gamma, and she knew the engine was bad, but she felt she had to start the race (in heavy fog, after waiting for the wreckage of a male pilot who crashed and was killed on takeoff to be cleared off the runway) lest the male contestants say the women wouldn't fly in bad weather. As she had feared, she was forced down over the Arizona desert.

But she was back in the race in 1937 and finished it; the next year she finally got her hands on a true racing aircraft. Historian Claudia Oakes explains the early Bendix years, saying, "One of the problems women pilots constantly faced was the attitude that they could not handle 'hot' aircraft built for speed, and therefore found their aircraft outclassed in the races." From the earliest days of aviation, women were denied access to the most innovative new technologies, and they would later similarly be shut out as propellers gave way to the jet age and then to space. In 1938, Jackie got to fly a Seversky P-35 with a twelve-hundred-horsepower engine and extra fuel tanks in the wings. And she got to fly it thanks to the now-enshrined belief that anything women could do must be easy. Designer Alexander Seversky was trying to sell his plane design to the Army Air Corps, and he figured that if he showed Jackie could fly it, the military brass would see the P-35 was a model of simplicity and reliability. Jackie was the only female entrant in the Bendix that year; she won the race, but did not stop at Bendix Field in New Jersey to collect her trophy. She kept flying to New York to establish a new women's west-to-east record of ten hours and seven minutes. By then, Jackie had embarked in earnest on record setting. In 1937, she set three—the women's national speed record, the women's world speed record and the New York-to-Miami speed record—and won the Harmon Trophy from the International League of Aviators. She won it the next two years as well, an unprecedented run.

She met Amelia at the 1936 Bendix, and later claimed, in typical Jackie fashion, "During the last years of her life, I was closer to Amelia than anyone else, even her husband, George Putnam." (Amelia's biographers make no similar claim about Jackie.) She and Floyd put up some of the money for Amelia's last doomed flight; Jackie later wrote that she could picture her friend alive and floating in the ocean for the first three days after the crash.

By the mid-thirties, Jackie was well embarked on her plans for great personal wealth. "I told Floyd that I wanted my own beauty business so I could end up at the top." She hired a cosmetic chemist away from a major oil company, found a consultant who understood perfumes, located the space for a small laboratory in New Jersey and rented an office in Manhattan. Within a year, Jacqueline Cochran Cosmetics rivaled the business of Helena Rubinstein and Elizabeth Arden. Jackie made much of her fortune with a then-revolutionary "greaseless" moisturizer called Flowing Velvet and the Perk-Up Cylinder, a three-and-a-half-inch stick that contained cleanser, foundation, eye shadow, rouge, perfume and face powder in one convenient tube. "I would take one on all my races," she remembered, and would refuse to get out of the cockpit until she had made up her face. The pictures of glamorous Jackie retouching her lipstick at the finish line were irresistible, and soon her cosmetics were carried in department stores across the United States.

In 1937, Jackie was invited to sit on the committee of the Collier Trophy, American aviation's premier award. She was the first woman given the honor, and it was a tailor-made opportunity for Jackie to solidify and demonstrate her own power base in Washington. From travels in Europe, she had a sense that war was looming and firsthand knowledge of how advanced German aviation was. She pushed the Collier team to recognize and thus bolster aviation medicine in the United States—only to discover that there was no government aviation medicine program. One of the few people working in the area was a young doctor at the Mayo Clinic, William Randolph Lovelace II. Jackie saw to it that Lovelace and his two assistants won the Collier that year, and when President Roosevelt went to present the trophy—a bit bewildered to be giving it to doctors rather than pilots—she delivered a half-hour lecture on Germany's superior air power. The next day, Lovelace had the funding for a formal research program—and the foundation of a lifelong friendship with Jackie, which would have a critical impact on his decision to test women for space twenty years later.

At the Collier dinner, Jackie got into conversation with men who were running pilot recruitment for the British Ferry Command. They asked her to pilot a bomber from Montreal to London, since the publicity might help drum up male pilots (if, after all, a woman had already shown she could do the job). It was the beginning of what was to be Jackie's greatest contribution to women in aviation. "I was also convinced that our own women pilots might be needed should the time come when our country needed to defend itself. . . . I'd heard that female pilots were ferrying planes in the English countryside and this was my chance to see firsthand." After overcoming almost violent resistance from male pilots, she safely flew the Lockheed Hudson to England on June 17, 1941. "Goddamn it, but being the only woman in the history of World War II to fly a bomber to our beleaguered British allies was exciting, and worth every ounce of energy I had spent manipulating my way into that airplane," she wrote.

Jackie's forceful personality, and her powerful position in society, would bring about extraordinary events in the next few years and change the lives of many American women. She came back from England with a plan: she wanted a women's ferry command just like that in Britain, where women were delivering planes and freeing male pilots for combat flying. Britain's Air Transport Auxiliary (a name that won the women the saccharine nickname "ATA girls") was organized six months after the start of the war, and the women were given full military status. The Australian Air Force had a Women's Auxiliary, and so did Canada, although few of those women actually flew. There were also extraordinary stories coming out of Russia about three separate divisions of female fighter pilots.

Jackie knew better than most Americans how badly the war in Europe was going for the Allies, and she thought the United States should be organizing its female pilots. Within days of her return she had drawn up a plan for a women's transport division modeled on Britain's and taken the plan to Roosevelt and his wife, Eleanor; to Gen. H. "Hap" Arnold, head of the Army Air Corps (precursor to the Air Force); to Gen. Robert Olds and to Assistant Secretary of War for Air Robert Lovett. Olds was putting together an Air Transport Command and was considering hiring the occasional woman as they were needed. That wasn't enough for Jackie. "I wanted a more organized program because I felt that a few good women pilots amidst all the men would simply go down as a flash in the historical pan."

Olds tried to quash her program; when she told Arnold about it, he objected too. In September 1941, Arnold formally wrote and told her that there was no shortage of male civilian pilots, for one thing; for another, he did not think there were enough qualified women to fly for the air corps, and even if there were it would be a huge burden to house and train them alongside men at army stations. He also hinted that the women would be taking jobs away from men. Jackie wrote back, refuting each of his points. Finally, Arnold said she should organize a group of American women to fly with the ATA group in England, who were desperate for pilots; if that worked, he said, he would think about her plans to have women ferry in the United States.

Jackie spent the next few months recruiting twenty-five experienced female pilots—women with more than five hundred hours in the air and who could drop everything for an eighteen-month contract to fly with the Royal Air Force. In September they flew to London, and the high-spirited and capable American women made headlines in war-weary Britain. Then Pearl Harbor was attacked and the United States was suddenly at war on two fronts. Overnight, there was a desperate need for pilots, and Arnold let Jackie know that if ever there were a female pilots' division in the Army Air Corps, she would run it.

Jackie had incomparable connections in Washington, both her own from flying and Floyd's from business interests. But while she was supervising her twenty-five pilots in London, she missed something big. In 1940, a pilot named Nancy Harkness Love wrote a letter of her own to General Olds. Nancy was the daughter of a distinguished Philadelphia family; she was a former test pilot for a small aviation company with fifteen hundred hours in the air, and she had married an air corps officer who became deputy chief of staff of the transport command. She too had proposed the creation of a ferry team of experienced female fliers to free male pilots for overseas flying. At first the army rejected her proposal (just as it would later reject Jackie's), but by 1942 the Army Air Corps had a critical shortage of pilots: they had recruited every last stunt pilot and crop duster, and they could not train new pilots quickly enough. Despite Arnold's assurances to Jackie, Nancy Love's plan was resurrected and she was given the go-ahead to start training a small group of women who had at least five hundred hours of flying time. They were called the Women's Auxiliary Ferrying Squadron (the WAFS).

Nancy knew the plan to have women flying for the military, even during the peak of the war, was going to be sensitive. She knew her pilots were going to be in the public eye, and she wanted them above reproach. While plenty of American women were pitching in for the war effort, they did so mostly in traditional roles, as clerks and secretaries and nurses. The WAFS were the first women to break out of that mold, and Nancy knew even a breath of scandal could shift the cautious public support right back the other way. She interviewed each candidate and demanded two letters of recommendation. And once they were in, she set the WAFS salaries at $250 a month—$130 less than male ferry pilots earned, so that the men would not be disgruntled.

Nancy pulled together a team of twenty-eight highly capable commercial pilots, including a vivacious society lady from Long Island named Betty Gillies, and Cornelia Fort, a Nashville debutante who was in the air above Pearl Harbor when the base was attacked. The women plunged into training, learning ferry routes, air corps terminology and formation flying. On October 22, they made their first ferry deliveries, from a Piper factory in Pennsylvania to a base in Long Island, and they barely stopped flying for the next three years.

Nancy wanted her group to be elite and professional, and she fought to have them fly bigger and faster aircraft. Before long, the WAFS had graduated from ferrying light trainers to transporting the heavy four-engine Flying Fortress B-17. So the WAFS attracted plenty of publicity—in fact, a hungry public couldn't get enough news about these female military pilots, and Nancy's elegant looks kept them in the magazines. That fall, Jackie arrived from England (summoned by Arnold, she says,

though it may have been reports of the WAFS that lured her).
She was furious. The day after she got home, she was in Arnold's
office, demanding an explanation: she had been made to wait
two long years to put her idea into practice, and behind her back
he'd given the project to Nancy Love? Nancy, of course, had
made a good proposal and had it accepted—it was only logical
that she head the WAFS. But Jackie didn't see it that way: all she
saw was that she wasn't in charge.

Arnold managed to patch it over, and when a new corps of
female pilots was created in September 1942 Jackie was its head.
The WAFS was left in place, with Nancy as its commander;
although no one was inclined to spell it out, she had become,
technically, subordinate to Jackie. The new head of the women's
air corps did little to disguise her distaste for the WAFS—she
called them "a bunch of society dames." Most of the WAFS pilots
were well-off, for only wealthy women had the money to rack up
the kind of flying hours Nancy Love wanted. But the WAFS felt
Jackie Cochran didn't like Nancy or her fliers because they were
women with serious hours in serious aircraft—the few rivals for
the kind of exclusive achievement Jackie claimed for herself.

Jackie's mission was to train female pilots—not the experienced women Nancy had, but women who were casual recreational pilots. She was given initial orders to train five hundred
women. But when word got out that the air force was going to
be training female pilots, the applications began to pour in.
Jackie soon had hundreds of letters: there would be twenty-five
thousand applications in all. Initially she asked for women with
two hundred hours of flying time, recorded in a detailed
logbook; eventually, as demand for pilots built, this was reduced
to thirty-five hours. She had letters from waitresses, nurses,
dancers, teachers and a blackjack dealer. Jackie tried to interview
each of the serious candidates personally, and she screened them
closely. Like Nancy, she knew that there would be plenty of
scrutiny of her pilots: their job would be both dangerous and

adventurous, and unlike the assignments of women in any other branches of military service, theirs was a job that many men would themselves want. She turned down one superbly qualified black pilot ("she understood perfectly," Jackie wrote blithely in her memoirs) but she accepted two Asian Americans. She told one of her assistants to weed out those who she thought might be lesbians as well: she wanted nothing to besmirch the reputation of her corps.

The applications kept coming, but Jackie didn't have an airfield, planes or a place to house her would-be pilots. She wanted her women trained before "the war would catch up to us, and the need for women would be over" (news was leaking out about the invention in Los Alamos of "the bomb to end all wars"). So she arranged that they be taken on as civil service employees—allowing her to skip the army's bureaucratic channels and giving them a strange hybrid status. Later, she thought, they could be militarized through an act of Congress. It was a fateful decision.

The air force sent Jackie and her pilots to Texas; first she operated from Houston, but later took over Avenger Field, a British training base, in Sweetwater. She had to pay to have the women's uniforms designed herself (at Bergdorf Goodman in New York) and fight with the air corps to pay for them. In November 1942, her first class of thirty women arrived. They were housed in makeshift facilities with just one washroom and flew a haphazard collection of battered old trainers. But Jackie was determined that her pilots were going to get exactly the same training given to male air corps cadets. It was a grueling program, designed to turn novice fliers into military transport pilots in a matter of weeks. The women started learning loops and rolls in light PT-17s, and before long they were expected to master nighttime navigation and instrument flying in heavy AT-6s. When they weren't in the air, they were in classrooms, where gruff air corps instructors taught them about engine maintenance, aerodynamics and meteorology. The days were long, the women were often freezing (for the air corps hadn't managed to find them flight suits) and spattered with the mud from the field. But they stayed up long into the night, trading stories and talking about flying. Word got out, and before long all kinds of male pilots were "forced" to land at Avenger with mysterious engine trouble. Jackie quickly banned any unscheduled traffic: she would not risk gossip or a "reputation" for her girls. The women sighed and declared themselves inmates of Cochran's Convent.

On April 24, 1943, the first class of Women Airforce Service Pilots graduated in Texas. The Army Air Corps didn't provide the traditional pilots' "wings" pin, and Jackie had to order and pay for them herself. She did, however, have General Arnold there to pin them on her pilots.

Immediately the WASPs started to show they could fly as well as men. Class after class graduated at Avenger, and they consistently outperformed groups of male pilots in ground school and flight tests. They tackled their assignments—dull or dangerous—without complaint. They flew Mustangs, the fastest pursuit planes the air corps had, and the B-29 Superfortress, the biggest. When male pilots objected to flying the B-26, a plane with such a powerful engine and such a demanding instrument panel that it was known as "the Widowmaker," Jackie sent women to fly them, part of a successful plan to embarrass the men into the cockpits. Within two years, WASPs were doing 70 percent of all ferrying of single- and twin-engine planes. One WASP, Ann Baumgartner, while working as a test pilot at Wright Field air base in Ohio, became the first American woman to fly a jet.

Cornelia Fort became a more grim "first": she was killed in a crash over Texas in March 1943 apparently when a reckless male pilot, trying to flirt, flew too close and cracked her wing. She was the first female pilot to die flying for the United States. Three months after her death, Jackie tapped twenty-five recent WASP graduates for a special mission: towing targets for artillery training at Camp Davis in North Carolina. It was dangerous work, pulling long muslin sleeves behind the planes while novice gunners shot live ammunition at them. Jackie told them it was a chance to fly bigger aircraft than women had ever flown. But when the WASPs arrived at Camp Davis, they found something Jackie had not warned them about. Those aircraft were in dangerously ill repair. They were old and the base couldn't get parts to fix them—but there was nothing else to fly for target practice. In August 1943, WASP Mabel Rawlinson's A-24 came apart in the air; she crashed and burned to death when the faulty latch on her canopy wouldn't let her out. A fellow WASP flying above her heard Mabel screaming as flames consumed the plane. The WASPs at Davis immediately summoned Jackie, who listened to their list of grievances but took no action. She was clearly afraid that any complaint about the perilous target-towing missions might scuttle the whole program. And Jackie was considering ways to get her WASPs militarized. (The women were doing life-threatening work, but as civilian employees they received none of the military insurance, death benefits or privileges that male pilots did. When WASPs were killed flying, the women had to collect money among themselves to send their bodies home. Their families received no flags for the coffins, no air corps escort.) In July 1943, the Women's Army Auxiliary Corps was militarized as the Women's Army Corps, but Jackie rejected a proposal that the WASP be brought in under that umbrella, apparently fearing she would lose control of the service if it was subsumed into the Wacs. But she began to press for a bill that would give the WASPs military status of their own.

And with that in mind, she stayed silent about Mabel Rawlinson's death and the complaints from the women at Camp Davis. Two WASPs resigned in protest. Jackie sent twenty-three more WASPs to Davis to join the target pullers, just five days after Mabel was killed. A month later, a pilot named Betty Taylor was killed in a crash; Jackie came back to investigate and found that someone had put sugar in the gas tank of Betty's plane. But once again, she would not make her findings public. The base administrators, however, now questioned the credentials of female pilots and insisted they have copilots.

In January 1944, a bill to militarize the WASP was introduced to Congress, and General Arnold expected the female pilots would soon be brought into the air corps fold. But the war department made two conflicting announcements that month: that the WASPs ought to be commissioned, and that thirty-six thousand male fliers and aviation cadets, including instructors, were not needed as pilots and would be made available for infantry duty. Men started to complain, and House members wanted Arnold to reconcile the statements. The fact was that the war was going well, and the army didn't need to train new pilots, but it needed troops. With no new cadets coming, they didn't need instructors either, and all those men were being redesignated for active duty. The men, Arnold told the House committee he lobbied, were simply complaining because they didn't want to do infantry duty (the WASPs, he added, never complained). Militarizing the existing core of one thousand female flyers was just a rubber stamp, he said.

But the public didn't see it that way: the air cadets lobbied their members of Congress, and so did the men who had been exempted from the call-up because they were instructing in the Civilian Pilot Training Program—now they wanted the jobs the already trained women were doing. There were editorials questioning why women were keeping male pilots from jobs and why Congress was indulging Jackie Cochran's "glamour girls." In June, the House Civil Service Committee headed by Rep. Robert Ramspeck of Georgia "recommended that the recruiting of inexperienced personnel and their training for the WASPs be immediately terminated" (even though the female pilot recruits had thirty-five hours of experience, compared with male recruits who had none). Two weeks later, the bill to militarize the WASP was defeated.

In late September, the nine hundred WASPs on active duty received a letter from Arnold: "I want you to know I appreciate your war service and that the AAF will miss you. I also know you will join us in being thankful that our combat losses have proved to be much lower than anticipated, even though it means the inactivation of the WASP." Jackie added a note, telling them they were to be deactivated on December 20. The last class who had begun training in June would be allowed to finish, but they would receive their wings with the knowledge they would never fly. Betty Gillies and forty-two WAFSs based at New Castle, Delaware, offered to keep flying for a dollar a year but were refused. On their last day as military pilots, some women got lifts home from men at their bases; others were left to make their own way. They had to give back their deep blue uniforms, and they were left with only a small pair of wings to take with them. In their two years, 1,074 women had qualified as military pilots. They had flown more than sixty million miles, and thirty-eight had died flying for the United States.

The end of the war brought a profound shift to American society. After three years of being exhorted out of their homes to contribute to the war effort, women were suddenly told their patriotic duty was to go home and resume the most traditional of jobs. The full force of propaganda was brought to bear, with movies and magazines that extolled the virtues of domestic life. The change was not merely economic: on the most personal level, women who had worn trousers and worked nightshifts suddenly found that this independence vanished as quickly as it had come, as Johnny came marching home.

The WASPs felt it. A small number found jobs with a pair of airlines willing to hire them, Transcontinental and Western Air. A few went to nonflying jobs in the air force. But most, like the vast majority of women who had gone to work in the war effort, were summarily out of jobs. But where a clerk or a nurse might find a civilian job, female pilots were stuck. There was a sudden glut of unemployed male fliers, and no one was going to hire a woman for a flying job. The WASPs had spent two years flying across the country on their own, hitching their way back to base with parachutes slung over one shoulder—or racing down ten thousand feet in a Mustang, simulating bombing runs. They were used to having passersby nod respectfully at the sight of the wings glinting on their lapels. And now they were ordered back to their prewar lives, which suddenly seemed hopelessly dull.

But for a handful of women, it was worse than dull. These were the women who scratched out a living in aviation before the war, when airline transportation was an infant industry and there were precious few jobs as test pilots or flight instructors. Now there were even fewer of those jobs. The government sold off surplus war planes, so the aircraft industry slumped—they didn't need test or corporate pilots. Certainly not female ones.

And aviation was changing quickly: the Army Air Corps was pouring money into the development of jets, of planes such as the B-52 bomber and the F-86 fighter. Just two years after the end of the war, a young captain named Chuck Yeager did something most engineers thought was impossible—he flew faster than the speed of sound. The future clearly lay in jet aircraft. But jets, like all the other cutting-edge developments in aerospace technology, were developed and flown by the military. The only places a pilot could learn to fly them were the air corps or navy training schools. And those schools were closed to women. Civilian aviation operations gradually began to employ jets—but female pilots had no way to get qualified and no way to keep up with the jobs.

If a woman were really determined to keep working, and to work in aviation, then she might find a job instructing. Or running a small airport. And every so often, there might be a dealership who would give her work demonstration flying— because, of course, if a woman could fly a plane, anyone could.

IN THE COCKPIT

Jerrie Cobb at home in the cockpit, 1959.

Into this, Jerrie Cobb, newly minted pilot, went looking for work.

She did all right, at first. In the summer of 1948, the owner of a local circus agreed that seventeen-year-old Jerrie could fly his plane if she rebuilt it and used it to promote his shows. The plane was a tiny red-and-yellow Piper Cub, and it needed just about everything fixed, but she got it running. Then she flew it from town to town dropping flyers and pulling a banner to announce the impending arrival of the circus. While the circus was in town she had to take the local dignitaries on flights as well, but if she took up enough spectators for rides, she could earn the money for gas to fly for hours on her own. She flew with a loaf of Wonder bread and a pound of bologna in the back of the plane, parked in fields overnight and slept in a bedroll beside the Cub to make sure the cows didn't lick the varnish off the thin fabric wings.

And that, as far as Jerrie was concerned, was her future settled: she would earn a commercial license and fly for the rest of her life. Her parents, predictably, had other plans. The fight erupted just after her high school graduation day. Harvey and Helena thought Jerrie would be best at their alma mater, the University of Oklahoma—where she could join her sister, Carolyn, in the Gamma Beta Phi sorority, Helena's old house.

Jerrie, on the other hand, planned to skip college and get right to earning the money to pay for the flight hours needed for her commercial rating. In fact, she had already lined up a job: playing first base for the Sooner Queens, a team in the women's National Softball League. In the era before television, women's softball was a big draw, and the really professional teams, such as the New Orleans' Jax Maids and the Phoenix A-1 Queens, drew thousands of people to their games. Jerrie was all set to go on the road with the team.

Her parents were stunned, and angry. "First horses, then airplanes, now baseball," her mother cried. "Geraldyn, you're already seventeen. When are you going to stop thinking about hobbies and games and start thinking about your future?"

Harvey understood a little better when his daughter looked at him, struggling to explain that flying *was* her future. But he had sobering words: "Of course, we know what flying means to you. But, honey, it's no career for a woman. The field today is overrun with highly trained men back from the war. A girl doesn't have a chance. Your mother and I don't want to see you break your heart trying to find a place in aviation that isn't there."

In the end they compromised. Jerrie could play softball for a year if she would agree to go to university the next autumn. She took to the field in the Queens' satin skirt and blouse (black with red, or blue with yellow-and-white trim). Fans filled the bleachers, but this was not a glamorous job. After a game, the team piled into two old station wagons to travel to the next town. And as the rookie, it was up to Jerrie to do the menial jobs, lining up the bases and cleaning the girls' spikes. But the job did what she needed it to: she had the money for flying hours, and on her eighteenth birthday she earned her commercial license.

Now she could fly for hire. "The one little thing was that no one would hire me." Her father was right. An airport manager told her, "Honey, I've got pilots running out of my hangar doors." He flipped through a file folder of job applications, rhyming off the medals the would-be pilots had earned in the war. "And I can't use 'em. Pilots are a dime a dozen today, and they've had thousands of hours in fighters and bombers, not just a few hundred civilian hours like you puddle-jumpers. You'd be about forty-sixth on the list if you want to apply."

Jerrie didn't earn a penny flying that year. She played a second season with the Queens, and then, "with the air of the condemned walking the last mile," went off to college— Oklahoma College for Women at Chickasa, which Jerrie chose in part because it was near the local airport.

Raised as an Episcopalian, she was, even then, deeply religious. "In the sky [even more than church] I had come to *know* that there is a God who designed this universe. In the perfect order of the heavens, I had seen that the stars and the planets could not be mere scientific accidents. Removed by two or three thousand feet from the little urgencies of daily life, I could sense the heights to which the Lord hoped we would aspire." She relished her college classes on philosophy and ethics; she walked out of one on public speaking.

All the girls at school wanted to talk about clothes and prom dates. Jerrie had plenty of friends, she says, but she had other things on her mind. She liked sports, for one thing—she came second in the state-wide women's golf championship. But all her spare time was spent at the airfield. She found a part-time job with a crop-dusting business, as "general flunky and grease monkey," but they let her make a few spraying runs, too. At the end of the year, she knew she didn't want to go back to college, and her parents gave in.

For the summer, she went back to the Sooner Queens. And she fell in love: with a war surplus Fairchild PT-23. She saw the plane for sale when the team made a swing through Denver, Colorado. The "PT" stands for primary trainer, a plane used for instruction. The maroon-and-yellow Fairchild had logged thousands of hours in the air—but it was in good shape nevertheless. And it was for sale, Jerrie's for just five hundred dollars.

The traveling softball player, of course, did not have five hundred dollars. So the Queens lent it to her, making her an indentured first baseman for the rest of the summer. When she struck out with the bases loaded and score tied in the last game of the season, she hung up her satin skirt—but she had the plane paid off. And she took the bus back to Denver, picked up her Fairchild and flew it home to Ponca City, Oklahoma, where her parents had settled.

Then she went looking for her first flying job. She found one, eventually, a job so boring that male pilots didn't want it: patrolling pipelines for an oil company. She flew low, sniffing for fumes, looking for telltale splotches on the earth. All that winter, 1952, she also went to ground school, determined to get licensed as a flight instructor. She even had a job waiting for her, at a flight school in Duncan, a small town in southern Oklahoma— just as soon as she turned twenty and could legally take the exam.

When she showed up in Duncan as a licensed instructor, she faced a class of leathery oil workers, veterans who "worked hard, played hard, cussed hard." They stared in disbelief as Jerrie began the first lesson.

"Lady," one of them finally said, "who's our teacher?"

"I'm the instructor."

"What? A *dame*?"

"But she ain't even a dame—she's just a kid."

Jerrie adopted as stern and professorial a demeanor as a young woman with freckles and blond curls could manage and began to lecture on the intricacies of meteorology. She was gruff and impersonal when flying, and she slowly won her students over. It was a fierce job: she earned two dollars an hour for flight time and nothing for the classroom hours; she flew sunrise to sunset seven days every week and earned no more than eighty-five dollars a week. She was ecstatic.

The flight school closed, but she soon found another job, this one with the airport in Oklahoma City where she had first learned to fly. Now she was a charter pilot, but it was a small operation, and she was recruited to wait tables in the airport restaurant at peak hours. Her passengers looked on bewildered when their waitress cleared their tables, took off her apron and climbed into the cockpit of their plane.

Then she discovered racing. By then, races were not the "hell-for-leather affairs of the thirties," Jerrie explains, when the gender of pilots was indiscernible beneath goggles and helmets and grease-spotted breeches. In 1953, women raced in skirts and heels, but they still raced flat out. Jerrie signed up first for a Sky Lady Derby, flying from Dallas, Texas, to Topeka, Kansas, and she placed third—winning $125 (including $25 as the youngest pilot in the field). She discovered she loved the challenge of racing solo, calculating the best speed and altitude for her plane.

So she signed up for the All-Women's Transcontinental Air Race (AWTAR), the most storied of all the women's races. Each year it drew a high-spirited but intensely competitive field of the best female pilots in the country. It was run on an elaborate handicapping system, based on size of craft and engine, so that even women in tiny planes stood a shot at winning. The only problem was getting planes: wealthy women flew their own, but women without that kind of money had to find sponsors, or someone who would lend them a plane, as Jerrie did. That year the race went from Santa Ana, California, to Tereboro, New Jersey. Jerrie made it over the mountains in New Mexico and over the desert in Arizona, running her fuel tanks almost dry but staying on course. Only in her last hour did she get lost, confused by the jumble of buildings and the heavy air traffic in New York—she had never flown in such an urban area. That last hour cost her, and she placed fourth, winning one hundred dollars. The prize money was put up by Jacqueline Cochran, although Jackie wasn't on hand at the finish line. For Jerrie, the real prize was the company of the other pilots who finished the race, women every bit as mad about flying as she was. Within days, she was making plans for the 1953 International Women's Air Race.

That race ended in Miami, and Jerrie came fourth. When she got to the finish line, she heard all the pilots talking about how many jobs there were in aviation in the city. She heard about a new airline advertising for DC-3 pilots willing to fly "for experience only." Jerrie figured that even a woman had a shot at a job that didn't pay—and she would love the chance to fly the slick twin-engine DC-3. Back home in Oklahoma, she sent off a telegram, and got word back that the company would consider her for an interview. She threw some clothes in her old Pontiac and drove straight through to Miami, eighteen hundred miles. But the airline owners hadn't realized the job applicant was a woman and when they saw her, they wouldn't consider her for even their nonpaying position. "We can't expect our passengers to fly with a girl copilot," the manager told her. "They're already scared of flying, and a girl in the cockpit will frighten them even more. You may have all the licenses and ratings in the world, and ten million hours of flying experience, but no airline passenger will ever fly with a woman in the cockpit." He suggested that if she really wanted to fly, she might try the stewardess training course down the hall.

Desperate for work, without even the money for gas to drive home again, Jerrie saw an ad for an apprentice airplane mechanic for Aerodex Inc., an aircraft company. Aerodex wouldn't give a girl a mechanic job, but they needed a clerk to type out work orders in the service department. This, at least, was a job *around* airplanes, if not flying them. For six months, Jerrie pushed paper. It wasn't much, but she would come in early to study the planes waiting for repair, and stand out by the runways on her lunch break watching the takeoffs and the landings.

And then one October morning she arrived at the office at seven, an hour before opening time, and found a surly, unshaven pilot waiting at the door, his plane parked at the ramp. She says she asked if she could assist him. "Where do you have to go to get a work order signed?" he snapped. It emerged that he was a ferry pilot, and the Peruvian air force was waiting for the plane he was transporting. His brakes had blown, and each day of delay was costing him a hundred-dollar penalty. Jerrie says she thought him insufferably rude—it was barely even light out and he was complaining about the service—but she signed Jack Ford's papers and off he went.

Midmorning, though, he was back: shaved, pressed, so tall and handsome he had every woman in the office craning her neck. And he wanted to buy the clerk a cup of coffee to apologize for barking at her. He was transformed in more than just appearance. He was charming, soft-spoken, asked if he could call her Jerrie. In the airport coffee shop he told her of the trouble he was having finding pilots for his company, Fleetway Inc. All their ferry jobs were to South America, and nobody wanted to take single-engine aircraft over the oceans and the Andes solo: his "big strong macho pilots" started making excuses when they saw the route.

Jerrie couldn't believe it: sitting across from her was a man who needed pilots. She choked on her coffee, trying to get the words out. "I'll fly your planes to Peru."

Jack thought he had misheard. She repeated the offer. And this is how she later recalled the next few minutes:

He began to chuckle. "Ha! A girl! A kid, yet. You some kind of student pilot? Forget it. I don't have time for wanna-be pilots."

Cursing her tied tongue, Jerrie reached into her wallet and laid her licenses on the table. Jack stopped laughing, but pointed out that she was working as a clerk in an office, not a pilot. "So?" she asked him, a little irritated.

"Just this: you're a woman and flying is a man's job. I'm not saying that women shouldn't fly—for fun or sport, if they have the time and the money." But women don't have the stamina or the temperament to fly as a career, he said, and few could hope to compete with men.

Jerrie was livid, and it gave her a rare eloquence. "Until recently, I *have* managed to support myself—if not luxuriously, at least adequately—in this so-called man's world of aviation!"

Jack acknowledged her thousands of hours in the air, but told her she still didn't understand. "Flying—as a career, that is—isn't a sometime thing. It's the whole works. A pilot is married to his job. The only home he's got is an airplane. He can't tie himself down. He has to be able to take off at a moment's notice and not have it matter when he gets back. He's got to be ready to go anywhere under any circumstances. He can't care about creature comforts. And the important thing is, he's got to *want* it that way. It's not just something he makes up his mind to. He couldn't live any other way if he tried. What woman can handle a deal like that?"

"I can think of one."

Jack and Jerrie were having for the first time a conversation they would have a hundred more times, a debate that would crystallize their future together.

He told her she would change her mind when she got a little older and found out that flying wasn't easy.

"Do you think I choose to fly because I thought it would be easy?" Jerrie asked him, almost disbelieving. "Do you think it's easy for me right now to spend my days glued to a desk filling out order forms, waiting for a chance to pilot a plane? You talk as though men have a monopoly on flying, not only commercially but emotionally as well!" She flew, she told him, because she couldn't *not* fly. She was as willing as Jack or anyone to live out of a flight bag and not know from one day to the next where she would be that night.

If that was true, he told her, she was one rare woman.

Again the normally reticent Jerrie erupted: it might come as a surprise to Jack, but there were hundreds of women like her, she said. "Not all of them make their living flying, but it isn't because they wouldn't like to. Many of them are married and have children. Probably every one of them has ties of some sort—a family, a dependent, someone she loves. They manage—not easily, perhaps, but as successfully as women in any other field."

She rose to leave the café, but he stopped her. "Jerrie—you put up a pretty good fight." She smiled, in spite of herself, and turned to remind him as she reached the door. "If you need a pilot . . ."

A week later her phone rang. It was Jack Ford, and he had a problem: "I've got a flock of T6s in Trenton, New Jersey, that have to go to Peru, pronto, and no pilots to fly them there. These guys won't touch anything with less than two engines and a rocking chair for a pilot's seat. I fired the lot of 'em." If Jerrie wasn't just talking before, if she meant what she said about doing any kind of flying, then he would give her a try.

"But fair warning. It's dirty, it's difficult and it's dangerous. Nothing glamorous about it. I doubt you can handle it."

The first trip was a blur: she had never flown formation and struggled to follow Jack. They landed in Cuba, then in Barbados, and Jerrie had her first taste of the Caribbean, its gardens and aquamarine sea so different from home in Oklahoma. In Jamaica, Jack gave her the blunt details of the flight to come: she had to fly 520 miles against the prevailing wind, with a fuel supply of four hours and fifteen minutes. The nearest stop, in Colombia, was four hours away—and everything else was shark-and-barracuda-infested water. "If you don't hit the coast right at Barranquilla right the first time, you have a fifteen-minute safety margin at best, and there's jungle on both sides. Be right or be wet."

Jerrie admits today that if she had been any older, had any more experience, she would have had the sense to be scared. She would have known why Jack could not get veteran male pilots to make the flight.

But she was young and blissfully innocent, and so she took off at dawn—and landed, just fine, four hours later in Colombia. At their next stop, in Cali, Jack hit a hole in the runway, damaged a wing and had to stay put waiting for spare parts. Jerrie offered to let him take her plane on, but he demurred. "It's your baby. You've brought it this far in good shape. You deliver it."

So on she went, on her first ferry job. She made it as far as Guayaquil, Ecuador: she had no sooner hit the runway than "what appeared to be the entire Ecuadorian army" charged the plane. They hauled her out, threw her down on the burning asphalt, one soldier jamming his boot in her neck. Before long she was in a jail cell, hands tied tight behind her, under heavy inter-rogation. Gradually, relying on fractured high-school Spanish, she pieced together the problem: Ecuador and Peru were having one of their not-infrequent skirmishes—in the middle of which she had landed in Ecuador in a Peruvian Air Force plane, equipped with bomb racks and .50-caliber machine guns.

"You come here to bomb Ecuador! To kill Ecuadorians! You are a spy! They dyed your hair and gave you a fake passport!" her interrogators screamed at her. Military and government officials trooped past her cell to get a look at the blond, 110-pound Peruvian commando bomber pilot. The days ticked by, and Jerrie imagined living out her life in an Ecuadorian military prison. She pictured her family, worried sick. She couldn't choke down the rancid food, but her Spanish improved rapidly. It took twelve days, but finally the United States Embassy managed to convince the Ecuadorians that the plane was the private property of a U.S. citizen until she delivered it, and they let her go. The army turned out again, this time to wave her off with big smiles. She landed in Lima, Peru, to a royal reception with the army's marching band: the young pilot who finally arrived with their detained fighter was a heroine.

It was an eventful first trip to South America, but it melted into a hundred others in the next year. Within six months, Jerrie says, she was in charge of the Latin American ferry route for Fleetway. She traveled with a parachute, a one-person life raft, emergency rations, a machete and a pistol in a shoulder holster. She flew twelve hours at a time over endless miles of jungle and landed at tiny rural airfields where the ground crews gaped at the *gringa* flying solo.

Flying a twin-engine amphibious PBY to Paraguay, she closed in on Asunción one night after almost twelve hours of flying, and the tower ordered her to land in the Paraguay River. When she touched down, government officials came out to meet her in a boat—to tell her that she must leave immediately for Buenos Aires. Exhausted, she refused: it was their plane now and they could do with it what they would, but she was going to bed. The men grew more agitated. A great man needed saving, they told her. She realized they wanted her to fly a rescue, and she wasn't getting mixed up in that. In the end, she agreed to wait until they found a military pilot and she ran him through the controls in the PBY. Then she went into town to find a bed; the pilot who replaced her took the plane on to pluck deposed dictator Juan Perón from Argentina.

The rebuilt T6s were still old planes, the route was dangerous, and Jerrie had dozens of near misses: engines cut out, propellers quit, and the Jamaica *Daily Gleaner* once ran her obituary when another pilot spotted a T6 in the ocean. One day in the summer of 1954, she and Jack were formation flying through a needle-thin pass in the Andes when the clouds and fog came in from nowhere: within seconds, Jerrie lost sight of Jack's plane and of the mountains that closed in on three sides. She says she took her hands off the controls, closed her eyes and gave the plane over to God. When she opened her eyes, she was in clear blue sky—and the plane had turned 180 degrees. Although Jerrie didn't know it then, that's the pilots' trick to get safely out of a fogged-in mountain pass: turn 180 degrees and fly back out the way you came.

The next disaster came a hundred miles off the coast of Jamaica: a prop seal blew on her engine, and oil began to pour out. She radioed Jack, who was flying behind her. With her engine pressure dropping by the minute, he began to give her instructions on how to ditch the plane in the sea: to stow all the gear in the cockpit so it didn't become a projectile when she crashed, to pull her raft out from under the seat and check the strings on her life vest. And, she says, he rather dramatically decided that he would ditch with her—because with her instruments out and her canopy smeared in oil, she couldn't calculate the best way down on her own.

She argued with him, shocked that he would ditch a perfectly sound airplane just because hers was going down.

But he just kept giving instructions: "Forget what the book says, slide your canopy all the way back and jam it with something. Or it'll slam shut on impact and you'll drown because you won't be able to get out. I'm with you all the way. Airplanes are expendable, good pilots are not."

Then, she says, he added hesitantly, "I didn't wait thirty-six years to lose the love of my life now."

He kept calling out instructions, but Jerrie was too dazed by his words to pay much attention. In the end, they stayed out of the sea: Jerrie managed to hold a glide into Montego Bay, and Jack talked her through a landing. When she climbed out of the cockpit, she was coated in engine oil and giddy; she says she and Jack embraced on the tarmac while emergency vehicles pulled up around them.

Jerrie Cobb makes Jack Ford sound like a hard man to resist. Devastatingly handsome (sort of a bigger, taller Clark Gable), he was charming, outgoing, witty, a bit of a rogue. A one-time movie stuntman, he had taken up flying, and when World War II began, he enlisted and flew bombers in the Eighth Army Air Corps in combat over Europe. He started Fleetway after VJ day, reckoning there were thousands of surplus aircraft and many countries that wanted to buy them; soon, he had one hundred pilots on his payroll—not that he did the office work himself. Jack kept flying. And Jerrie knew her competition for his affection was airplanes as much as it was other women.

She says her feelings for him had caught her quite off guard. He was, first, her teacher—he taught her how to fly the bulky T6, how to salute the army officers who met their planes, how to tie her company tie. Then he was a friend. And then, in feelings she did not like to admit to herself until the emergency above the Caribbean, something more: she knew all about his glamorous Hollywood life, and she never thought he would be interested in her. But Jerrie's calm spirit, and fearless flying, had moved him as the starlets never had.

By the end of 1954, Fleetway had her ferrying B-17s (the huge, four-engine Flying Fortresses) and making deliveries to France, Germany, India and Scotland. Jerrie says they had an international romance, spending a stolen day or two together in London, Paris or the Caribbean, but mostly relying on telegrams and transatlantic phone lines. Then, in the summer of 1955, she went to work as a test pilot at Fleetway's base in Burbank, California. The work was even more difficult than ferrying, she says, because the rebuilt DC-3s and PBYs were full of bugs, and

Jerrie had to fly them until she had found them all. She loved the
job, simply because it was flying. But sometime around then,
things went wrong with Jack. It's not clear what happened, for
Jerrie later told this part of the story a number of different ways.
Sometimes she says they were engaged, that he had proposed on
a beach in Jamaica. But when she quit ferrying, they started to
argue about his wanderlust, and it exacerbated the differences
between them: she wanted a church wedding and he wanted a
quick ceremony with a justice of the peace; he wanted a honey-
moon ferrying and she wanted to walk on the beach in Florida.
In one version of the story, she finally decided that it wasn't going
to work, and she told Jack it was over.

At other times, however, she said that they were together for
years before Jack was killed in an aircraft accident over the Pacific
in 1959. "Jack was a great guy but was overcome with jealousy at
times," she said recently. "I considered that a lack of trust in me
and an infringement on my independence. . . . But we could
never stay apart for long."

Whatever happened, it left her unhappy. She quit Fleetway
and went home to her parents in Ponca City, morose, keeping to
herself, stick thin, refusing even to go flying. Finally, Harvey and
Helena hatched a plan to cajole their daughter back to life:
Harvey arranged for a local oil company to sponsor her to fly
their twin-engine Piper Apache in the International Women's Air
Race, running that year from Hamilton, Ontario, to Havana,
Cuba. Jerrie didn't place in the race, after losing an hour circling
above another pilot's wrecked craft, but by the time she was
down over the finish line she was thinking about flying for a
living again.

Some things had not changed: there were still few jobs for
female pilots, and she sent off more than a hundred letters before
she was hired on as chief pilot, running flight operations for the
Executive Aircraft Company in Kansas City, Missouri. It was
round-the-clock flying work, and she was delighted to be earning

a paycheck again, but it didn't have the excitement of navigating the Andes or being pressed into rescue efforts for deposed dictators. And so Jerrie went looking for a new challenge: she wanted to set a world record. The handful of famous female pilots flying then—Jacqueline Cochran, Ruth Nichols—all had records to their names, and Jerrie wanted that distinction, too.

The problem, as she recalls it, was a bit like the old recipe for making rabbit stew. "First you get a rabbit." To set a record, she needed a new, maximum performance aircraft, and people weren't exactly lining up to turn those over to twenty-year-old female pilots who fancied they might like to break some records. But by now, there had been some press coverage of Jerrie's exploits, and her break came when the Oklahoma Semi-Centennial Exposition Committee decided it would make for good, nationwide publicity to have her break a record in an Oklahoma-built aircraft—a Rockwell Aero Commander.

She decided first to go for a nonstop distance record in a midsize aircraft, flying from Guatemala City to Oklahoma City; 1,504 miles. The Fédération Aéronautique Internationale in Paris, the world governing body for aeronautics, said the existing record was held by a Soviet Air Force officer, for a 1,237-mile flight. The idea of beating the Russians was, Jerrie says, "irresistible."

On the appointed day, she loaded extra fuel into the Commander and took off from Guatemala City. There were mountains, endless open ocean, tornadoes and a hailstorm along the route—but the worst part, she says, was trying to shimmy out of her flying suit and into stockings, dress and heels, while still flying the plane, as she neared the exhibition grounds. She landed, appropriately dressed, after eight hours and five minutes in the air, and she had her record.

Then she wanted another: three weeks later, she set out to break an altitude record in the Commander, this time at the opening of the exhibition. She planned to fly well above the plane's designated maximum of twenty-seven thousand feet—so high that she would need oxygen, and the temperature would be minus ten degrees Fahrenheit. It took her an hour and a half to get up there, pushing the red-and-white Commander. As she passed the five-mile mark, she found another world.

"I saw the bluest sky I'd ever known. I could barely breathe, and not from lack of oxygen. It was the stillness, the Godliness of it all. There was no horizon, no boundary, no limit to the ways one could go. I felt I could reach up to the sun or touch the stars that were hidden in its glow. I wanted to go on and on, up and up."

She pushed the plane to 30,361 feet and landed to great acclaim, with a world altitude record. But it turned out that one of the barographs, the small sealed instruments that record the altitude, had not functioned, and a week later she had to make the flight again. On July 5, 1957, she got to 30,560 feet, just short of six miles, 199 feet higher than her first flight. The barograph captured this record just fine.

Back on earth, however, she faced a familiar problem: record setting did not pay the bills, and she needed a job. Her old firm had "reorganized" her out of a position, and no other company was keen to hire her since she had made national headlines setting a record in an Aero Commander. In fact, it quickly became clear that Aero was her only hope of a job. The company had a new sales manager, Tom Harris, and while he admired Jerrie's ambition he didn't see how Aero could use a female pilot. Women might have been getting more jobs with distributors and dealers those days, but he didn't know of a single aircraft manufacturer in the country with a woman working as a company pilot. "This is a man's industry," he told her frankly. "With the exception of Olive Ann Beech [who ran Beechcraft after her husband and partner died in 1950], aircraft manufacturers' front offices are womanless. And I'm afraid it's going to continue that way."

"At least," Jerrie says, "he was honest."

And she was tenacious. She pitched him continually—a hundred ideas, she says—on how vital she was to Aero's future. He listened politely. He didn't hire her. She worked out a complex plan to fly around the world crossing the two poles, the first ever such trip (and making her the first woman to set foot on Antarctica), and Harris liked that one, but the company's engineers said the plane couldn't be counted on to fly in arctic temperatures.

Finally, at the end of 1958, she sold Harris on an idea and got herself a job: to set a world speed record in a Commander at the World Congress of Flight in Las Vegas the coming spring. She was after the speed record on a two-thousand-kilometer closed course (twelve hundred miles), another record held by a Soviet pilot. The company stripped the plane down, lightening it by removing everything but the paint. Shortly after she left the ground on record day, her radio quit; her flare gun (so she could be identified from the ground as she passed over checkpoints) jammed, suggesting it might go off at any moment into the fuel tanks; her ADF (automatic direction finder) went out, so she had to navigate by dead reckoning; she was slowed by heavy clouds and had to pour extra fuel into the tanks from cans in the cabin while she flew. After five hours of this, she got her record—by twenty-six seconds.

And she got a permanent job at Aero. Harris wanted her to keep right on attracting this kind of attention for the company. She flew at air shows and conventions all the next year. Aero was pleased, and recognition came from outside the company as well: she was the Woman of the Year in Aviation in 1958, and the next year she was honored by her peers as the Pilot of the Year chosen by the National Pilots Association.

She went to Paris that year to fly at the huge biennial Salon Aéronautique Internationale. She was the only woman flying in the show, and so the officials gallantly replaced her green armband reading *pilote* with one in lavender. She zoomed the

Commander over spectators with both engines at full throttle, and then, to show how reliable the plane was, she did her trick of deliberately shutting down an engine. She buzzed the crowd at fifty feet, and "landed her on a *sou.*" On her last night came a surprise: a banquet where the FAI presented her with its Gold Wings. She was the first woman to wear them.

INSTANT HEROES

Courtesy of the National Aeornautics and Space Administration

The Mercury 7 in 1959. Back, l to r: Alan Shepard,
Virgil "Gus" Grissom, Gordon Cooper. Front, l to r: Walter Schirra,
Donald "Deke" Slayton, John Glenn, Scott Carpenter.

The men were uncomfortable, standing around in the civilian clothes they had been ordered to wear. And they were more than a little confused about what they were doing there. Each of the thirty-five United States military test pilots had received a mysterious telegram marked "Top Secret," and it ordered them to report here, a government meeting room on a chilly day in early February 1959.

Then a couple of high-level bureaucrats arrived and got right to the point. The brand-new National Aeronautics and Space Administration was looking for volunteers. They wanted pilots who would agree to be strapped into a small metal capsule on the top of a rocket and shot into the airless void of space.

They wanted astronauts.

The word—Greek for "star voyager"—was new to the men in the room. And it was an almost unbelievable idea. Everybody knew there was a contest to put a man into space—and that the United States was losing it. The Soviets had three satellites in orbit around the earth, and the United States had yet to get one up. But now NASA was looking for volunteers who were ready to climb up to the top of one of those unreliable rockets and fly into the complete unknown.

All the men at that meeting were military test pilots: those were the ranks from which the space agency intended to draw its first astronauts. But that had not always been the plan. NASA started off with a wild, almost comical list of places where it might find a few good men. An astronaut was going to have to be brave, obviously, so NASA thought about where to find brave people—or at least people who sought out danger. The first list included mountain climbers, sky divers, even bullfighters. Then they thought about what an astronaut was facing, besides simply personal peril, and they put polar explorers and deep-sea divers on the list—people who had experience in isolated and hostile environments.

But NASA was in the middle of a race, with a public clamoring for achievements, and the agency did not have time to wade through the ranks of daredevils and adventurers, weeding out what one engineer called "crackpots." They thought about scientists (physicists, astronomers, meteorologists), but there was another consideration: the first plans for the mission called for the capsule to be controlled from the ground, but no one knew how the systems would hold up in a space flight. Robert Gilruth and the men of his Space Task Group started to think that they better have somebody in the craft who knew something about flying. The person who went into space was going to have to be able to monitor the systems functions, evaluate them and report back to earth. Pilots: they needed pilots.

Many of NASA's new engineers had come from the civilian aircraft industry, and they knew what kind of pilots were required on a project like this. Test pilots, guys who had experience with new and unknown ships, who could be part of the design process—and who had nerves of steel. "Test pilots," Gilruth later told a historian, "are used to altitude, the need for oxygen, bends and acceleration. They are used to high discipline and to taking risks . . . the test pilots would be best because they also had the technical knowledge to understand the ins and outs of the space capsule and the rockets and navigation."

So NASA started to map out a plan for screening the country's civilian test pilots: the men running Project Mercury were sure they would have to recruit from civilian ranks, given President Eisenhower's emphasis on keeping the space program separate from the military. But at a meeting with the president on December 22, 1958, NASA's first administrator, Keith Glennan, raised the subject of military pilots. Eisenhower liked the idea: military men were already cleared for classified projects, the test pilots were the elite of the military flyers, and they were already on the payroll. He cleared NASA to confine its search to the ranks of military pilots; the armed forces could second the men to duty with the civilian space agency. "The President agreed on getting the men from the military services, so that they would have had their disciplinary training behind them," reads a summary of the meeting.

Glennan and his men were relieved: this would speed the selection process considerably. The Space Task Group drew up a list of qualifications for these pilots: a university degree in the physical sciences or engineering; a minimum of fifteen hundred hours of flight time, including jet experience; an age of less than forty years; optimal physical condition, with "physical and psychological attributes suited for spaceflight"; and height of less than five feet eleven inches and weight of less than 180 pounds (because the pilots would have to fit in the space capsule, and every extra pound would be one more for the rocket to lift).

The list was sent out to all branches of the service, and by late January 1959 NASA had 108 names. They invited the men to Washington in three groups; they looked them over, sent the too tall or too heavy ones home (for not all the personnel files were accurate), and told the others the speculation in the newspapers was true. They wanted volunteers for suborbital and orbital flight. The program, unlike the Soviets', would be public, but no one would know if the men chose *not* to volunteer; no note would be made in their military files. NASA knew some ambitious pilots would not want to leave their jobs for an uncertain civilian project and that others were not going to be interested in consigning their lives to an agency that could not get a rocket into the air in one piece. But far more men than they anticipated said yes—the men were, after all, pilots, and if there is one thing every pilot wants it is to go higher and faster than he or she has gone before. By the time NASA had reviewed the first two groups, they had thirty-two candidates, which seemed like plenty, so the last group never even got to Washington.

NASA told the pool of thirty-two men that before they could officially volunteer, they needed to pass some tests. Brig. Gen. Donald Flickinger, the expert in aeromedical research who had helped NASA make its first assessment of whether a human could survive the trip into space, was part of those first discussions about qualifications. And he wanted to see that these volunteers had a thorough medical exam. Sure, they had to be in top condition to fly for the military. But the demands of spaceflight would be enormous: the G-forces, the pressure drops, the weightlessness. A tiny undetected problem in a heart valve, for example, could be instantly fatal when a pilot was put under pressure six times the force of gravity. And so, at Flickinger's recommendation, the thirty-two candidates were to be given a thorough medical screening. But where to do it? It had to be secret, for one thing. All the obvious hospitals for this kind of work were military establishments, but NASA was trying to keep this a civilian operation.

Flickinger suggested the Lovelace Clinic in Albuquerque, New Mexico—an operation run by his friend Randolph Lovelace II, who chaired NASA's Life Sciences Committee. The clinic was established by Lovelace's namesake uncle, a doctor who first went west to treat his own tuberculosis in 1922. He passed the mantle to his nephew in 1946. The younger Lovelace, a dark-eyed charismatic man known as Randy, had trained at the Mayo Clinic and was a widely respected doctor. He was also a pilot, with a fascination with all things to do with flight. He had served as a flight surgeon and colonel in the air force and pioneered aviation medicine in the United States. He did groundbreaking research into the effects of aeronautics on the human body; he helped invent the oxygen mask, and then in 1943 made a land-mark parachute jump (his first ever) from a record forty thou-sand feet, holding a jar of oxygen to prove that portable oxygen could allow pilots to fly to new heights. Randy created the Lovelace Foundation in 1946 to do research and education in support of the clinic and set up an innovative department of aerospace medicine.

The Lovelace Clinic was a logical place to screen the test pilots. Lovelace himself was intimately involved in the emerging aero-space industry, and for the previous ten years the foundation had been extensively involved in clinical examination of airline and industry pilots. In 1955, the clinic was awarded a top secret contract to select and monitor the pilots who would fly the U2 spy plane missions, and its professional work had won Randy points in Washington. Dr. Lovelace had also assigned a lab to develop a test protocol for space pilots and received a government grant in 1958 to pay for it. NASA had asked him to act as chair of its Life Sciences Committee the year before—he knew what NASA needed in its space pilots—and his aerospace medicine department was headed by a retired air force general, Albert Schwichtenberg, who would know what to look for in these fliers. The clinic was a civilian institution, and shipping the men out to Albuquerque might help to keep the secret. Lovelace it was.

The astronaut candidates were divided into groups of six or seven, and the first group arrived in New Mexico in February 1959, once again ill at ease in civilian clothes and trying to remember the aliases they were assigned to keep things secret. In 1959, no one had ever traveled beyond the pull of gravity, and nobody knew what being in space would do to the human body: would the heart cease to beat and the control of the other muscles fall away? Would eyeballs lose their shape, perhaps drift out of sockets? Would food stick in the throat, refusing to be swallowed? The doctors at Lovelace had no idea, and so they did every test they could think of. They tried to shake the men's bones with blasts of sound, sat them under pulsing strobe lights, induced vertigo, plunged them from light to dark and counted how long it took their eyes to focus again. They analyzed every bodily fluid they could wring out of the men, baked them in saunas and pushed them to the point of exhaustion.

The staff at the foundation observed the order of secrecy, although Lovelace himself later recalled "a special electricity" in the air while the astronaut candidates were being screened. But the nurses and doctors paid close attention to their subjects: NASA wanted men who saw the tests as a challenge, not an ordeal. It was noted who was jumpy or abrasive, and a little flag was put beside the names of those who kept their heads regardless of what the doctors did to them.

Only one man was weeded out at Lovelace: the rest were ruled without flaw. "We were used to seeing all different kinds of human beings," says Donald Kilgore, a clinic doctor involved in the screening. "But these men were intellectually, physically and psychologically extraordinary. We were dealing with something we had never seen before." The thirty-one surviving candidates were directed to Wright-Patterson Air Force Base in Dayton, Ohio, for psychological, endurance, altitude and isolation testing. It was another grueling ordeal: they were sent to a simulated height of sixty-five thousand feet without oxygen or pressure suits, left in dark rooms for three hours and then subjected to a barrage of questions: "Who am I?" over and over, for example, or "What do you see here?" (on a blank sheet of paper).

Finally a board made up of senior NASA engineers, flight surgeons, psychologists and psychiatrists made the selection. They were meant to winnow the list down to six, but they couldn't get past seven, and in the end they gave Robert Gilruth seven names.

With rockets blowing up all over the place, NASA needed some good publicity, and on April 9, 1959, it introduced the word astronaut—and the seven men to whom it gave the title— to a hungry public. But nobody in NASA or the government predicted the wave of national fascination that greeted these men who were ready to leave earth.

The press conference was jammed with reporters, and the usually jaded group actually applauded when Keith Glennan introduced the seven men at the table. Glennan outlined the astronaut selection procedure, emphasizing the large pool from which this team was drawn. He introduced Randy Lovelace, the doctor who had supervised the medical screening, and the media seized on the details of the examinations, breathlessly describing the ordeal.

The reporters hustled the NASA types through the technical details of the Mercury program, because they wanted to get to the men. They wanted to know everything about them. Did they go to church? What did their wives think of this? Weren't they afraid?

There were three air force pilots: the sharply intelligent Deke Slayton, a relentless racer called Gordon Cooper and a reticent loner named Virgil "Gus" Grissom. There were three navy pilots: the joker named Walter Schirra, Alan Shepard, the big-picture guy, and the dreamer, Scott Carpenter. Plus one marine, the straight arrow, John Glenn. The reporters could tell just by looking at them—spines ramrod straight, hair buzzed almost to their scalps, reactions like lightning—that these men were impervious to fear. Asked which of them would be the first in space, each of the seven immediately raised a hand. Glenn raised both hands. The astronauts were clearly stunned by the force of the media attention that was suddenly trained upon them, and most of them were more than usually reserved—except for John Glenn, whose skill with media quickly became apparent. They were nonetheless irresistible, these men, in their laconic, casual bravery.

Lined up behind the table, they were a remarkably homogenous group. All were white, Protestant men from small towns; four were named for their fathers; three were graduates from military colleges; all were married and had children. This, America was told, was what an astronaut looked like.

The seven were instant heroes. Their families were besieged by reporters, and in acres of media coverage they were held up as the embodiment of American virtue: decorated war veterans, fearless pilots, husbands, fathers, churchgoers, devoted to their country and prepared to risk their lives for its greater glory. The astronauts reduced the space race and the competition with the Soviets to the level of single combatants: these were America's warriors, and the country pinned its hopes on seven pairs of broad shoulders.

The United States needed heroes. The Soviets were still leading the race, and it seemed as if every few months there was another triumph. In September 1959, the Soviets launched *Lunik 2* from the end of a rocket and the small sphere hit the moon. In October, they shot *Lunik 3* around the moon and past it. The capsule sent back astounding photographs, the first ever taken of the dark side of the moon.

America's astronauts reported for duty at the Langley Research Center in Hampton, Virginia, where NASA had established its astronaut training facility, and very quickly established a culture of unadulterated machismo. They raced on the long country roads around the space center in their signature Corvettes; they played elaborate practical jokes on one another, and they caroused, creating a "wild boy" ethos that would endure for twenty years. The men were womanizers, all but John Glenn, and soon there were women around who claimed to have bedded six of the seven.

Now NASA had its star voyagers, but it did not have a craft to get them to the stars. The plan called for the rocket to carry the capsule to the edge of the atmosphere, where the arc of flight would propel it through the atmosphere and into orbit around the earth. The pod would be equipped with small retro-rockets that would push it down far enough for the force of gravity to pull it back for a splash down in the ocean.

The rockets were still a problem: they were exploding on the platform or going awry a few minutes after launch. And NASA's engineers were struggling with the design of the capsule. It had to be small—really small—because the Atlas rocket could launch a maximum payload of twenty-seven hundred pounds. The Space Task Group's first priority was this orbital vehicle, one that would protect a human passenger through all phases of a space-flight: launch, weightlessness above the atmosphere, reentry deceleration with its furnacelike heat, and descent to parachute deployment at about ten thousand feet. The capsule had to keep its occupant alive in the wild temperature extremes of space (two hundred degrees Fahrenheit above in sunlight and two hundred below in shadow), and then the fiery reentry (where they believed the heat might reach four thousand degrees Fahrenheit). It had to protect the astronaut from the intense radiation, the huge aerodynamic stress and the forces of massive acceleration. The designers had decided on a cone-shaped pod made of titanium, the curved wider end of which would be covered with a heat shield made of fiberglass and resin composite that would burn away during reentry.

The Mercury capsule, when they finally built one, was nine feet five inches high and barely six feet two inches across at the widest point—because that was the width of the rocket that would launch it. The astronaut would have to slide in on his back between the seat and the instrument panel. Packed in around his contoured seat were the systems to keep him alive (water and oxygen), the radio, the impact bag, the mechanical and electrical systems and their backups—before long, the capsule's weight had crept up to more than twenty-seven hundred pounds, not even counting the 180-pound astronaut.

Meanwhile the Space Task Group was grappling with a crucial question: would the man in the Mercury capsule be a pilot or a passenger? The original design gave the pilot virtually no control over any of the systems: he would, in effect, be lobbed up and wait to fall back down. McDonnell Aircraft Corporation in St. Louis won the contract to build the capsule in 1959, and they had initially proposed a craft whose primary flight control systems were entirely automatic. Rumors about the pilot as payload had spread in test pilot circles, leading Chuck Yeager and the guys out at Edwards Air Force Base who were testing the transonic X-1 aircraft—very much a ship controlled by its pilot—to dub the astronauts "Spam in a can."

But NASA's engineers began to argue that if something were to go wrong with that automatic system, the pilots should have the ability to take over. And once the Mercury 7 were involved in the process, they added angry voices: they intended to fly the capsule just as they had their jets. They had experience under great stress and with what pilots call G-loads, the pressure of forces many times greater than gravity, which come with acceleration or sharp banking maneuvers. They had started doing some testing during brief moments of weightlessness when planes were in steep dives, and they were confident they would still be able to fly in space. They made technical recommendations: for the rearrangement of the control panel, an escape hatch they could open from the inside and a window. And they pushed for a conceptual shift—that the astronaut was not just there to survive the trip, but also to control at least some of it.

But in truth, the astronaut remained largely a passenger. When the capsule design was unveiled in the autumn of 1959, the astronauts had their window and their escape hatch. And while the attitude thrusters (which turned the capsule) and braking rockets (which would slow the capsule down to take it out of orbit) had an emergency override system, they would primarily be controlled by engineers on the ground. The astronaut could fire the thrusters to change the capsule's roll, yaw or pitch (its three axes), but he could not alter the trajectory or the speed at which he traveled. He could fire the retro-rockets in an emergency (but only once—and if he was pointed in the wrong direction, he would go into higher orbit with no means of coming home). He wasn't a straightforward passenger, but he sure wasn't a pilot—not that you heard that assessment around Langley.

Work progressed on the capsule, and the astronauts trained in everything from desert survival (lest they come down somewhere unplanned) to astronomy (so they could navigate by the stars). But there were significant obstacles standing between the men and space. In Washington, there was by no means consensus on the urgent need for a staffed spaceflight: Eisenhower's advisers were still not convinced it would work, and they were sure it was going to cost too much. And the astronauts had to deal with a stern team of flight surgeons. The doctors put the men through repeated rounds on a centrifuge that simulated eight or more G-loads, and they shot them up in a parabolic flight in a C-135 jet that produced a bit less than a minute of weightlessness, but none of it was enough to convince them that space travel was going to be safe for humans.

The first Mercury flights, they insisted, were going to have to be made by monkeys. The suborbital flights of two chimpanzees, Ham and Enos, went fine, but the doctors were not certain. They wanted more tests.

While NASA was struggling with the science, there was also a political battle under way. The United States was not, in fact, doing that badly in the space race: in 1959, NASA had launched eleven satellites that made major scientific discoveries about solar flares and radiation, the first communications satellite and several probes that passed by the moon. The Soviets, in contrast, launched only three satellites.

But it didn't matter: the Soviets had the firsts. And while the average Americans weren't too excited about solar flares, they certainly understood the goals that Nikita Khrushchev was setting for his space program. In August 1960, the Soviets sent up two dogs, Belka and Strelka, who orbited the earth several times before returning, alive and well, and proving for the first time that a living creature could go into the weightlessness of space and survive reentry. It was obvious the Soviets were closing in on the goal of sending a human.

It was an election year, 1960, and space figured large in the contest. John F. Kennedy, the Democratic challenger, hammered his Republican opponent, Richard Nixon, on the issue, alleging that under Eisenhower's watch, a perilous "space gap" had been allowed to open. He warned of Soviet superiority in missiles and their delivery. And he spoke of a global struggle in which the uncommitted nations of the Third World would soon choose between the East and the West, saying the Soviet Union was winning the race for hearts and minds. He promised that his administration would see the "American giant" stir once more. Kennedy won, in what was then one of the country's tightest election races.

But while the space race was a major plank in Kennedy's election platform, in truth the subject was not of great interest to him. Once he was in office, he turned over the portfolio to his vice president, Lyndon Johnson, the only member of his cabinet who knew much about it. Johnson, for his part, had sensed the public interest in the space race early on and, as an adroit politician, had fashioned a position as a supporter of bold American action. Kennedy saw it as a good way to keep Johnson occupied and away from the social policy matters of his "new frontier."

Meanwhile the new president appointed Jerome Weisner, a professor at the Massachusetts Institute of Technology, as his science adviser. Weisner had been highly critical of NASA during the election, and he was a major opponent of staffed spaceflight, saying it would be too costly and too dangerous, and that the United States was better off probing the military uses of satellites. He urged Kennedy to dissociate himself from Mercury.

But on April 12, 1961, something happened that forced Kennedy to pay close attention: the Soviets announced that a Russian named Yuri Gagarin was orbiting the earth. Launched in a capsule called *Vostok* ("East"), he traveled at seventeen thousand miles an hour, 203 miles above sea level. He orbited the earth once, passing from day to night and back again, a trip that took him 108 minutes. Gagarin, the twenty-seven-year-old son of peasant farmers, was a major in the Soviet Air Force. He was the first person to see the spines of mountains and twists of rivers from above, the first to discern the delicate blue halo around the earth, and to see the endless black reach of space. On his return to earth, Soviet premier Nikita Khrushchev greeted him with the words "You have made yourself immortal because you are the first man to penetrate space."

"Now let the other countries try to catch us," Gagarin replied.

It was Sputnik all over again: the United States had been humiliated, beaten, and the Soviets had shown themselves to have a new and threatening technology. The whole world was heralding their achievement. Kennedy tried to downplay Gagarin's flight, saying the United States would "go into other areas where we can be first." But Congress was demanding inquiries and reviews—and Kennedy already had a crisis to worry about, for U.S.-backed Cuban forces were anchored off the Bay of Pigs.

Two days later he gathered his closest advisers and the administration's experts on space. "Is there any place we can catch them?" the young president demanded impatiently. "What can we do? Can we go around the moon before them? Can we put a man on the moon before them?" NASA's Hugh Dryden and newly appointed administrator James Webb suggested a crash program, like the Manhattan Project to build the atomic bomb, that might beat the Soviets to the moon. But Kennedy's budget director, David Bell, warned of the cost of such an effort. The president ordered the group to put together more information on projects that might beat the Soviets. "There's nothing more important," he said as he left the meeting.

NASA's designers knew a moon mission was one area where they might beat the Russians. Bob Gilruth met with the president, and told him, "You've got to pick a job that's so difficult, so new, that they [the Soviets] will have to start from scratch." If both countries had to start from zero, he said, the United States could probably win.

Meanwhile Gagarin's flight had silenced the doubters, the doctors who had insisted on more flights with monkeys—or at least the Soviet first had given the astronauts and their backers the political force to overrule the flight surgeons.

On May 5, 1961, American pride was salved when Alan Shepard was successfully launched in Mercury capsule number seven, on Redstone rocket number seven. Shepard had given his craft a name, too: *Freedom 7,* for the seven astronauts. Forty-five million Americans, an astonishing number for the time, leaned close to grainy black-and-white television screens to watch the slender Redstone shoot into the air on a cushion of fire. The capsule came away from the rocket just as planned, and Shepard flew 116 miles high. He was well below the height needed to orbit, but he was weightless for about five minutes. And he felt fine: he could see, he could radio back to Cape Canaveral, he could monitor the systems. As the capsule began to fall back, the parachutes opened and *Freedom 7* splashed down three hundred miles off the Florida coast. Within minutes a helicopter had lifted the spacecraft onto an aircraft carrier, and Shepard stepped out, grinning broadly.

At last the United States had its hero. Thousands turned out to see Shepard ride in a parade down Pennsylvania Avenue, he was received at the White House, he was on the cover of every newspaper and magazine. Now the space race had the heart and imagination of every American.

Kennedy knew he had to capitalize on that energy. Three weeks after Shepard's flight, on May 25, 1961, the president addressed Congress. He spoke passionately about the worldwide struggle between "liberty" and Communism. He addressed the difficult social and economic problems of the developing world and the military challenge presented by Soviet expansionism. Then, two-thirds of the way into his speech, he turned to the space race.

"If we are going to win the battle that is going on around the world between freedom and tyranny, if we are going to win the battle for men's minds, the dramatic achievements in space which occurred in recent weeks should have made clear to us all, as did the Sputnik in 1957, the impact of this adventure on the minds of men everywhere who are attempting to make a determination of which road they should take."

Kennedy's voice, strong and controlled, took on a new urgency as he got to the climax of his speech, words so fantastic that his audience could barely conceive of the plan he described.

"I believe that this nation should commit itself to achieving the goal, before this decade is out, of landing a man on the moon and returning him safely to the earth. No single space project in this period will be more exciting or more impressive to mankind, or more important for the long-range exploration of space; and none will be so difficult or expensive to accomplish."

Unspoken, of course, was one other word: *first.* Landing a man on the moon, first. The Soviets had the first satellite and the first man in space and they would go on to have any number of firsts. But with Kennedy's public pledge, the space race suddenly had a finish line. The Americans had tried to hit the moon with a small probe three times, and the Soviets had quietly tried four times—they succeeded with *Luna 2*, in 1959. But now it was out in the open. The broad ideological and political contests between two rival world powers had been acknowledged, and the prize hung on the evening horizon for the winner.

It is hard to recall now, when Neil Armstrong's first words as he stepped on to the lunar surface are some of the best known in the world. But when Kennedy spoke to Congress in 1961, his dream of a moon landing looked impossibly far off. Robert Gilruth marveled at it years later, saying that if the president had been any older, any wiser, he would never have taken the risk of committing to going at all, let alone within a decade. When Kennedy made the pledge, the United States space program had to its credit fewer than fifteen full minutes in space.

"Kennedy's 1961 challenge can only be fully appreciated if we remember that 23 days prior to Shepard's flight the Soviet Union put Yuri Gagarin in Earth orbit aboard a Vostok spacecraft," wrote Buzz Aldrin, the second man on the moon, in his memoir *Men from Earth.* "The Russians were beating us, hands down. They had huge leads in every element of manned spaceflight: propulsion, life support, and flight control. For Kennedy to dare the Soviets to a moon race in 1961 remains one of the classic examples of chutzpah in modern history."

The space agency adopted the goal enthusiastically. "The manned lunar landing . . . is the largest single effort within

NASA, constituting three-fourths of our budget, and is being executed with the utmost urgency," administrator James Webb wrote in an assessment memo to Kennedy on November 30, 1962. When Kennedy was assassinated a year later, the goal became a covenant. Webb constantly reminded the engineers and technicians of the ticking clock, of the need to honor their fallen president by meeting his goal of a moon landing within a decade, and the agency became increasingly streamlined, focused on this single objective.

The whole world heard Kennedy's pledge before Congress that warm May day in 1961. But thirteen women took it very much to heart.

UNIT ONE, FEMALE

Jerrie Cobb at the controls of the MASTIF at a NASA test center, 1960.

After that fateful meeting on the Florida beach in September, Jerrie Cobb could not get thoughts of space out of her head. She would lie in the backyard at night and look at the stars and imagine what it would be like to be flying up there. She was tantalized by the thought that there might be a way for her to get there, and she was eager to start. She waited for a call from General Flickinger or Dr. Lovelace.

Flickinger, an air force general and flight surgeon, was best known for a series of jumps he made in the Pacific theater in World War II, when he was parachuted in to tend to survivors from plane crashes and then lead them out to safety. In 1951, his friend Randy Lovelace recommended him for the job of chief of Human Factors (official speak for pilots) in the Air Research and Development Command (ARDC), the experimental branch of the air force. "Flick," as the doctor was known, was an innovator in aerospace medicine, and he rose rapidly through the ranks at ARDC. He was particularly interested in the emerging field of space medicine and how his human factors were going to survive in this new environment. He was also a big supporter of NASA. When the air force lost the fight to lead America's space program, Flickinger was one of the few "men in blue" who advocated total cooperation with the new agency. This in turn led to appointments on advisory boards within NASA. He was running the show in bioastronautics at ARDC by 1959, and he and Lovelace had together developed the idea of testing women, a logical step in the study of human survival in space.

The United States knew the Russians were close to launching a human, but NASA designers could not come up with a capsule big enough to hold a pilot and still light enough to be boosted by the best rockets the air force or the navy could produce. And nobody knew what it was going to be like in space, but they were sure it was going to be tough. Lovelace and Flickinger suspected that female pilots would be smaller, lighter, use less oxygen, less food and less water, so they would be far easier to launch. Studies had proven that women were more tolerant of pain, heat, cold and isolation. Certainly they did not have the same degree of physical strength as men, but then strength was not a job requirement for a pilot who was going to be strapped into a Mercury capsule. Women might be the answers to all of America's astronaut problems.

Discovering Jerrie Cobb on a Miami beach was just the spur they needed. Her pilot ratings checked out with the records of the Civilian Aeronautics Authority (the precursor to the Federal Aviation Authority), and so did those of the women she suggested. Flickinger and Lovelace gathered eight more names from their own flying sources and were set to begin testing. Jerrie was itchy with anticipation.

And then in November 1959, ARDC brass quashed what Flickinger called his "girl astronaut program." Jerrie could not know it, but the abrupt reversal was a grim harbinger of problems that lay ahead. For now, she was startled, and she wrote to Flickinger asking what had happened. They hadn't even started, so what could the objections possibly be? On December 7, 1959, he replied: "please realize that I am even sorrier than you on the unfavorable turn of events in my original plans. The unfortunate 'Nichols' release did much to 'turn the tide' against Air Force Medical Sponsorship of the program, and to this day I cannot find out the individual responsible for approving the release."

The infamous Nichols release: it doesn't survive, but one can guess what it said. In the autumn of 1959, Ruth Rowland Nichols went to the air force's Wright Air Development Center in Dayton, Ohio, and underwent a series of astronaut tests. (After NASA's creation, the air force did not get out of the space game entirely, and researchers at Wright were considering the defense applications of launching humans.) Ruth Nichols was fifty-eight, and she was one of the great female pilots, a trailblazer from the earliest days of flying. Born in 1901, she was a "society girl," as the papers called her, who learned to fly as a student at Wellesley College in 1923. Six years later she set a record as the first woman to land a plane in all forty-eight states. After the historic Lindbergh flight, she set out to be the first woman to cross the Atlantic solo—it was Ruth who smashed five vertebrae crashing into a field in New Brunswick; Amelia Earhart had made the flight by the time she recovered. Ruth flew in the first Powder Puff Derby in 1929, and she was one of the first two women, with Jackie Cochran, to enter the legendary Bendix race in 1933.

She kept up a glamour girl image, but like Earhart she also wrote widely about the safety and promise of aviation. In 1940, Ruth, who was a devout Quaker, started an organization called Relief Wings to transport humanitarian assistance to civilians affected by war and to use airplanes as ambulances; during World War II she merged Relief Wings with the Civil Air Patrol.

Ruth had air force connections through her brother, and in 1958 she set a women's record by flying an air force TF102-A jet faster than one thousand miles an hour at fifty-one thousand feet at Suffolk County Air Force Base in Long Island, New York. It may have been through those connections that she was invited to do some astronaut tests. There is no surviving record in air force archives to explain how it came about, and Flickinger made no further mention of it. Ruth killed herself less than a year later. But she definitely went to Dayton and took part in isolation, centrifuge and weightlessness experiments. She did well—and she urged the air force scientists to incorporate women in their spaceflight plans. "They thought of this with horror, and they said under no circumstances," Ruth later recalled to an oral historian. The scientists at Wright told her they "knew nothing about a woman, physiologically, which I thought was an extraordinary statement. . . . I suggested a crash program to find out how a female reacted." Women are tough, Ruth argued—their bodies were "meant to withstand a crisis in childbirth." And a woman was also "more passive than a man, and could therefore endure long isolations. From every viewpoint, she could hold her own in a space situation and be of tremendous service."

The air force scientists, apparently, did not agree. Someone made the Nichols tests public, and the publicity was enough to scare off ARDC. The differences between men and women had rarely been more sharply defined in American society than they were in this postwar period. Women were defined by a domestic role, as wives and mothers and consumers whose lives in new suburban tract houses embodied the American dream. Women's moves into the war-era labor force, and into the military services, had reversed by the early 1950s, and the deepening Cold War was a strictly male battleground. The air force could only open itself up to condemnation by involving a woman in its most innovative defense program: testing Ruth Nichols had freak value at best; the underlying implication was of weakness, the suggestion that Wright couldn't find a way to make its most advanced technology work with men.

"The concensus [sic] of opinion . . . was that there was too little to learn of value to Air Force Medical interests and too big a chance of adverse publicity to warrant continuation of the project," Flickinger wrote to Lovelace in late December. One of the major objections from researchers, he explained, was that the air force could not afford the price of remodeling the partial pressure suits (tight coveralls that put pressure on a pilot's torso, upper legs and arms to keep blood flow to the head during maneuvers that pulled against gravity) for female bodies. "Since there was such great unanimity of opposition I did not see fit to overrule it and do not plan on re-opening the issue with anyone at [the School of Aviation Medicine] or at Air Force level."

And so Flickinger reluctantly turned his "girl astronaut" file over to Lovelace and his private institution. "I continue to have a keen personal interest in it and believe it should be done on as scientifically sound a basis as possible, " he wrote to Lovelace. "I feel (by instinct perhaps) that if carefully done with a large enough series, there would be some interesting differences between male and female responses noted."

Lovelace, too, was intensely curious about this question of women and their capacity for endurance. Randy Lovelace and his wife, Mary, had five children—but the first two, boys, died of polio within days of each other in 1946. That left Lovelace with three daughters. Like their mother, they were hardy girls. They hunted, fished and hiked with their father in the mountains outside Albuquerque. And then, of course, Jackie Cochran was one of his closest friends. Lovelace was used to tough, capable women who did the things men did. He had followed Jackie's experience with the WASP closely, and the limited research from that program hinting that women were in fact hardier than men intrigued him—Jackie herself certainly bore out the idea.

Lovelace was not a social reformer, seeking to alter the position of women in society, not at all. But he was a curious researcher who did not think politics should get in the way of genuine scientific inquiry. "Randy was a futurist; he was always one hundred years ahead of everyone else, " says Donald Kilgore, who was then an otolaryngologist with the clinic and who knew Lovelace well. Kilgore says Lovelace was largely unconcerned by contemporary ideas of gender roles and simply saw in women a potential solution to a grave national problem. Kilgore notes that the pioneering doctor was likely also motivated by his personal curiosity and his fondness for assuming a leadership role. *He* had no interfering bureaucrats to deal with, so he took Flickinger's files, talked to Jerrie about the list of women to examine and arranged to start the tests. Just before Christmas 1959, Jerrie got a letter from the clinic: finally, things were starting to happen. She was told to report to the clinic in New Mexico in February. In the meantime, there was advice: "start training." She was to run and swim and cycle and get plenty of sleep.

Jerrie didn't know how long the tests were going to take, but she knew she needed time off—from an already shorthanded aviation company where her boss regularly muttered, "My job does not include philanthropy." Tom Harris listened to Jerrie's request a little stunned. The guys at Aero teased Jerrie about her dreams of going to the moon, but as she made her pitch from across his desk, one look at her told Harris she was completely serious. He asked if she realized that this might not go as she planned, that it could even damage her career. Was she willing to risk her job as one of the few women in a senior position in aviation? How much did this mean to her?

"Everything," Jerrie replied simply.

So Harris told her to go. "If it means so much to you, and if this is a way our company can help toward American space achievements I'm for it."

Jerrie launched herself into her new regimen, running a couple of miles around and around the vacant lot next to her house each morning, and a couple more each night. She worked up to cycling twenty miles a day on an exercise bike in the house, and she lived on "man-sized steaks." She fell into bed each night—no trouble getting the Lovelace-recommended nine hours of sleep. She had orders to keep her plans quiet, and so she could only smile weakly at colleagues who puzzled over her weariness.

Then on February 2, *Look* magazine put out an issue with an extraordinary cover. It showed Betty Skelton, a three-time national aerobatic champion turned auto racer, posing in a silver space suit in front of an Atlas rocket. "Should a Girl Be First in Space?" the cover line demanded. Inside were four pages of pictures of Betty spinning in a centrifuge, sitting in a jet cockpit and splashing in the neutral buoyancy tank. Beside her, in all the pictures, were the Mercury 7, laughing it up with the petite redhead in an oversized flight suit.

The article explained that there was "at this writing, no announced program to put women in space," and that Skelton, thirty-three, had done the Mercury tests at *Look*'s behest. In her four months of researching the Mercury program, however, she had heard some extraordinary ideas, the magazine said. "Both American and Soviet experts agreed that women would respond as well as men (some thought possibly better) to the physical and psychological stresses of space travel. No conclusive data is available, but the requirements as now conceived are so specialized that specific individual qualifications far outweigh any difference based on sex." In the end, however, *Look* made it clear that while the Mercury 7 astronauts called her "No. 7½," the aerobatic champ wasn't going into space. "Though Betty Skelton would love to orbit, she does not believe she or any American woman her age has a chance. Even if she could qualify, a very large 'if,' she thinks she will be too old by the time the program gets around to using women."

The *Look* piece was a public relations exercise designed to get NASA some good press. Jerrie Cobb's assignment was rather different. On Valentine's Day, 1960, a crisp cold night, she arrived in Albuquerque. There was nothing romantic about the instructions that awaited her: have nothing to eat or drink—not even chewing gum. Do an enema at night, another in the morning and report to the lab at 8:00 A.M.

She was "unit one, female." That first morning, as she waited for her instructions, she felt a heavy weight of responsibility: this wasn't just about how good her eyes were or how strong her heart was. If she wasn't up to this, Lovelace might never test another woman. He would have no reason to suggest it to the NASA committee he chaired. "Here was the chance, perhaps the only one, to prove a female space-worthy." Jerrie says she prayed.

The first hour of the first day brought a complete blood count, a hematology smear, a blood sugar test, a nonprotein nitrogen test, serology, sedimentation rate, cholesterol test, Rh factor test and urinalysis. It continued from there. There were X rays—more than a hundred pictures of every bone Jerrie had. She blew into tubes while doctors listened for the smooth flow of blood between the chambers of her heart (tiny defects could explode in a rapidly decompressing space capsule). They strapped her to a table and hung her tilted at sixty-five degrees while every five minutes an electrocardiogram recorded the function of her cardiovascular system. And when she sat back in an innocuous-looking chair in the otolaryngologist's office, he used a huge syringe to inject supercooled ten-degree Fahrenheit water deep into her ear. The water froze her inner ear bone, destroying her sense of balance and inducing vertigo. "I felt the water hit my inner ear and almost immediately the ceiling began to whirl and became a multiple of spinning blobs. My right hand fell off the chair and I couldn't lift it back. I knew what was going on, but I couldn't focus my eyes or control my equilibrium." A nurse with a stopwatch stood by, waiting for her eyes to stop spinning.

Next they put her on an exercise bicycle, covered her in electrodes and had her pedal in time to a metronome—and every minute, they added drag to the rear wheel, so that it felt as if she was going up an ever steeper incline. She puffed into a gauge that read the amount of oxygen she took in and of carbon dioxide she expelled, while a ring of doctors stood around watching. The metronome kept ticking, and she kept pedaling. And pedaling. Sweat poured off her and her vision narrowed. The wheel got heavier. She kept pedaling. Finally, as her pulse rate hit 180 (the point just before unconsciousness), they told her she could stop. Her legs were numb. The test determined how far a person could continue once the point of exhaustion was reached—that extra "push," as Jerrie describes it. She found it, deep within herself, knowing the Mercury men had beaten this bike.

Toward the end of the week they took Jerrie out of the clinic and put her on a government plane for a quick flight up into the mountains to Los Alamos, a destination shrouded in slightly sinister secrecy, home of the United States nuclear research effort. Her papers were checked, and then she was led into a fenced-off laboratory that housed a "total body counter," one of just two or three in the United States at the time. The test would calculate her radiation count, then determine the amount of potassium in her body: that told the doctors how much of her was muscle in relation to fat and total weight. She was led through a series of basement hallways to a room containing a machine that reminded her of an iron lung—a big tank with a tube protruding from one end. She was sent to an adjoining room to scrub (removing "the top layer of skin, if possible"), then dressed in big white pajamas and helped up on to a long tray that was then slid into the tube—like a cookie tray into an oven, except with so little room she had to fold her arms over her chest. Before the door was closed, sealing her in the dark, she was handed the "chicken switch," a button to push should claustrophobia set in before the count was done and she needed to be pulled out. Jerrie decided she wasn't going to use it. (Anyone who hit the switch, of course, would immediately be out of the running for astronaut training: the space capsules were certain to be small, tight and dark.) The count showed Jerrie's body mass to be much more muscle than the average female: the trips around and around the vacant lot had paid off.

On Saturday morning, at the end of a week of tests, Jerrie had one more appointment, this one with Dr. Robert Secrest, a flight surgeon who supervised the medical examination. That meeting, she says, made her more nervous than any of the tests.

Secrest greeted her with a smile. "Let me sum this up quickly, Miss Cobb. You're a remarkable physical specimen. I wish there were more women like you . . ." Here he stopped and looked down at papers on his desk, and Jerrie could hear her heart pounding in her ears.

"You've passed the Mercury astronaut tests, Miss Cobb. And we've gained valuable firsthand information on a woman's performance in the tests. Thank you."

So she'd passed. What did *that* mean?

Dr. Albert Schwichtenberg, the head of the aerospace department, had written an assessment. "She is a very highly motivated, intelligent and stable adult female who created a very good impression throughout the clinic." Jerrie had had astonishingly few accidents or ailments in her life, he added. Jerrie says she was later told that she tested in the top 2 percent of all the people, men and women, who took the exam.

"It is considered that from all information available and tests done here that she would qualify for special missions," Schwichtenberg concluded. "It is recommended that she proceed on to the aeromedical laboratory for stress tests followed by a final evaluation based upon all available test information."

Dr. Lovelace, it seemed, did not intend to stop with the medical screening. Jerrie's performance thus far had fueled his curiosity about how women would perform in the stress of space: now he envisioned this process in three stages, just like those through which the Mercury 7 were selected. He wanted to test additional women—and he had plenty more in store for Jerrie.

Next Lovelace arranged for her to "fly" the Multi-Axis Spin Test Inertia Facility (MASTIF), built for NASA and housed at the Lewis Research Center in Cleveland. It was a huge gyroscope, the size of a two-story house, with three separate steel frames nested one inside another so that each could spin independently. It was designed to test a pilot's ability to control roll, pitch and yaw, the three axes on which a plane or spacecraft turns. Yaw is side to side, like a car fishtailing. Pitch is up and down (as in extreme turbulence) and roll is the horizontal wallow. A pilot sometimes fights against one or maybe two, and the ability to gently stabilize a plane is the sign of a gifted flier. Spinning in space, a capsule could oscillate on all three axes, and the pilot would have to fire rocket thrusters burning hydrogen to still the spinning.

Jerrie reported to the lab that housed the monster, christened the Vomit Comet by the Mercury 7 (Alan Shepard, they say, hit the chicken switch on his first flight). She was outfitted in an orange flight suit and a helmet. She climbed up into a rig about the same size as the Mercury capsule and slid on the contoured seat, facing an instrument panel. NASA technicians strapped her to the seat with a chest harness, then tied down her legs, waist and helmet. She put one hand on the control, and the men fired up the MASTIF. The machine began to move, faster and faster, until it was spinning on all three axes at once, thirty revolutions a minute.

"First the thing started to pitch, and if I hadn't been fastened in, I would have been tossed right off the couch," Jerrie recalled. "Then as the pitch reached peak speed, I felt the roll start. I was twisting, twisting like a toy, and going head-over-heels at the same time." When yaw set in, all she could see was a "dizzying blur." Her stomach churned, as if she were on a combination of a dozen of the amusement park rides she avoided.

She forced her eyes to focus on the instruments. Using her hand control, Jerrie had to guide the capsule out of each spin— but if she pushed too far or too fast, or didn't push enough, the spinning became wilder. One by one, she stopped the gyrations, until suddenly the machine was tamed. "Want to try some more?" the technicians asked over her headset. "Why not?" she replied, waiting for her stomach to climb back up from her feet.

She rode it for forty-five minutes. At the end, the MASTIF handlers told her, "Your response was exceptionally quick. And don't worry—the space capsule won't be nearly as bad as the ride you just took."

And then she went back to work, determined to start earning her keep again for Aero. Tom Harris wanted her to go show off (and sell) the Commander in Africa, where it would be popular for its ability to take off on short runways and survive with little service. She flew 13,170 miles that summer, from Oklahoma to Brazil, then across the ocean to Liberia, South Africa, Kenya and Zanzibar. It was her favorite kind of flying—a chance to show off her plane, and even better, endless hours alone over the seas and the vast African plains.

Lovelace, on the other hand, had a very public plan for that summer. He decided to reveal the results of Jerrie's tests at the Space and Naval Medicine Congress, an international convention of aerospace scientists held in Stockholm in August. He gave a cautious presentation. In tests done under his own auspices, he said, he had found that the preliminary results for one female candidate showed she would hold up well in space. And, he explained, there was reason to consider using women: his female subject had used less oxygen per minute than the men tested, so less oxygen would have to be carried for female crew members.

She tolerated heat as well as men, and pain better. Her reproductive organs were internal, obviously, and so that lowered her risks from radiation. "We are already in a position to say that certain qualities of the female space pilot are preferable to those of her male colleague." He told the audience that the tests to date were purely research, but that they would continue.

It is unlikely that Lovelace made Jerrie's results public without first talking to the Space Task Group at NASA. With Jerrie, he was already using terms such as "woman-in-space program," and describing a broad testing process. She believed he was talking to NASA about the formal inclusion of women in the Mercury program. But he was cautious in Stockholm. He might have been at odds with his colleagues on the Life Sciences Committee about his thoughts on women in space. Perhaps, in going public, he was playing politics. "Nobody else was doing it, except maybe the Russians," says the clinic's Donald Kilgore. "He wanted to be on the record about there being something special about female candidates."

Whatever his reasons, Lovelace gave an understated presentation. Jerrie wondered if there would be any reaction at all. There was a polite reception from the other conference goers, and a bland little item went out on the Associated Press news wire. Written from the conference press release, it said a scientist had tested one female pilot and found she might hold up in space. It wasn't press-stopping material.

But in 1960, the words "female astronaut" had an irresistible allure. The story was picked up by newspapers all over the world. Randy Lovelace was a name instantly associated with the astronaut program, and look at what he had said—that women weren't just as good as men in space; in some ways, they were better! "Woman Qualifies for Space Training," *The Washington Post* reported on August 19.

Lovelace had sworn Jerrie to secrecy until he made this speech. And she had told only her boss at Aero about the tests. But somehow *Life* magazine had caught wind of her trip to Albuquerque. The magazine had signed a controversial deal with the Mercury 7 in August 1959 for $500,000 split among them, giving *Life* exclusive access to their stories. The astronauts, who earned only a comparatively paltry military salary, were relieved to have the money—and to have a reason to avoid the media mob, whose interest hadn't abated much since the men were first introduced. But the result of the deal was that scarcely a single issue of the magazine came out between 1959 and 1962 that didn't include at least a page or two of pictures and a few lines on how John Glenn kept fit or the Schirra family spent their weekends. *Life* was very big on astronauts.

And now the magazine wanted the scoop on Jerrie. The editors told Lovelace they would hold off making known that he was testing women—or at least, a woman—if they could have an exclusive on her, too. She agreed, she says, because she knew that any publicity about the tests done without the doctor's approval would be sensational. This was deadly serious for her, and she didn't want it to look like some silly stunt.

As part of that deal, she had to be "unavailable" if anybody picked up the news of Lovelace's speech in Stockholm, until *Life* had introduced her at a press conference. So she was in Manhattan the night of the Stockholm news release, staying with a friend. The story went out on the AP wire at 6:00 P.M. EST, and in the dead of night the phone began to ring. And ring. Somehow, reporters had tracked her down there. The friend kept telling callers that she didn't know where Jerrie was ("driving back to Oklahoma, I think") while Jerrie, clad in her bathrobe, stood and listened with disbelief and growing apprehension. The phone was ringing at her parents' house in Ponca City, too, and the next day her office got hundreds of calls, from as far away as Japan and Australia. Jerrie couldn't believe the intensity of the press interest: she was about to take her first steps into the spotlight, and the glare would become ferociously bright in the year to come.

Bound by the pledge to *Life,* Jerrie spent three days hiding while the team at Aero fought off increasingly hostile reporters. A British reporter threatened to write that the Russians had kidnapped Jerrie unless Aero produced her. The media wanted this story: space was big news. And this wasn't a complicated story about rocket boosters or communications satellites. This was about an astronaut, and America loved astronauts. This was about a twenty-eight-year-old female astronaut, a *pretty* astronaut, and that made for juicy headlines. In truth, all Jerrie had done was some tests, and she had done them for Lovelace, not NASA—but to the media, that didn't matter. Lovelace's post as head of a key NASA committee was enough to make her an astronaut.

Finally, on August 21, *Life* was on the newsstands—complete with pictures, shot earlier in the summer, of Jerrie tilting on tables and puffing on bicycles. Now other reporters got to meet their female astronaut. For Jerrie, as shy at twenty-eight as she was at six, this was an ordeal more painful than anything at the Lovelace Clinic. She stood trembling outside the meeting room, listening to the bustle as the television and radio crews set up inside, and she thought, I can't. "It's not space that scares me. It's the lack of it."

The interviews went okay, at first. "Aren't you afraid of space-flight, a total unknown?" She answered frankly that no, she wasn't. "Aren't you afraid of anything?" a reporter asked.

She thought fast. "Grasshoppers," she replied. In truth, bugs didn't bother her, but the reporters were satisfied.

Jerrie answered all the reporters' questions about why women were suited for space, in her grave low voice. But that was dry stuff—and so the personal questions started, questions she didn't expect. Was she married? Could she cook? Well, *what* did she cook? Chickasaw Indian dishes, she said. She liked to bake yonkapins. That stumped them. "It's a water lily root growing in the mud bottoms of lakes and ponds. Best way to pick them is with bare toes," she said. "They taste kind of like sweet potatoes."

Jerrie the space woman was a headline writer's dream. "Moon Maid's Ready!" said one. "Astronette!" said another, and "Woman Astronaut Down to Earth about Space Flight." The fact that she had long blond hair made the first paragraph of every story. *Time* helpfully put her measurements in the second: "The first astronautrix (measurements: 36–27–34) eats hamburgers for breakfast, is an old hand at airplanes, with more air time—over 7,500 hours—than any of the male astronauts." A wisecracking male reporter asked if she would object to sharing a space capsule with a male astronaut; she said no, and that made plenty of headlines too. "'Spacewoman' Would Let Man Come Along on Trip," trumpeted *The Sun* in Baltimore.

When it was over, she flew home to Oklahoma, hoping to relax with her parents. Instead she arrived to celebrity status. Governor Howard Edmondson and just about every other dignitary in the state were there to meet her at the airport; she was given a sash proclaiming her Oklahoma's "Ambassador to the Moon" and armloads of flowers. When she got into the office at Aero, there were stacks of letters and telegrams from well-wishers all over the world. She tried to plow through them, sending an earnest thank-you to each. But to a flood of endorsement offers and pitches for billboards, magazine and television commercials— that would sell mattresses and cigarettes, among other things— she sent a resounding no. This was serious business for her.

In late September, NASA sent out a sign that it wasn't pleased with the flurry of publicity Jerrie had earned: a short story moved on the United Press International wire. "The National Aeronautics and Space Administration says it never had a plan to put a woman in space, it doesn't have one today and it doesn't expect to have one in the foreseeable future," the story ran. "Any story that you may have read or heard to the effect that NASA is selecting and training girl astronauts just isn't true, a spokesman said." The article noted that there had been a couple of "girl astronaut" reports in recent years (apparently a reference also to the Betty Skelton *Look* cover). "In each case, NASA officials quietly denied the story, sometimes at first with a trace of irritation. 'Now we must shrug them off,' a spokesman said. . . . A national magazine called [Cobb] the first U.S. lady astronaut. It said she might ride a rocket into space in late 1962. If she does, it won't be a NASA rocket, and NASA is the only U.S. agency that has scheduled any rocket riding in the next few years."

But Jerrie didn't see the article, and if Dr. Lovelace saw it, she says, he didn't tell her. She had a great many other things on her mind: in September another summons from Dr. Lovelace arrived. He wanted to duplicate the stress tests the astronauts had done at Wright-Patterson, and he wanted to know everything there was to know about Jerrie's brain. The psychologists working on the space project were focused on the effects of isolation. They knew that people deprived of stimulation, communication and movement were prone to greater suggestibility, depression, loss of organized thinking, possibly delusions or hallucinations. Weightlessness might further add to the disorientation. A space voyage would be isolation on a scale humans had never before experienced. An astronaut who cracked in space might panic— start pushing the buttons, vent all the oxygen, fire the rockets too soon, spin off into the abyss. With that kind of stress, the doctors said, an astronaut would have to be an excellent psychological as well as physical specimen.

Phase II, the psychological testing, was close to home. For a week, Jerrie took afternoons off, and reported to Dr. Jay Shurley behind the heavy, locked doors of the psychiatric wing of the Veterans Administration Hospital in Oklahoma City. Shurley and his team gave her ink blots to stare at and sentences to complete, then asked her to talk aloud for five minutes about a personal experience. (Jerrie fumbled and hesitated, awkward as always when called upon to speak about herself.) They took electroencephalograms of her brain when she was awake, and then lulled her to sleep and took more. There were pages and pages of intelligence tests and personality quizzes.

And at the end of the week, they told her she was deemed sufficiently psychologically healthy to go on to an "isolation run." The Mercury astronauts were tested for three hours in an empty room, but the military facilities where the men were examined did not have the test that Shurley pioneered in his studies of patients and research subjects. The psychologist had concluded that the best way to mimic the experience of being alone in space would be to suspend the subject in water (which would be the nearest thing possible to weightlessness) and remove all other sensory stimulation. The water was calculated to the exact temperature of the subject's body, and the tank had thick walls that blocked out all sound, vibration and smell. Many subjects who held up to all the physical tests would crumble on this one: with hours alone, they would hallucinate, lose touch with reality or be insupportably uncomfortable without stimulation.

Jerrie arrived that Saturday morning feeling a certain trepidation: she had read about this test, and she knew it could produce unexpected, surprising and often quite embarrassing results for the people who took it. She had spent plenty of time alone— she preferred it—and she had faith in her sound mind, but she wondered what kind of secrets it might reveal in Shurley's big steel tank. But she put on her bathing suit, let the doctors wire on their sensors and climbed in. "If my confidence was unfounded, if the results were dire, better to find out now than someday in the isolation of outer space."

They put an inflated rubber collar under her head and another piece of rubber around her waist to keep her face above the water. They told her to talk whenever she liked—no one would answer, but it would all be recorded. Microphones would pick up her every breath, in fact. And she was simply to tell them when she wanted to come out. Then they closed the eight-inch-thick doors, and she was alone in the pitch-black and the silence.

Her mind wandered. Is this what it was like to be blind? How was she going to get all that mail at the office answered? She began to wonder if she was falling asleep, if she'd already been asleep. If she had snored into the microphone. She grew accustomed to the tank and the peaceful feeling. Every so often she reported in that she was fine. She thought about flying, about what it would be like to fly in space, and she let her mind drift. Finally, she told them she would get out. Shurley's voice came over the speaker: why did she want out now?

"I don't have any particular reasons for coming out or staying in, I'm so used to it in here—I don't know," she said with a laugh. "I don't think my feelings are going to change by staying in here any longer, so I don't see any need in doing so—but I'm perfectly happy and willing to and I just feel calm and relaxed."

Shurley greeted her outside the tank. "What time do you think it is?" She guessed two o'clock, but it was seven in the evening—she had been in the tank for nine hours and forty minutes.

The doctor told Jerrie she "excelled in loneliness." She later added that it came as little surprise since she had been practicing all her life. None of Shurley's previous female subjects had lasted more than six hours, and no men, more than six and a half. "Probably not one in 1,000 persons would be capable of making such a lengthy isolation run," he wrote later. "We have had extraordinary people as subjects. Among them she still stands out. . . . She would be in the top 1 per cent or 2 per cent to adapt," he added, noting that she had not even gone to the limit of her endurance. All in all, the Phase II assessment Shurley gave Jerrie was as glowing as that from the first phase:

It is our opinion that Miss Jerrie Cobb not only possesses no significant liabilities, but also possesses several exceptional, if not unique, qualities and capabilities for serving on special missions in astronautics, viewed from the standpoint of her personality makeup and functioning. Among these are: a ready acceptance of direction or a ready assumption of responsibility, as circumstances dictate. An exceptional ability to remain passive and relaxed when action is unavailable or unwise. An unusually smooth integration of psychophysiological functioning, a stable ego, and a strong, healthy motivation. Her pleasant personality would lend itself as well to nonsolitary missions. I believe she has very much to recommend her for selection as an astronaut candidate.

That same week, just to round things out, Jerrie set another world record: in altitude this time, taking a stripped-down Commander 680F up to 37,010 feet, wired to an oxygen mask and wearing a set of military-issue arctic long underwear under four layers of clothes. To practice, she took test runs in an altitude pressure chamber that shot up to the equivalent of forty thousand feet. Then the technicians took away her oxygen mask and had her write her name repeatedly, the test for anoxia. Jerrie says she more than tripled the time it normally took for a pilot to get drowsy and confused.

That winter she set out on the "chicken and peas" circuit, much in demand as a public speaker. She didn't like it much, she says, but she made the speeches, figuring all of it was good for the space program, and maybe even good for women in the space program.

Lovelace, meanwhile, had surveyed the thick file of her results with satisfaction. Jerrie had proved him right: she had phenomenal endurance, she had lightning-quick reactions and she had set a record in isolation. Her scores were so good that members of his team were quietly asking if she was not, perhaps, an aberration. Maybe he had some sort of superwoman on his hands.

Jerrie was clearly an extraordinary pilot—her world records attested to that. But Lovelace was eager to get his instruments on other women: maybe it wasn't just Jerrie. Maybe all women had her tolerance of pain, her ability to resist the delusions induced by isolation. And if they did, the scientist in Lovelace, who knew all about the struggles in the Mercury design lab, saw immediate possibilities. That capsule, already too heavy for the rocket— imagine if it had a hundred pounds less of astronaut in it.

He went back to the list that he and Flickinger had first compiled with Jerrie, and the one with the names of the dozen women from their search of the 99s records. (Among them was Betty Skelton, who had graced the *Look* cover in the silver space suit.) He double-checked the Federal Aviation Authority ratings and narrowed the list to fourteen names.

His first batch of queries went out in September, brief but official letters on clinic letterhead sent to fourteen female pilots. "Will you volunteer for the initial examinations for woman astronaut candidates? The examinations will take one week and are done on a purely voluntary basis. They do not commit you to any further part in the Women in Space Program unless you so desire. . . . We should like to hear from you if you are interested." He enclosed a detailed questionnaire, and his qualifications were stringent—he wanted at least fifteen hundred hours of flying time, perfect health, age under forty, a commercial rating and experience in pressurized flight. Seven of the women he initially contacted did not make this first cut.

Right about then, Randy Lovelace had a fateful conversation: he told his friend Jackie Cochran about his women-in-space program.

Jackie, by then, was the most famous female pilot in the world. She had kept right on flying at the end of the war. She bought a surplus P-51 Mustang and flew it ninety thousand miles a year on business for her cosmetics company. She went back to racing, coming second in the 1947 Bendix. She set more world records. She spent a year on a public relations campaign with Gen. Hap Arnold to have the air force recognized as a separate branch of the armed forces. She was voted the national

Business Woman of the Year in 1952, and again the next year, by the Associated Press.

But she felt the jet age was passing her by, and Floyd watched her get increasingly wistful. He bought her a surplus Canadair F-86, and then Jackie lobbied everyone she knew in the air force and the government to let her friend Chuck Yeager teach her how to fly it. Yeager started her in a T-33 jet trainer, and then moved her up to the F-86. They began with short courses and dives. Finally, on a hot, clear morning in May 1953, Jackie dove the F-86 through the sound barrier above Edwards Air Force Base in California, the first woman in the world to fly past Mach 1.

"You're part of the plane on a flight like that," Jackie wrote later. "Attached to it in ten different ways, strapped into your seat, to your parachute, to the oxygen system, to your radio for listening, talking, reading the Mach meter aloud." Yeager's voice on the radio asked what she was feeling as she put the jet into a steep dive and the Mach meter climbed. "Shock waves look like rain," she told him, as the plane shook and blood rushed into her head and her body ached. Later, she added that she had wanted to say it was "like flying inside an explosion" but she couldn't find the words.

Jackie and Yeager received the Harmon trophies that year from the president, her friend Dwight Eisenhower. She had set eight world records in 1953, but the sound barrier was the one that mattered. "The greatest thrill of my life," she called it.

After that, Canadair, Northrop and Lockheed all hired Jackie to test fly their prototype jets. In 1956 she decided to run for Congress as a Republican from Indio, California. She flew herself around the district, trying to meet everyone, but she wasn't a natural politician. Folks in her district didn't know what to make of a woman as driven as Jackie, one who lectured far more than she listened and jabbed her elbows into the ribs of people standing near her to make a point. At a rally, a teetotaler asked her if she drank (and she did, prodigiously). "Well, sir," she replied.

"Yes, I drink, but just two years ago I flew an airplane faster than the speed of sound, so I guess I don't drink too much." She campaigned hard for nine months, but lost by fifteen hundred votes. It was a rare defeat, and she took it hard.

But it didn't slow her for long. Eisenhower sent her to South Korea, heading a mission to bring food and supplies to the American partner against Communism. But when, over tea, the South Korean president, Syngman Rhee, began to criticize the United States, Jackie called him a "nasty-minded, dirty old man" and said she was leaving before she gave him "a knock right on the nose." In 1958, and again the next year, she was elected president of the Fédération Aéronautique Internationale (FAI), and she was the first woman to hold the post. She traveled into the Soviet Union for the FAI's annual convention and while there, she used several unorthodox methods, including demanding pee breaks by the side of the road near military bases, to spy on Russian air power. She debriefed Eisenhower and his advisers on her return.

Jackie was by then a powerful woman—in business and politics, and in particular in aviation. In 1953 she published her autobiography, *Stars at Noon*. The list of people she drew up who were to receive an autographed copy reads like the *Who's Who*. Mr. and Mrs. Pierre Cartier in Geneva, Gen. James Doolittle in New York, Mr. Howard Hughes in Los Angeles, the Hon. and Mrs. Lyndon Johnson in Washington, plus a dozen generals and ambassadors. By then Jackie believed, with some justification, that she belonged at the center of every new development for women in aviation. And that included any moves toward putting women into space.

Jackie and Randy Lovelace, of course, were old friends. Their friendship had been cemented in 1940, when Jackie had made sure her choice (Lovelace and two of his colleagues) won the Collier Trophy. She had not only demonstrated to Lovelace the extent of her Washington muscle, but also won his loyalty.

When he established a foundation to support his clinic and research, he asked Floyd Odlum to chair the board, and Floyd gave the clinic millions over the years. Jackie's husband was by now a central figure in the aviation industry—his interest was fueled by Jackie's convictions about how air transport would grow and by her fascination with high-performance aircraft. And the three of them shared a keen interest in the newest technologies. By the mid-1940s, Lovelace was Jackie and Floyd's personal physician: he managed the care of Floyd's crippling arthritis and Jackie's often precarious health. The doctor named his youngest daughter Jacqueline, and Jackie showered her goddaughter and Lovelace's other two surviving children with presents and pampered them on visits to the ranch. She and Lovelace's wife, Mary, were also extremely close; Mary was one of the few female friends Jackie had. Don Kilgore, who later treated Jackie for almost fifteen years, says, "She had an unstinting admiration for Randy and for Floyd Odlum—those were the two most important people in her life."

Some time in the autumn of 1960, Randy told Jackie that he was testing women for space. Jackie, as she was wont to do, later said the whole thing was her idea from the start—and she repeated this idea so loudly and so often that to this day many people involved still believe it. "I had every intention of following my high performance aircraft adventures with a trip into space," she wrote in her autobiography. "So I got myself teamed up with my good friend Randy Lovelace, M.D., working at the Lovelace Clinic in Albuquerque, New Mexico, to test women for astronaut abilities." In truth, the documentary record shows that Flickinger and Lovelace had been at work on this project for at least a year before Jackie got involved. They met Jerrie in September 1959, and she started the tests more than six months before Jackie ever knew of it. But Jackie was to spend the next three years making sure that this venture became hers.

She wanted, of course, to be the woman who went into space herself. But Jackie was in her late fifties by 1960, and her health was poor—she was frequently troubled by abdominal pains, the result of a botched surgery for appendicitis as a child, and she had aches in her legs from blocked arteries. She later said on some occasions that she took the tests and on others that she didn't: "I did not try to become one of the candidates, partly because my age barred me under the ground rules laid down by Dr. Lovelace but mostly because I was consulting with respect to what Dr. Lovelace was doing and did not consider it proper under the circumstances to become a candidate and therefore in a sense a competitor with the others." She might have taken at least some of the tests. In a letter to Lovelace in late December 1960 she discusses a schedule ("I'll take that bicycle test Monday"), but on that visit Randy likely gently delivered the news that she was too old, and she was not going to pass.

Jackie Cochran was not accustomed to being told she could not do something. If she couldn't be part of this program, then she was going to run it. She told Lovelace that she would help him find his female pilots, and furthermore that she and Floyd would pay all the expenses of the candidates. She was used to leading things, and she assumed (not without reason, given her experience with the WASP) that if Randy was getting her involved, it was so that she would run the operation. In November 1960, she wrote to him as his "special consultant" about his "women in space program . . . still in its formative stages" (although in fact it was well under way). Jackie, of course, had suggestions. Lots of suggestions. For one thing, Lovelace should broaden his search pool. "Some of the remainder [of the initial candidates] will not pass the physical tests and still others, for one reason or another, will drop out. The consequence is likely to be that the group carried on into succeeding phases will be too small to reach adequate conclusions as to women as 'astronauts', per se or compared with men. . . ." And in this letter, Jackie gave the first hint of what would be a vicious enmity toward Jerrie Cobb. Her comments made it clear that she didn't like one bit the kind of attention Jerrie was getting as the first "astronaut candidate." Emphasizing that she sought to avoid the criticism that would accompany an appearance of favoritism, Jackie wrote, "there should be care taken to see that no one gets what might be considered priorities or publicity breaks." A month later, she wrote to Randy to say she was on her way to take the tests herself and returned to this subject. "As you know I think it important to have a group operation with each participant individually anonymous until the whole group can be talked about without priorities or precedence." Jackie was reading the coverage of Jerrie's testing closely: "What is the 'isolation chamber' that Jerry [*sic*] Cobb talks about?" she asked Lovelace. "Has she been advanced to Wright Field or was this one of the routines of the medical tests which took place at Los Alamos?"

Once she knew she stood no chance of being the first female astronaut herself, Jackie began maneuvering to put a rival lead candidate in place of Jerrie. She knew a pair of pilots in California, identical twins named Jan and Marion Dietrich. Marion was a hobby pilot, but Jan had eight thousand hours of flying time—more than Jerrie. Jackie wrote a bossy letter to the clinic asking why Marion had been invited for testing when Jan had more hours. "On September 14, 1960, letters were sent out to the women suggested by Miss Cobb," replied Lovelace's long-suffering secretary, Jeanne Williams. "At that time a letter was sent out to Miss Marion Dietrich and since Miss Jan Dietrich had telephoned us and already had the information required, we did not write her a letter as it would have been repetitious. Their applications are both being considered and Doctor Lovelace was quite interested when he realized that they were twins and they will be given the utmost consideration." In January, Jackie made a first donation of five hundred dollars to the clinic to cover the cost of astronaut testing. And she brought Jan out to stay at the ranch with her and Floyd for a few days, and then flew her to Albuquerque in her Lodestar.

Lovelace was used to dealing with his domineering friend. "Dear Jackie," he wrote to her on January 31, 1961. "Several of us here have gone over your letter about broadening the test program for the potential woman in space pilots. We would like very much to have the names of some additional girls that we could contact. We are enclosing a list of the girls that have met the preliminary requirements and will be going through the Clinic beginning within the next 2½ months."

There were fourteen names on his list; Jackie supplied eleven more. Nineteen of the women took the gamble and turned up at the clinic for the tests, and twelve, plus Jerrie, emerged as candidates for the final phase of the women-in-space program.

"I'VE GOT TO FLY"

Irene Leverton begins work as a crop duster,
Tennessee, 1950.

If Randy Lovelace had lined up his thirteen candidates all together in his office, he might, at first glance, have thought them a startlingly diverse group of women. They ranged in age from twenty-one to forty, and they came from all over the country. One had eight children, while a couple of others were staunchly single. A few were struggling to keep a roof overhead, and one was a millionaire's daughter. But beneath the surface differences, one thing united them: these women fell in love with flying the first time they climbed into a cockpit. As little girls, they begged and cajoled their parents to let them "go up." If coaxing didn't work, they lied and sneaked out to the airfield. Once they were licensed, they realized women weren't going to get the glamorous test pilot or corporate jobs, and they turned instead to instructing and ferrying. They took advantage of the Civil Air Patrol and the WASP to get access to planes, sometimes to heavy, fast planes. They paid lip service to the rules, flying in shirtwaist dresses and pastel pumps. But they always found ways to keep flying.

The pilot strode down the aisle of the plane in his navy wool uniform and stopped at her seat. Geraldine Hamilton, just four, was looking at his knees.

His voice boomed from above. "Want to come up and see the cockpit, little lady?"

It was 1932, and Jerri was flying with her father Watson Hamilton, an oil man, to a meeting in Austin, Texas. They left home in Amarillo in a Lockheed Electra that belonged to a family friend, and when the plane leveled off at about five thousand feet—these were the days before pressurized cabins—the pilot came back and made his offer to Jerri, all starched and shiny in her best dress. She most certainly did want to see the cockpit: she scrambled out of her seat and followed him back up to the front of the plane.

The pilot let her sit in his lap and hold the control column, which she called the steering wheel. He showed her the compass and told her to keep the little needle right in the middle. And she "flew" the plane until they were close to Austin; then a stewardess led her back to her father.

"Jerri, when you grow up, if you study real hard and become a nurse, you can fly all the time," Watson told his daughter as she clambered back up into the seat beside him. "You can be an air hostess."

Jerri shook her coal-black curls, unimpressed. "I don't want to do that," she informed him. "I'm going to *fly* these airplanes. I've been flying this one and I'm gonna fly 'em."

Watson corrected her. "Honey, gals just don't fly airplanes."

Telling this story almost seventy years later, Jerri lets out a rich laugh. "I guess I showed him."

Her father was the son of a powerful Texas rancher and a prominent figure in the booming oil patch. Her mother, Prissy, was a daughter of Texas society; both sides of her family traced their roots in America to back before the Revolutionary War. Jerri, born in 1928, was their only child, and the focus of Prissy's considerable attention. Her third birthday party was written up in the social pages. She had tap dancing lessons, and she was never allowed to leave for school until her mother had painstakingly brushed her hair into thirty-two perfect Shirley Temple curls. (As soon as Jerri was allowed out the door, she crammed on her toy pilot's hat and goggles, squashing the curls, and pedaled off in her little red-and-yellow airplane on wheels.)

One day in the middle of World War II, Jerri was in the car with her mother when she saw two women coming along the sidewalk in Amarillo. They wore trousers and caps and had shiny gold wings pinned to their shirts. They walked with confident strides, parachute packs and duffel bags slung over their shoulders. Jerri pressed her nose up against the window: "Mother, look! They're letting women in the air force!" She had never heard of the WASP. Her mother started to explain what the women's air corps did, but Jerri wasn't listening. "I said, 'Oh, that's what I'm going to do, I'm going in the air force.'" But the WASPs were disbanded eighteen months later.

When she was fifteen, Jerri and a friend went out to the Amarillo airfield and persuaded a young man who was just out of the navy to take them up in his Waco open-cockpit biplane.

She had fifteen minutes in the hat and the goggles—for real, this time—with the wind slamming into her face and the air thick with the smell of gas. That was it: she had to have flying lessons.

She knew better than to ask her parents for the money: a premium was put on "ladylike behavior" in the Hamilton household, and there was nothing ladylike about flying lessons. Jerri had had her driver's license since she was thirteen (that part wasn't so unusual in Texas at the time) but she started charging her friends for rides in her car. She squirreled away her allowance and money from her parents that she told them was for sodas at the drugstore or trips to the drive-in. She could scrape together five dollars, enough for one lesson, each week. She found an instructor who was willing to teach her, though there weren't any other girls taking lessons. And she started to build up the time for her license.

Then—disaster. One day Prissy was home to catch her daughter coming in the door in her coveralls. "Somebody ratted," Jerri says. There was no plausible excuse for the oil beneath her fingernails, the wind knots in her curls. "How could you do such a thing without telling me?" railed her mother. Prissy had ambitions for her daughter: college, a good marriage, a membership at the country club and a position in society. Hanging out at the airport with Lord knows what kind of men was *not* part of that picture.

She was so angry that she called Jerri's father. Although the two had been bitterly divorced after Prissy caught him cheating with Jerri's piano teacher, they managed to agree on one thing, and within a week their duplicitous daughter was on a train bound for the convent school in San Antonio. "We were Episcopalian, we weren't even Catholic!" Jerri snorts, recalling the depth of her mother's horror. "I spent a whole year on my knees plotting how I would get back into a plane." After that one year, her mother relented and she was allowed back to the local high school in Amarillo—but nowhere near airplanes.

But within hours of her return, Jerri was sneaking out to the airfield. One oppressively hot day in June 1945 she was hanging around the tarmac with friends. The war in Europe had just ended; she was seventeen and newly graduated. That afternoon, a B-25 thundered in and touched down beautifully, and Jerri and all the other spectators turned to watch the huge bomber as it coasted down the runway—and kept going. "Amarillo is up at three thousand feet and there's not a tree, shrub, bush or bump on the whole place, and the plane just went right off the end of the runway," Jerri recalls. Jerri and everybody else chased after the plane, and she was standing a few feet from the cockpit when a tanned, dark-haired pilot jumped down, grinning ruefully.

"He was *gorgeous*," Jerri says, the power of that first glimpse undimmed by fifty-five years. The pilot stood watching a truck hook up his plane to tow it back toward the airport. Jerri took a deep breath.

"Your brakes gone?" she asked the pilot, searching for conversation.

"Sure are," he said. "I hadn't planned on a trip out the highway."

His name was Lou Sloan, and he had stopped to refuel on his way from Europe to the Pacific coast, as America shifted its forces to the last battles of the war. A few days later, he took his plane west, but he was soon back in Amarillo, come to visit the petite, blue-eyed teenager from the airfield.

"He was never one to waste any time," Jerri says, laughing at the memory. "He said, 'Let's get married and go on up to the university together.'"

Jerri hesitated—she had only known him a couple of weeks.

"Look, I'm twenty-seven, you're seventeen," Lou told her. "You got time. I don't." The war had left him feeling far older than his years, and Jerri was won over by the force of his conviction. Her mother reluctantly consented when Jerri promised she would go to college. They were married a month later, and come September they headed off to the University of Arkansas.

They moved into Veteran City, a community of ex-soldiers and their wives. "Nine months and thirty minutes" after they were married, Jerri gave birth to their daughter, Candy. Now she could resume her flying lessons—it was a bit of a strain on their budget, but she and Lou both wanted to fly. When they graduated from college, they moved to Memphis, where Jerri's father helped Lou get an engineering job with an oil company. In 1952, their son, David, was born. And as soon as he was toddling, Jerri got a nanny to watch the children and concentrated on getting her private license.

The FAA inspector for her exam had never licensed a woman, and he didn't like the idea much. He put Jerri through a brutal check ride, going around and around the field, screaming at her that she was doing everything wrong, obviously intent on rattling her. She looped, spun, stalled as directed. When they landed, she got out of the plane and started to walk to her car in tears. "I knew the way he yelled at me I wasn't about to get my license." He asked where she was going. "And I said, 'What, you son of a bitch, I know you're not going to give me a license.' And he said, 'Well, I never thought I'd see the day I'd give a woman a license to fly an airplane.'" But he gave Jerri one.

Now she told Lou she was going to get the rest of her certifications: she wanted instrument, instructor and commercial ratings. She wanted a career.

They moved to Dallas, and when Jerri met a couple of other women who flew out at the airfield they got together and started a chapter of the 99s. Within months, she was flying in local air races, building up the two hundred hours she needed for a commercial rating. On one of those races, she met a quiet Oklahoman who shared her sense of humor; she and "Jerrie C" quickly became friends. Then Jerri got some work ferrying planes for a Cessna dealership. She gloried in it, making money for being in the air. "Only another pilot knows what I'm talking about. It's an exhilaration, you're free, you're in control, you're up in the heavens, nobody can get to you if you don't want them to, the phone doesn't ring, the kids don't cry, the world can go to hell. You're floating in the clouds and then you grab hold of that machine and you go play. Just go play. Go play with the clouds."

But at home, things were grim. Lou was drinking, all the time. He was haunted by demons that had followed him home from the war. And now drinking was in his job description: two-martini lunches, then rounds of whiskey with colleagues after the eighteenth hole in the evenings.

"He was such a gentle, kind man until he was drinking. Then it was absolutely 180 degrees in the other direction: he was mean, he was loud." Jerri's voice is raw with pain as she recalls the disintegration of her brave, young pilot. She emptied his gin bottles into the hyacinth bushes outside the kitchen door, and when Lou was on a tear, she barricaded the children in her bedroom with a dresser in front of the door. She knew about the memories that haunted him but despaired of how to help. She had two small children who were terrified of Daddy, and she sensed that she had better make sure she had an income of her own. She had been raised to imagine herself cared for as some-body's wife, but Jerri didn't see that in her future.

In 1959, she heard that several test-piloting contracts were coming up at the nearby headquarters of Texas Instruments, and she wanted them. But she was certain she wouldn't get them as a woman on her own. She knew a pilot named Joe Truhill, a slight, reticent man who also worked for the Cessna dealership. He had taught Jerri for her instructor rating. Joe was an experienced pilot and an airplane and engine mechanic—she persuaded him to go into business with her, and they opened Air Services Inc. Then she called her father and asked if he would help with the purchase of their first plane, and he agreed to sign for a loan. She and Joe earned military security clearance, won the TI contracts, and before long they had a fleet: three DC-3s, four B-35s, two B-26s, a DC-6—most of these war surplus planes that Joe refurbished.

Jerri loved the flying: most of it was military equipment, top secret work. She tested the first airborne radar systems, the first "smart bombs" and the first powered navigation systems, flying just a few feet above the waves out on the Atlantic. Sometimes they flew all day and often all night, too. The cockpits were freezing cold, the flights so long her muscles would ache. At home, things were difficult, but her business was booming, and out over the sea, or above the clouds, she felt free.

Then, in the summer of 1960, there was a strange phone call. Jerrie Cobb, her pal from the races, wanted to know if Jerri could get away from work to take part in "a top secret government project." Jerri thought for just a minute, then replied, "Sure, yeah, I think I can get away." She didn't hear anything more for almost a year, and she didn't ask. "We were doing secret work, too, and it was need-to-know. If you needed to know you did, and if you didn't, you didn't get told."

She had just about forgotten the whole thing until one day in early spring of 1961 she found a letter in the mailbox. "It said, 'We understand you have volunteered for the preliminary astronaut tests.' I said, *Huh?* I kept wondering when the hell I had volunteered." She laughs uproariously. "And then I thought, 'Oh this must be what Jerrie was talking about.' Jerrie never has been one to give out a hell of a lot of information." The letter gave her a date to be at the Lovelace Foundation in New Mexico. Jerri went back into the house and began to think about how she was going to tell Lou—she was going.

Jane Cameron Briggs came in from riding in the woods on a gray Saturday afternoon and sat down on the edge of the sofa where her mother reclined. Janey was about fourteen, and the Briggs family was on an extended stay in England, where her father went for business each year. Janey had made a decision about her future that afternoon, and she confided it to her mother: when she grew up, she was going to be a spy. She had heard the tales of intrepid female spies who carried out covert missions in World War I, just before Janey was born, and this struck her as just the life of adventure she was looking for.

Her mother was alarmed, and made her promise she would give up the idea. "Mother said, 'You're just dumb enough to believe that you're smart enough to do it,'" Janey recalls. Her mother was adamant, so Janey agreed, with considerable reluctance, that she would forgo life undercover. "But in my head I thought, Okay, fine. But I *am* going to learn to fly."

Janey's father, Walter Briggs, was a self-made millionaire auto industrialist, who married Jane Cameron, a young lady from a good Detroit family. They had five children. The youngest, named for her mother, was always known as Janey. As a child, Janey had a governess. Then, in fourth grade, she was sent to the convent at Grosse Point. She hated it, and made it known. The nuns gave up after a year and sent her home to her mother. She did better at boarding school in Philadelphia. But she was happier outside—playing tennis, swimming, sailing or riding. She regularly competed in horse shows and regularly shattered bones. She also followed the adventures of Amelia Earhart with great attention—her records and her Atlantic crossings and the horrible day when the radio said she had disappeared.

After high school, Janey went off to Manhattanville College in New York, but at the end of her first year it was apparent that the United States was about to enter the war. Janey went home to Detroit and signed up as a volunteer with the Motor Corps. She looked tall and strong in her trim uniform, and she wore her sandy hair cut short. She was often sent out to the city airport, which had been converted into a base, to ferry pilots to their billets in town. At the airfield, joking with the young air force fliers, Janey remembered her childhood plan. "I was out there with all those guys in those planes and thinking, Well, that's what I want to do."

But when she broached the idea at home, her parents were disapproving. And so, like Jerri Hamilton Sloan, she secretly saved up her allowance for the five-dollar cost of an hour-long lesson. She took the streetcar out to the airport, coming up with excuses for where she had been. "I just wanted to *fly*."

One day when Janey was nineteen, she was bedridden with the German measles. Downstairs, she heard her father come home—and with him was Capt. Eddie Rickenbacker, the World War I flying ace. Janey did not intend to miss this opportunity. "I thought, if anybody in this house should be meeting Eddie Rickenbacker, it's me." So she got out of bed—and on the way down the stairs, heard her father telling the pilot that his youngest daughter was "secretly" taking flying lessons. And he sounded proud, not furious. Her mother later confided that yes, they knew about the lessons. Rather than try to stop her, "Mother just turned me over to a guardian angel."

About the time she got her private license, Janey read about the WASPs in the papers. At twenty-one, she wrote to apply. The WASP flying sounded like hard and often tedious work, she says—ferrying and target towing. But it seemed like a good way to be "useful," to be part of the war effort. "And you'd get to fly some planes that you never could get your hands on any other way." She passed the interview and was about to enlist when something happened to change her plans.

Phil Hart was a serious young lawyer from Bryn Mawr, Pennsylvania, the son of a bank chairman. He roomed with Janey's brother Walter at Georgetown University, and was sometimes invited home at holidays. Janey had known him since she was nine and he was eighteen. In 1942, she met him again at a party in Detroit. He was gentle and kind and funny, and he began to court her intently.

Phil had joined the army reserves at Georgetown, and he was called up after the attack on Pearl Harbor. In the spring of 1943, it was obvious he would be sent overseas imminently, and Janey wanted to be married to him first. They joined the legions of couples who wed that June, weeks before he was dispatched to England. She wrote to the WASP office and said her circumstances had changed. She could still have flown with them as a married woman, but months after the wedding she found herself pregnant and that ended her plans to join the pilot corps.

Phil was wounded in the invasion at D-Day; after recuperating and another tour of duty in Germany, he came home in 1945, deeply disturbed by what he had seen in Europe. Shortly after his return, there was tragedy at home. The Harts were spending the first of what would be many summers on Mackinac Island, the seasonal enclave of Michigan's wealthy. One morning in 1946 their firstborn, Phil Junior, just three, toddled down on the dock when everyone's back was turned and drowned. "It's awful," Janey says, simply, about losing a child. Sixty years later, she knows without pausing to calculate how old her son would be had he lived.

Phil left the law to try his hand at public service—at politics. The day after Janey gave birth to their third child, Phil showed up to tell her he had been to the county Democratic convention and had signed Janey up to be the vice chair of the Democrats in sprawling Oakland County. "I said, 'Are you out of your mind? What am I supposed to do with these two little girls?' And he said, 'You'll be able to figure that out, you'll manage.' And I thought, I don't know anything about this." But she and Phil had similar ideas, including a sense of responsibility for society's poorest, and as she got involved she found she loved the inner workings—organizing, campaigning, seeing the party grow. The state Democratic chairman was a veteran politician, and at his side Janey learned how things worked.

She was still flying, in the spare time she managed to carve out of being a politician's wife and the mother of, before long, eight children. In 1953, Janey bought her first plane, a twin-engine

Bonanza. The same year, she and another female pilot were asked by the military to do a test flight in a Thunderbird jet. Recruiters were having trouble signing up pilots for the Korean conflict and thought it might be because anxious mothers and wives were holding men back. The military brass figured that if they showed the jets were so safe that women could fly them, it might allay their fears. Janey found that idea a little wry, but she was willing to help—and glad for an hour in a jet, something she wasn't likely to get any other way. The speed and the pull of gravity were a revelation. On steep turns, she took deep breaths and clenched her muscles to try to keep blood in her head; "my arm weighed six times what it should have."

She flew the All-Women's Transcontinental Air Race three times in the 1950s. The race winner was calculated with a complex handicap formula that included not only the pilot's finishing time but also the size of her aircraft and her fuel efficiency. "I didn't pay any attention to worrying about the handicap and flying intelligently," Janey recalls of her first race in 1956. "I just put the throttle to the wall and wanted to be the first to finish." Phil was up for election that year and she knew that if she landed first at the finish line in Boston, it would make news—and that most people wouldn't know the AWTAR rules or that she had not actually won the race. The odd person, as usual, told Phil he should be controlling his unruly wife instead of letting her race airplanes, but mostly, as Janey had intended, the publicity helped Phil's campaign. She went on to serve on the board of the AWTAR, and in the years she could not compete she lent her Bonanza to women who could not afford their own planes.

Phil served two terms as lieutenant governor, and then, in 1958, he ran for the Senate. But he had a problem—a poll said that despite almost ten years in public office, he had a very low recognition factor. Janey thought there had to be something she could do to help, so she earned a helicopter license, the fifty-eighth woman in the world to do so. There were only two helicopters in all of Michigan then, and this ensured press attention. Soon she was flying her husband to campaign events. "I picked Phil up and we would go to picnics or county Fairs and I'd land right there [on the grass]. . . . That certainly helped."

He won the election, and in the fall of 1958 Janey moved her clan to the capital. She made a lousy Washington wife. "Washington at that point was a southern city, and you had to get your calling card and then you were supposed to call on all the other wives, one after the other, and you wore your white gloves. And then the women—the volunteer work for the Senate wives [was] still making bandages for the Red Cross. I said, 'You make the bandages and I'll deliver them anywhere in my helicopter or airplane.'"

Commuting to their home in Michigan in her helicopter, she would fly over the highways and revel as she passed above the lines of traffic. And with so few people flying helicopters, there were few rules about where she could land. Janey would touch down next to restaurants for dinner. Inevitably, crowds would appear, drawn by the machine and the doubly astounding sight of its female pilot.

In the spring of 1960, she went sailing in the Caribbean with a couple of friends. One of them, B Steadman, was an old pal from the 99s, a flight instructor who taught Janey for her instrument rating. B had heard about a program for female astronauts, and in the warm sun on the deck of the boat near Martinique she confided that she was going to try to take the tests—and she thought Janey should try to get in, too.

On December 3, 1943, Jean Hixson stepped off the train in Sweetwater, Texas, and into the rigors of air force life. "I'll tell you my schedule," she wrote home to her parents that first week. "6:00 A.M. reveille, it is darn cold. 6:50 mess, good swill, 7:45 to 1:00, flight [training], 1:15 mess, 2:30 class call, aerodynamics, it is tough, I thought this stuff would be a pushover. Tests are already beginning to come up. We have seen some government films on it. We need a little geometry in this class but I haven't come to that part yet. It's based generally on general sciences and a little physics. 3:30, engine class—this is really tough. We have a test Monday, there are a lot of physics formulas and stuff we studied in texts. 4:30 to 5:30 math, we start at the beginning and go clear through the problems, a lot of tricky ones. Physics, so far we are only on the ones dealing with volume density and formulas. Physical training: this is really something. I am having a little trouble with drill. 7:50 mess, 10:00 P.M. lights out."

In her first letters home, in scratchy handwriting on thin onionskin paper, Jean sounded awestruck. "Almost all the army personnel you see in this town are officers and most all the officers are pilots," she wrote. "I have never seen so many different types of pilots—ferry, transport, everything—not to mention the girls who are everywhere." Her pride was palpable too. "One of the officers told one of the girls that when a WASP walks down the street, even in civvies, you can tell it is a WASP. There is just a certain distinction."

Slim and strong with short, dark curls, Jean was determined to win her wings. Like so many of the other women who would be WASPs, she had been in love with airplanes since she saw her first one courtesy of a barnstormer who buzzed Hoopeston, Illinois, on a summer Saturday in 1931. The pilot was taking thrill-seekers up for a ride for a few dollars. Jean, age nine, begged her parents and finally struck a deal with her father: she would go to Sunday school every single week without complaint if she could take the flight. He gave in, and Jean got her few minutes in the sky. On the very next trip, with Jean looking on, the barnstormer cracked up the plane. He was not badly hurt, and Jean was undeterred.

Jean was born in Hoopeston, "the corn capital of the world," in 1922. She was the eldest child of Pearl Hixson and her husband, Robert, who sold insurance. The town was thirty miles from the nearest airport, so when, at sixteen, Jean persuaded her parents to let her start flying lessons, she had to take them on Sundays. She was immediately, instinctively good at flying and earned her private pilot's license at eighteen.

The next year, America entered the war, and suddenly all the boys in Hoopeston were going off to fight. When Jean heard about the WASPs, she immediately wrote to the *Chicago Daily Times* for information. She soon learned that she was too young to enlist: WASPs had to be twenty-one. Jean anxiously put in the time, working as a secretary at the food rationing office and the canning company, taking extra classes at the high school and flipping over pages on her calendar.

From her first day at Avenger Field, it was hard work. The classes were rigorous, and friends from home washed out. "After going several months, some girls who were crazy about flying even hate it, the classes and the regimentation," she wrote home. "Our courses get tougher all along, I think they are as tough if not tougher than the [male] Air Cadets. We have to be able to send code faster than the cadets. It is an odd business—one day you may be here, the next you may be eliminated. . . . It all adds up to a devil of a life."

She graduated in June, her wings pinned to her uniform by Jackie Cochran. The next day, Jean was dispatched to Douglas Air Force Base in Arizona, a bomber base. At Douglas, she test flew B-25s from 11:00 P.M. to 3:00 A.M., checking out their navigation systems in the dark. It was risky flying, in battle-fatigued aircraft. One night, a thousand miles away from Douglas over mountainous terrain, she lost all navigational aids, radio and lights. She was alone in the dark at the controls of the heavy plane, reaching for the instruments from memory as she turned by instinct to avoid the mountains and head back toward the base. She followed the lights of the towns until she recognized the landing field, but she could not radio to tell the tower she was coming in, so she took a deep breath, gripped the steering column, came in straight and brought the B-25 down. She parked it, reported the loss of the instruments and went to catch a few hours' sleep before the sunrise.

When Jean had been at the base six months, she had the chance to go back to Texas for an advanced instrument course at Avenger. The political furor over the WASPs was growing and Jean wrote to her parents that she thought she should seize the chance to get this training normally closed to women. She spent six weeks in Texas and had been back at Douglas for only a couple of months when word came from Washington: the WASPs were to turn in their uniforms and make their own way home.

Jean came back to Hoopeston for a little while, but she soon qualified as an instructor and got a job in Akron, where a flood of veterans was taking flying lessons on the GI Bill. She had a roster of twenty students and worked from 8:00 A.M. to sundown on a bustling airfield. But she didn't think flight instructing would be enough of a career—for one thing, the work might dry up when the vets were gone, and as a female instructor she'd be the first one fired. And she saw limited room to advance. So in 1948, she enrolled at University of Akron. She earned an education degree in two and a half years, going to school year-round, and teaching flying on the weekends, then got a job as an elementary school teacher.

In 1949, the WASPs were belatedly given the right to be commissioned into the Air Force Reserves as second lieutenants, and Jean accepted the commission. She took her reserve duty seriously, going back to Douglas to do research every year, and was soon promoted to lieutenant. She saw the reserves as the best way to keep up with the latest developments in aeronautics.

Jean was also intensely patriotic—in a firm, committed way that was common in the years before the Vietnam War. She was a staunch supporter of the American military and believed that each citizen should contribute to building the nation. It was a

sense of patriotism forged in World War II and undiminished by
the Cold War standoff with the Soviet Union. She took Russian
classes at the local college, thinking it might be useful in her military career. She read all she could about the Soviet education
system and worried that the Russians were producing far more
scientists and engineers than her country. She wanted to keep
abreast of developments in aeronautics so that she could pass on
the most up-to-date information to her students and inspire in
them an interest in aviation and the military: even out of
uniform, she saw herself as part of a national effort to safeguard
the American way of life.

The desire to bring aviation into the classroom led Jean to one
of her great adventures. "I had been holding forth in front of my
third graders about flying, about how important it was as both a
civil and military preoccupation, how it would mean even more
in their time than it does to my generation," she wrote in a
personal memoir. "A student asked if I'd been in a jet. I hadn't."
That, she felt, was undermining her credibility with the tough
crowd of eight-year-olds, and so she wrote the head of the
Eastern Continental Air Defense Command a persuasive letter—
and he agreed to get her a jet.

She reported to Youngstown Air Reserve Base in Dayton for
instruction with fifteen air force jet pilot trainees. Jean planned
to go through the sound barrier—something only one other
woman, Jackie Cochran, had done. In the lectures, she learned
what happens when Mach 1 is "broken," then had the conditions
of flight at forty-two thousand feet simulated in an altitude
chamber. She learned how to use the ejection seat. And finally
she had to pass a 109-question exam she called "plenty tough."

Then they took her to her plane. The pilot in the Starfire
F-94C jet fighter was Capt. Don Chaplin, a war veteran a year
younger than Jean at thirty-four. The takeoff was standard—but
they shot up, higher than Jean had ever flown in her multiengine
prop planes. "At 42,000 feet, we leveled off in that special 'purple

plain' of which pilots speak." Jean described her flight in an essay for a national education association. "The sky above was never bluer, and I never felt so divorced from the other earthbound beings. It was exhilarating. . . . Then with the afterburner on giving us an extra shove, we went into a 60-degree angled dive down toward the lake. The captain counted the speed off for me. 'Point eight,' he said. 'Point nine. Mach ONE (the speed of sound).' There was a slight buffeting, or tremor, nothing like I had expected. Gravity assured me it was there, and I squashed real hard into the seat, weighing about 400 pounds at this point. 'All right?' he asked as we turned back to Youngstown. 'Fine,' I said."

The flight made her philosophical. "Men, once schoolkids like mine, had built it, every bit of it, all the 8,000,000 or so little wires, rivets, connections, rotor blades, gadgets—everything, and then pulled this glistening aerodynamic skin over it all to 'clean' it for speed. Why such speed? Well, for one thing, an attacker could come right now against the U.S. in present planes owned in numbers by our possible enemies at 10 to 12 miles per minute. Every minute that could be saved in getting up to intercept and shoot these intruders down would keep them 10 to 12 miles farther from my home, or yours."

In the national awakening that followed Sputnik in 1957, Jean lectured about the need for drastic changes in the American education system. "The Soviet Union's ten-year school demands five years of chemistry, four of physics, and mathematics through trigonometry," she wrote that year. "When a boy or girl walks through the door the first day of school, they know a decade later that they will have spent 40 per cent of their time on these compulsory activities. This system of preliminaries, of forced feeding in math and science, now produces three to one more engineering graduates for their universities than we graduate annually. What used to be a peasant people, which could only copy our B-29 after World War II, was able 10 years later to show their long range jet bomber, the Bison, equal to or maybe better than our B-52. It was no copy. It was their own."

That first jet trip was extraordinary, but Jean was not content to be a passenger. In July 1958, she was the pilot, the second woman to fly the F-102 Delta Dagger fighter-interceptor (Ruth Nichols was first). Again, Jean arranged a flight through the air force. A squadron pilot did the takeoff, then gave her the controls and she "put it through every manoeuvre they would allow." A reporter for the *Akron Beacon Journal* noted that she showed "no trace of excitement" as she clambered out of the cockpit in her heavy flight suit. He gave her a nickname that would follow her all her life, one she disliked—"Akron's flying schoolteacher."

Jean learned to fly gliders and blimps and balloons, and received a master's degree in education in 1959, with a thesis on attitudes toward aviation. Her commitment did not go unnoticed. That year, she won a National Education Association contest as "a teacher who had made outstanding use of travel and aviation experience in her classroom." She also raced the AWTAR almost every year and did stunt flying for Warner Bros. at the Akron Airport. She later told friends how once she was instructed to fly low over the camera. "I looked back over my shoulder to see the camera apparatus and the cameraman flat on the ground. I was only following orders." The remark was typical—Jean was reserved and unassuming, but also funny and gregarious, prone to undercutting those who irritated her with wry remarks they often missed altogether.

She followed America's first, faltering steps in the space race with great interest, and she was quick to pick up on rumors at 99s meetings that women were taking the astronaut tests. Jean mailed Dr. Lovelace a letter in August 1960, after laboring over several rough drafts:

I understand that you are in the process of selecting women for the astronaut tests.

I have an extensive background in aviation, education, science, and educational writing. If feasible at all I would like very much to participate in this program for two reasons. First, being, any help that I can give my government in the space race, I want to do. Secondly, I hope within several years to work on my Ph.D. in the area of space psychology, and this background would serve as an excellent stepping stone toward this field. . . .

I would like very much to have the opportunity to undergo the program for purposes of educational dissemination as well as the fact that I would have no aversion to an orbital shot, because I have seen the precautions our country goes to insure safety.

Dr. Lovelace responded promptly with a questionnaire—and then, it seems, he read her letter more closely and noticed her age. In November he wrote a polite letter declining her participation. "After reviewing all the applications and consulting together, we have decided that thirty-five will be the upper age limit for candidates in the Women Astronaut Testing Program." But Jean really wanted this opportunity: she still had a copy of the questionnaire, and she sent it back to Lovelace with her date of birth changed from 1922 to 1924, bringing her in just under the limit. Lovelace either didn't notice the deception or tolerated it. Jean must have been an alluring candidate—a military veteran with test-pilot experience, jet time, a half-dozen ratings, altitude and compression experience and a graduate degree. Jean's qualifications were reminiscent of Jackie Cochran's. In August 1961, Dr. Lovelace summoned Jean to Albuquerque.

Janey Hart and Jerri Sloan had money behind them as they made their way into flying: an allowance that paid for those first clandestine lessons, a comfortable middle-class life that allowed for someone to take care of the kids while they went flying. They could afford to pay for flying time and to earn ratings. For women without family wealth, it was much more difficult to get into aviation. For Jean Hixson and the select group who wore the WASP wings, there were rare and great opportunities. But other women also managed to take advantage of the changes that swept in with the war years, as new jobs opened up and the social restrictions that kept women away from airfields began to ease.

When Irene Leverton started flying, there was no family money to pay for lessons—her father had drunk himself to death, and her mother was working dawn to dusk scrubbing floors just to pay their rent. But in her senior year of high school, the war effort was enlisting every possible pair of hands, including those of seventeen-year-old girls. Irene got a good-paying job at the Douglas Aircraft plant in Chicago, working as a riveter on the assembly line. The war ended three days after she graduated; three days after that, she and all the other women were sent home from their factory jobs. It was the first of what would be a lifelong experience for Irene, losing a satisfying job because she was a woman. But those few months of work paid for a first, crucial set of flying lessons.

She had wanted to fly, just to be flying, for as long as she could remember. She loved things that went fast: as a tiny child, she eschewed dolls in favor of a toy train. She was fascinated with airplanes: air shows were a popular diversion in the Depression, and there are grainy pictures of a two-year-old Irene pointing at the planes overhead. Her father, Curly, indulged her, and bought her balsa models from the time she was six. She would toss them over the third-floor railing at their apartment house, then race down the stairs to catch her gently descending planes.

Irene was headstrong and bossy, and other mothers didn't like to let their children play with her. Her mother, Frieda, was her best friend. "She was always climbing trees and walking on fence rails"—that's how Irene remembers her mother. Curly fought with the Canadian army in France in World War I and told his daughter stories about lying in his trench, watching the dogfights between the Tiger Moths and Sopwith Camels. He came home from the war with medals, and a body riddled with shrapnel. Frieda was German; she came through Ellis Island when she was thirty-five and met Curly at a pub where she was a waitress. They married in 1926; a year later Irene, their only child, was born.

Curly was an ironworker, part of the team that erected the first high-rise in downtown Chicago. But his war injuries tormented him and he took refuge in liquor, going on week-long benders and selling his medals to buy booze. As Irene got older, she would regularly come home from school to find the furniture piled out in the yard by an angry landlord, and they would move into another, smaller, darker apartment. "The city sent trucks around with boxes of food. They'd put them in the snowbank outside the doors of people who really needed it. We were in *bad* shape." By the time Curly died in 1940, they were in a basement apartment with a shared bathroom and a tide of cockroaches her mother could not stem. Frieda worked for a while, tutoring middle-class children in German. But when the United States entered the war against Germany, her services were no longer required, and she started scrubbing floors.

Irene too got a job, at twelve, washing dishes and carrying trays at a private girls' school a few miles away. In exchange for several hours' labor each day, she was given a hot meal. "Everybody seemed to be in the same boat. Going to school, kids didn't have clothes to change into and their shoes had holes in them." She also started working weekends at a stable, grooming horses and cleaning stalls. She was saving for something special: she wanted desperately to join the Civil Air Patrol cadets, who marched and learned about flying and were trained by real marines. But she had to be able to afford the uniform, the royal blue jacket and trousers and cap. Finally it came to a choice between the flannel trousers that went with the uniform and a replacement for her school skirt, so patched it could no longer be made to serve. Irene chose the uniform—and so had to wear her uniform trousers to school. Outrage ensued—girls did *not* wear trousers—and Irene was suspended. The rule was only relaxed after the parents of her fellow students protested (they couldn't afford long coats to keep girls in skirts warm in winter).

Now Irene had the uniform, and she could join the CAP. Every Saturday, she took the bus four miles out of town to the assembly hall and joined five hundred other cadets. There were lessons on flight and meteorology, and on military techniques as well—a burly marine taught the group how to slit the throat of a sentry. And the cadets could learn to fly, if they could come up with six bucks—four dollars for an hour in an airplane and two dollars more for the instructor. In June of 1944, Irene took her first flight, going up in a Piper J-5 with a CAP captain and the only other female cadet. The girls were buckled into the backseat, and the captain set out on a hair-raising series of banks, steep climbs and rolls: if the cadets couldn't hack it, they were weeded out early. Irene was unfazed. "I felt—just—that this was where I belonged."

She had an ambition: she was going to be a fighter pilot. "Howling around, upside down, firing those machine guns." She had the stories her father had told her, and the images of the bold Tiger Moth pilots fighting for America over Europe. And even though she had to fight just to be allowed to take the high-school aviation class, she was sure she would one day fly a fighter jet. She never believed the world was going to stay the way it was. "It was all going to change and I was going to get to do this."

Once she had started proper lessons, funded by her factory job, she heard about the WASPs, and was desperate to join. When she called to ask about the specifics of recruiting, she was told candidates had to be nineteen. She borrowed a birth certificate from an older friend and faked a logbook that showed the requisite thirty-five hours of flying time (in truth, she had about nine). But the recruiters saw through her and sent her home again.

She finally saved up the money for enough hours to get her private pilot's license and got a job working on the line crew at Elmhurst Airport. She was the only woman on the crew; the others were all students at Northwestern University. But the guys admitted her easily to the fraternity that washed, gassed and propped the planes, and smoothed down the snow for ski landings in winter. "They were so nice," she recalls wistfully. When the weather was too bad to fly they played poker in the hangar. Irene studied every plane that came into the field and traded labor for fifteen minutes of flying time here and there. She earned her commercial license in 1948.

She was up for a job as chief of the line crew, but an old war vet gave the job instead to a pretty girl in a sweater set. Already, Irene was getting the sense that she was going to have a real struggle to work in this business, despite the conviction that she could do these jobs as well or better than anyone else on the airfield. "I never even knew about [discrimination] before, and I think as a child, whatever I did, I just wanted to do better than anybody else—sort of a big ego thing."

In the summer of 1948, the airport at Meig's Field was inaugurated, and a pilot friend told Irene that she could get her a chance to fly a crop duster—another woman knew Jackie Cochran and figured she could get a couple of gallons of Jackie's trademark Tailspin perfume. They thought it would be fun to spray the crowd at a 99s air show at the field. She agreed immediately—but had a little trouble gauging the crowd and wind and wound up liberally dousing a line of Chicago cops in perfume. "People said it was the first time the Chicago police ever smelled good," she recalls; the memory still makes her giggle. In the crowd was a man with a crop-dusting business, who asked the woman sitting next to him who that was flying the duster. The woman happened to be a friend of Irene's; when the man said he was having trouble finding "ag" pilots, she said, "You should hire Irene! She's real experienced!" That was an overstatement, but within days Irene found herself on her way south, at twenty-one, to her first real job as a pilot.

On her first ag flight in a Piper Cub with a huge tank loaded with DDT, she came in too low and tore the propeller off on a power line. But she managed to land, and her next flight was without mishap, and so began six years of crop dusting. She sprayed and dusted wheat and cotton in Tennessee and Arkansas and Mississippi, and she reckons she was one of just three or four women in the whole country doing the job. In Arkansas, all the men turned out to see her do her first field, just a foot above the cotton, her wheels thocking against the branches—but she did fine, and after that she was just one of the team.

The third season, she flew for a company that had almost two hundred pilots dusting; they flew from before dawn to after dark, following each other in to the airfield on the dark blue trails of exhaust in the night sky. That year, on the best days, she might make as much as two hundred dollars—a fortune. She bought her first car. The ag money paid for her instrument, multiengine and seaplane ratings. She remembers that season, 1951, as the happiest year of her life. "I love the heavy smell of the air at sunrise and the way the dust swirls in the vortices," she wrote in her scrapbook above pictures of her favorite planes, "and I love the way the exhaust blows blue on the way home after dark."

In the winters, she went back to Chicago and scrambled for jobs, instructing, flying charter, working on an assembly line at the Ford plant. Irene had started racing shortly after she got her license. She founded a race in 1948, the Illinois Women's Air Meet, although to her irritation she did not manage to win it until 1954. She competed in the Transcontinental in 1954, and then again in 1956. But she didn't do well because she couldn't afford a decent plane and couldn't muster good sponsors. "The rich women were the ones who won those races," she says a little bitterly.

In 1956, she decided to head west, with her two hundred dollars in savings. She got as far as Kansas City when a female pilot she met at the airport restaurant told her a DC-3 pilot was scrambling to find a replacement first officer. The cargo plane was five times bigger than anything Irene had flown before, but the pilot said that if she could do three takeoffs and landings unassisted, he would hire her. She did, and he did. She made a flight as first officer that afternoon.

For a year she flew the company's contracts, ferrying military personnel across the country. Then, she says, she ran into "a real S.O.B." of a captain, who tried to take off with the flaps still down, which meant the plane would never have the lift to clear the hill at the end of the runway. Irene fought him for the controls; when they landed, he said the fault was hers, and she was fired. The pilot was ex-military with war buddies in management, and no one was going to take the word of a female pilot over his, she says. But almost immediately, she met the pilot of a C-46, a huge cargo plane, who needed a first officer on a route to Fairbanks, Alaska. She went with him and that same day landed a job with a small charter outfit based in Fairbanks. She rented a room in town and came back to start work—to find that the boss had called the owner of the DC-3 operation, learned the flaps-down story and was reneging on the job offer. The same C-46 shuttled her back south. Now, however, she was stuck—in Oregon, she flipped through the yearbook of the 99s and relied on their generosity for a meal or a night's hospitality here or there as she made her way down to California.

The next years brought a string of jobs, a year at a flight school, a year with a charter company. Irene was restless and dissatisfied, and nothing seemed to go right. Men, she says, kept getting in her way, when all she wanted to do was fly. By 1960, she was flying air taxi in Santa Monica, when the phone in the hangar office rang, and a man's voice she didn't recognize asked if she was free in a few weeks' time to come and take the astronaut tests.

Wally Funk never imagined she would fly. Trips in airplanes were for rich people.

"Commercial aviation was—we didn't talk about it much, it was really for the elite. You had to be dressed. The men had to have coats and ties, and the women had to have heels, hose and gloves and that was what was expected." When Wally was growing up in Taos, New Mexico, in the 1940s, there was one plane in town, a Cessna 195 that belonged to a photographer. She liked to go and watch at the little airport, in case other planes stopped in, and she loved the tiny model airplanes that her father, Lozier, sold in Funk's Five and Ten. But she never thought she would fly a plane.

Lozier and Virginia Funk had a son, Clark, in 1936, and Mary Wallace arrived three years later. Wally (as she insisted everyone call her) was a tousle-haired tomboy who spent much of her time off in the mountains with the Tiwa, the local aboriginal people, who taught her to hunt and fish. She used her twenty-five-cent weekly allowance to buy bullets. She played at being Joan of Arc, carrying out a bold plan to save her people, and Lawrence of Arabia, urging her imaginary camel forward. She was thin and strong and her smooth cheeks were perpetually sunburnt. "Mother wanted a froufrou girl with frills, and all I wanted was an Erector set."

At five, Wally was jumping off the barn roof into a haystack, holding a Superman cape behind her. On the sidewalk outside her father's store, she sold live rabbits, fresh vegetables, bows and arrows and furniture she had made to visitors passing through town. And she excelled in sports. When she was a teenager she was a fearless skier, and her parents let her leave school for weeks in the winter to train for the national team in Colorado. Her sights were firmly set on the Olympics; she would ski, and possibly shoot, for she was an expert markswoman.

In 1956, when she was sixteen, her parents decided she had exhausted the educational opportunities in Taos, and she was enrolled at Stephens College in Missouri, a two-year junior college that prepared young ladies for university. The Wabash Cannonball pulled into town, and Wally got on, fidgeting with her new gloves. She made her way to the car where the Stephens girls were gathered and found a group of young women in fashionable hats and high-heeled shoes, smoking cigarettes—and thought, I'm not going to belong here. That first semester, she was uncomfortable, coming down to dinner each night in her requisite skirt and embroidered sweater. When she went home for Christmas, she rushed to the ski slopes—and had an accident with a tow line one day on ski patrol, crushing two vertebrae. At first the doctors said she would never walk, but Wally, ferociously stubborn, wasn't particularly interested in that diagnosis. Within weeks, she was back at Stephens—but she was in a half-body cast and could not sit down. A guidance counselor suggested aviation class as a distraction.

The classes were indeed interesting, and then came the day when the instructor led the girls out to the airfield for their first flights, in a Cessna 172. Wally went up with the teacher and one other student in the four-seat, single-engine plane. "What impressed me the most was that the airplane just kind of took itself off, and the ground was so beautifully packaged as north, south, east, west—it was all fields we flew over, near the Missouri River. The earth was so pristine, and I was up there looking down at the perfect pattern on the ground, at the cows and the cars and the houses and the river and the town. The bug bit and that was it."

She had to have lessons, and her parents agreed to pay for them. She didn't find out until ten years later that it was a huge financial burden. "It was fifteen or twenty dollars an hour. I had to do one hundred hours, which was about three thousand dollars, which was as much again as my tuition at the college." There was a fringe benefit to the lessons: only two groups of Stephens students were exempt from the dress code of skirts or dresses at meals—the fliers and the horseback riders could wear trousers on days they had classes. Wally carefully arranged her schedule so she had a class every day. She soloed at sixteen, won her license at seventeen and promptly joined the Flying Susies, Stephens' intercollegiate flying squad.

That was wonderful flying—alone in a tiny Cessna 120 or 172. "I took a plane with a radio to listen to radio stations, because we couldn't have radios at school. . . . I snuck out the window from a formal one time to go night flying and snuck back in by midnight so I wasn't caught." Another time she accepted a ludicrous dare to land on a sandbar in the river, where she could easily have been stuck with the plane crippled; she pulled that off, too. The student pilots would take their Aeronca Champions, with just sixty-five-horsepower engines (roughly equivalent to that in a vintage Volkswagen) and deliberately fly into a fifty-mile-per-hour head wind, so that they floated stationary, like hawks on an air current.

At the 1958 National Intercollegiate Flying Meet in Minneapolis, Minnesota, Wally won the Outstanding Female Pilot trophy. And she got her first sight of the Oklahoma State University's flying team—the legendary Flying Aggies—who won all the other trophies. She decided she had to go to OSU to fly with them. In 1959, she was the university's top female flier. She studied for an education degree that qualified her to teach junior high, but she was never much of a reader (she got through school relying on comic books that described historic events) and freely confesses that she took as many aviation courses as she could because she always got A's in those. At the end of her senior year, Wally was named the top female pilot at an international air meet in Columbus, Ohio, and won the Alfred Alder Memorial trophy as the most outstanding pilot. As airport manager Hoyt Walkup presented her with the trophy, she says, he told the crowd, "This young lady has one of the brightest futures in aviation that I have ever seen. Mark my word, if ever a woman flies into space, it will be Wally, or one of her students."

In the summer of 1960, she earned her instructor's license. The day after graduation, she went home with a friend from college whose parents lived on the military base at Fort Sill. The girls had envisioned doing some lounging around, but the friend's father quickly informed them they had better find jobs. That afternoon, Wally landed a job instructing at the Red Leg Flying Club, teaching servicemen who wanted to fly recreationally and, sometimes, their wives. She was paid four dollars an hour. She says today that she was immediately welcomed as a flight instructor by her soldier students. "Oh, they loved me. I had forty [students] waiting; I could only take ten to fifteen at a time. And all of the instructors would say, 'Are you going to go to that girl? She doesn't know much.' That's what I heard later." On the base, she watched the marching, the roll calls and the tank drills and reveled in the military atmosphere. She nursed a secret desire to join the forces, but women would not be allowed to fly for the military for another twenty years.

By then, she knew Jerrie Cobb, whose senior job with a major aviation company made her something of a star for young women fliers. "She was premier with Aero Commander," Wally recalls. "They loved her. She knew her stuff, she had flown a lot of airplanes, she had a lot of hours. Personality wise, she was probably as painfully shy as I. I remember going to Aero Commander and being escorted in by her secretary and sitting down and fidgeting in my chair, and I suspect we probably had two or three moments of niceties to say."

Leafing through an issue of *Life* magazine at the flight club one day in October, Wally saw a picture of Jerrie, all wired up and floating in the isolation tank under the headline "Damp

Prelude to Space." That same afternoon, Wally sent off letters: to Jerrie, to the doctors quoted in the article, to staff at the hospital that ran the isolation tests. "I am most interested in these tests to become an Astronaut, this has been ever since I started to fly," she wrote to Dr. Lovelace. "It would be greatly appreciated if you could send me some information on the field, or who to contact immediately. I can arrange for an interview most any time." If women were being trained for space, Wally was going to be part of it.

B Trimble Steadman knew that somehow she would be part of it, too.

In 1937, when B was twelve, she conned her parents into paying the two dollars for a brief ride with a barnstormer named Clarence Chamberlin, the daredevil pilot who had crossed the Atlantic just weeks after Charles Lindbergh. Strapped into the wicker seat between the broad expanse of the double wings of his Curtiss Condor, B felt almost drunk on the smell, a mix of gas and oil and leather. "I could see the whole world passing below my wings."

At the end of high school, B badly wanted to go on to college and dreamed of becoming a doctor. But her stepfather, an electrician at the car factory, said there wasn't money for that. "Go to work and learn the value of a dollar," he told her. It was wartime, and she quickly found a job on the assembly line at the E. C. Sparkplug factory. It was dull work, but she could finally afford flying lessons. At seventeen, she was tall and strong with dark curls. She earned her private license in weeks. She bought a war surplus bomber jacket and saved up for the chunky chronograph watch that pilots wore. At the airport, B met a couple of women, one a flight instructor, the other the owner of her own FBO (fixed base operation), and began to consider a new idea: women could make a living at this. *She* could make a living at this.

Then the war ended and suddenly there were floods of young men, pilots with hundreds of hours of flying time, all hanging around the airport hoping for a job. And the GI Bill was sending more veterans to college who were now graduating and hoping for jobs in aviation. The men, however, wanted to fly charters, or airliners—not teach amateurs. Nothing glamorous about that. So B earned a commercial and an instructor rating and soon got work teaching ground school at the junior college. The guys called her Miss B, and a breathless article in the *Flint Journal* in 1947 reported that "glamour has been added to flying lessons at Bishop Airport" where the "tall, statuesque" B was teaching flying. By then, she had soloed thirty students, all men. "This is my career," she told the reporter.

For eight years, B flew and instructed for the FBOs in Flint, working from first light until long after dark. One day one of her students, a businessman, gave her an appraising look after a lesson and said, "If you're gonna work so hard, why not work for yourself?" Friends leased her a pair of war surplus Taylorcrafts, and she opened a school of her own. "I hired another instructor, and a secretary," she says with a grin, "a man secretary." At twenty-four, she was CEO of Trimble Aviation. She took on dealerships for Piper and Cessna, did aerial photography and taught. She taught Marine Corps vets, Janey Hart the Senator's wife, and even a nun, who wanted to be able to explain airplanes to her pupils. One student, a lawyer named Bob Steadman, convinced her to marry him. She started coming first in the national races, and at one she met Jerrie Cobb. B began to hear rumors—that women were being tested as astronauts, that Jerrie was at the center of it.

Dr. Lovelace called her in the spring of 1961. B says she had no reason to think she would be chosen for his program—she was just a young woman with a small business in a little town in Michigan. But still, "I'd been waiting for this."

Sarah Gorelick, on the other hand, was caught totally off guard. On a Saturday afternoon in May 1961, Sarah was in the beauty parlor at Macy's in Kansas City, having her blond bouffant set when the hairdresser beckoned her out from under the hood of the dryer for an urgent phone call. It was Dr. Randy Lovelace—Sarah certainly knew the name. He wanted to know if she could be in Albuquerque the next day to take the astronaut tests.

Her mother died when Sarah was just fifteen and left her a small inheritance. She used it to buy a plane—a Cessna 120 with a silver body with a red stripe, blue fabric wings and yellow numbers. She named it *Baby*. Sarah's parents were Russian Jews who emigrated at the turn of the century and bought a pawn shop in Kansas. She joined the Civil Air Patrol in high school and knew from the first time she went up in a surplus World War II T6 trainer that she wanted to be a pilot. "Just to feel the freedom," she says, struggling to explain what was so intoxicating about that experience. "And getting everything in perspective in your life: one little old building down there couldn't cause you all that trouble. The world was so much vaster than that . . . to be tied down nowhere, to be controlled by no one, just to be me, no one telling me what to do or when to do it. Just feeling truly free, and being able to rise above my problems."

Women who learned to fly in that era raise this idea again and again: flying was an escape. It lifted them out of the tight social strictures of American life in the forties and fifties, and it offered brief moments of freedom from the roles they were under great pressure to fill. "My sister stayed home to learn to be a good housewife and all that good stuff," Sarah says. But she went to work in her father's store, helping with the filing, doing the taxes and saving up for flying lessons. At eighteen, she flew off to the University of Denver in her own plane, weighed down with everything a young coed needed to take away to school. "To arrive at college in an airplane is something different. I didn't have any trouble making any of the rush parties." The curvy blonde with a sassy pilot personality was immediately popular, and she met lots of boys: she was the only girl in the math and physics classes.

She earned a math degree—and instrument, commercial and seaplane ratings. But she didn't intend to instruct. "I could make ten times as much money in engineering. I worked my way through college partially teaching people how to fly, but there were so many pilots at that time. . . ." Instead, she returned to Kansas City and went to work for AT&T, calculating circuitry loads for the telephone system—but she flew every weekend, in races and to 99s meetings.

In April of 1959, she saw the barrage of press coverage as John Glenn and the others were introduced, America's new heroes. "I remember watching. And wishing it was me up there on the stand." There were new horizons out there: "to be a pioneer, that's what appealed to me." And her résumé clearly appealed to Dr. Lovelace: he could not wait to test this multirated pilot who was also working as an engineer. Sarah was on a plane to New Mexico the next day.

Gene Nora Stumbough heard about the tests from Wally Funk at a 99s meeting in April in Oklahoma City—the same place, in fact, that Sarah Gorelick first heard the news. Gene Nora (pronounced Janora) was a flight instructor at the University of Oklahoma in Norman. She was twenty-four, and she had one thousand hours in the air. She worked her way through college, dropping out after every semester to make the money to pay for more flying time. "I thought, Well, the only thing you could do as a girl in aviation was be a flight instructor—that's it." When Wally told her about the tests, however, it suddenly seemed as if there might be something else a girl could do: Gene Nora wrote to Dr. Lovelace immediately, offering one more volunteer.

While Gene Nora was writing, Rhea Hurrle was making her way stoically through the tests in Albuquerque. A farm girl from Minnesota, Rhea ran away from life as a teacher in a one-room schoolhouse, learned to fly in Texas and by the mid-1950s was working as a corporate pilot in Houston. She was twenty-nine and flying seven days a week when the first mysterious letter arrived from Jerrie Cobb, whom Rhea knew from racing. Rhea signed up immediately. "Being a pilot, I thought that going into space would be great. And I knew I was good."

And K Cagle went to the clinic a week after Rhea. Just five foot two and a self-described Southern doll, she was christened Myrtle, but that sounded too much like turtle; she preferred the snappier sound of K. When she was twelve, her brothers taught her to fly in a little beat-up plane on a "runway" cleared in the family tobacco field in North Carolina. Too young to be a WASP, K trained as an airplane mechanic in the war and later opened a one-woman airport in Selma, Alabama. When she heard about the astronaut program, she had forty-five hundred hours and an airline transport license, and she was flying out of Robbins Air Force Base in Georgia. She wrote to Jackie Cochran—and "they phoned me immediately. I was ready to go into orbit right then."

NORMAL WOMEN

Jerrie Cobb at the controls of an Aero Commander, circa 1960.

Jackie Cochran made the women-in-space program public with a splash. The April 30, 1961, edition of *Parade* magazine that arrived with the Saturday newspaper across the country had an extraordinary photograph on the cover. Two women posed in orange flight suits, holding pilots' helmets, the sky vast and blue behind them. Their black curls were tousled by the wind, and they had identical red-lipped grins. The cover proclaimed them "Jan and Marion Dietrich: First Astronaut Twins."

That was something of an overstatement—but a two-page spread inside showed the twins puffing into machines and strapped to exam tables at the Lovelace Clinic. And in the accompanying article by Jackie Cochran, readers learned that a whole program was under way to find more women like them. "I myself, while not an active participant in the present program, expect to fly into space before I hang up my flying gear," Jackie advised *Parade* readers. She described the tests and noted Jan and Marion had passed "pretty much as if one person were taking the tests twice." But Jackie stressed that she needed a large pool of candidates and asked for volunteers. (This was the article that prompted K Cagle to write immediately and offer her services.) Jackie concluded the article with a snide shot at Jerrie Cobb: "You might become the first woman astronaut who really earns that name."

Jan and Marion, the Flying Dietrich Twins, were identical, so similar that boyfriends confused them and not even their mother could tell who was whom from the back. Their physical resemblance didn't carry into their personalities—where Marion was outgoing and boisterous, Jan was quiet and reflective. About flying, though, they thought with one brain.

Born in San Francisco in 1926, the twins were intrigued by the first plane they saw overhead on the walk to school one day—what would it be like to be up there? They started saving for flying lessons in the first grade, putting birthday money and leaf-raking earnings in a flying fund. At sixteen, they began the paperwork they would need for student pilot certificates. They got letters of recommendation and photos and forged the signatures on the permission forms to avoid any possibility of parental interference. Then they went to take the medical exam.

"You passed the physical for the airline transport rating," the nurse announced brightly. "But of course those certificates are never issued to women." She gave them the second-class medical rating.

In 1943, the twins joined the local squadron of the Civil Air Patrol cadets; they traveled to Nevada for practice flights because the air space along the Pacific coast was closed to all but military air traffic. The next step was to get into the aviation class at Burlingame High School—it, like many others, taught the basics of ground school in the war years. "When we entered that senior aeronautics class," Jan recalled, "a room full of forty boys turned and looked at us and chorused, 'You've got the wrong class!' "

"Oh, no, we haven't!" the twins replied together. They received the top grades each semester. That Christmas vacation, they worked fourteen-hour days in the post office to earn the money for their flight lessons. After high school, they enrolled at the University of California at Berkley, and immediately joined the UC Flying Club. They soloed that year, a day apart. "Except for the tremendous exhilaration, it felt the same as other flights. No doubt. No fear," Marion recalled. "Now I could fly alone! Now this wonderful airplane was all mine." Jan was president of the club by second year, Marion the next. In 1947, they entered the inaugural Chico–to–San Mateo Air Race in California, a handicap race for stock model aircraft. It was a brash move: the twins had barely one hundred hours of flying time, and they were flying against thirty-six experienced pilots, almost all of them men. They won.

The prize money paid for flying time to get their commercial pilot licenses and flight instructor ratings. Then they placed in a few other local races. That gave them the confidence to tackle their big goal, an All-Women's Transcontinental Air Race—a chance to see the country and to compete against some of the most experienced female pilots in the country. A sponsor lent them a twin-engine plane. They had fewer than two hundred hours of flying time when they got to the start field; many of the other competitors had five thousand hours. The night before the race, panic set in—what had they been thinking? They knew that if they didn't acquit themselves well in this race, they would have trouble ever getting sponsors for another. But they were a sensation from the start: vivacious, bubbly, startlingly alike. "The twins in a twin!" the announcers would blare. In this race, as in all others, they flew together, refusing to compete against each other. Up against the best female pilots in the country, they placed second, taking home eight hundred dollars.

The twins graduated in 1949, and Jan soon landed a job as chief pilot at a flight school in San Mateo, where she supervised three male instructors. Marion, however, had another love: writing. She got her first real newspaper job in 1950, on the social pages of the *Sacramento Bee*. She was thrilled to be working for the daily paper, but she didn't much like covering fashions and dieting—although it was the only kind of reporting a young woman was permitted to do. She moved to larger papers, and slowly her beat widened. She angled to be allowed to write aviation stories, she took photographers up in her own plane for aerial shoots and she flew herself to stories in remote locations.

In the spring of 1952, Jan had an interview for a very big job, the kind she had daydreamed about for years: chief pilot for Cessna's operations in Long Beach, California. Cessna was then the largest light-plane distributor in the world. Their chief pilot would deliver multiengine aircraft from the factory in Wichita, Kansas, test fly for the shop, fly charters and supervise the flight and ground schools. Jan longed for a job like this, but she was anxious when she turned up to see the boss, Larry Hunt—she had grave doubts that Cessna would put a woman in charge.

She need not have worried. "I want to hire a lady pilot," Hunt announced in a booming voice as Jan was shown into his office.

She was caught off guard. "Commercial women pilots were about as acceptable as female ship captains," she explained later.

"I had never heard of anyone deliberately wanting to hire a woman pilot. This seemed amazing if not downright charitable."

She took a deep breath and started to give Hunt her credentials. "I have been chief pilot for a flight school, I have three thousand hours—"

"What do you wear flying?" he interrupted.

Jan thought she must have misheard. "What do I *wear*?"

Hunt nodded.

"Um," Jan stammered, "a nice slack suit, made to order. Slacks and a jacket with my initials on it." She gave her head a little shake and returned to listing her qualifications. "I have a commercial pilot's license with flight instructor and instrument ratings—"

"What about those French things?" Hunt waved his hand, searching for the right word. "Divided skirts—uh—culottes."

Inwardly, Jan marveled at the breadth of Hunt's knowledge of female apparel. "I could wear skirts," she offered. "I have flown charter and raced planes—"

"What shoes would you wear?"

Jan gave up and spent the interview discussing wardrobe options with Hunt. He gave her the job. She bought a couple of straight skirts to fly in (full ones would have blown back over her head on the runway) but soon found she ripped them climbing in and out of high-wing planes. After three weeks, her tailor resigned in frustration over the daily repairs. She tried a dress, but ripped it all the way up the front when she was climbing out of a cockpit. Her stockings tore, her high heels jammed in the rudder pedals, her earrings got caught in the radio earphones. On a day when she wore a sunny yellow frock out on the tarmac to watch a soloing student, an irate army sergeant tried to chase her off the field, assuming she was a lost passenger, not the person in charge. Why did Hunt insist she dress this way?

Jan got the answer the day a new shipment of planes arrived, and she showed them off to a crowd of prospective buyers. She worked hard, making the tires whisper on to the runway. And as she came in, she heard a passenger remark, "Why, the airplane practically lands itself!" Hunt beamed at her, and suddenly Jan understood. "If a girl does something well, especially a small one who dresses and looks like a girl, it looks easy."

Jan was made a designated flight examiner for the FAA, the second woman in the United States to have the title. She kept playing the game: she was poised and aloof, and she kept high heels stowed in the cockpit for when it was time to climb down. A local newspaper said, "She is probably the only woman in the United States to hold such a job," then passed on Jan's assessment of life as the lone woman in a male world: "Though a woman is a good pilot, she gets further if she is 'humble and discreet' in her dealings around the airport. 'You just quietly do your job. Your boss knows your talents but you don't advertise them.'" Her favorite hobbies were listed as decorating and antique collecting. "She herself tumbles out of an airy canopy bed each morning."

In 1960, Jan earned her airline transport rating, the top class of pilot license. She was the ninth woman in the United States to get the rating, and she set her sights on an airline job. Then, in the beginning of January 1961, she received a letter asking her to be at the Lovelace clinic in a few days' time.

Jan had written to the clinic four months earlier, when Jerrie Cobb first appeared in *Life*. But the arrival of actual orders to report to Albuquerque left her uncertain. She had just landed a chief pilot job in Los Angeles, the first woman at the airport to hold the post, and it was going to be hard to get a week off. And she wondered if, really, there could be much point—would women really get this chance? She wired Marion for advice.

Marion typed out her impassioned reply on January 13, 1961:

Dear Jan,

Your hesitating to go to Lovelace absolutely shocks me. You don't seem to realize what is involved. Yes, I can get away for a week—no one would possibly refuse me. Jan, we are poised on the edge of the most exciting adventure man has ever known. Most must watch. A few are privileged to record. Only a handful may participate and feel above all others attune with their time.

To take part in this adventure, no matter how small, I consider the most important thing we have ever done. To be asked to participate, the greatest honor. To accept, an absolute duty. Exploration of the last physical frontier—space—will contribute knowledge and literally open another world to all mankind. Being in space, thus having some control of it if others would also be there, is essential to defense. Space achievements are presently the most recognizable feature of a successful society to many turmoiled societies teetering between communism and democracy. Thus the space race [. . .]

The easiest ready standard for selecting women for preliminary testing is aeronautical experience. The number of women they have to choose from using this standard is pitifully small. That is why, if you are asked, you MUST go. You, probably more than any other woman, because of your superior aviation experience, control and character, good health and small size (in sharp contrast to Jerrie [Cobb]) are presently most qualified. So go, Jan, go. And take your part, even as a statistic, in man's great adventure.

Good luck!

Love,
Mare

Man's great adventure, indeed. Marion brimmed with enthusiasm, but Jan had good reason to be hesitant. Women could not fly for the United States Air Force. NASA gave no official indication it intended to employ women in the space program. As Jan was fast finding out, she couldn't even get a job as an airline pilot: the airlines told her that passengers wouldn't be comfortable with a female pilot—and they were unabashed about the explanation. There were no laws against discrimination on the basis of gender.

It was against this social backdrop that Jan, Marion and the other women went first to work in aviation and then attempted to break into the most male of bastions, the space program. World War II had changed many things about American society: in 1938, for example, only 20 percent of Americans (men and women) believed that women should work outside their homes. By 1942, that number was up to 87 percent. The twins and the other Lovelace women were teenagers or in their early twenties in this era, when social restrictions suddenly eased, and women could work, wear trousers, travel by themselves and have nobody think less of them. But the changes didn't last. The war ended and the government mounted a huge propaganda effort to convince Rosie to give up riveting and go home. Women who continued to work saw their wages drop by almost a third by 1946, from the war level, and they were forced for the most part into pink-collar jobs. Suddenly the emphasis in America was on family life: this is what the boys fought for overseas. The baby boom began—it would prove to be the single largest demographic leap in U.S. history. The middle class expanded rapidly, and white American families began a massive exodus to the suburbs, to tract homes with subsidized mortgages (often cheaper to buy than renting), stocked with dishwashers, televisions and other modern miracles. The nuclear family, gathered around their backyard barbecue, was the American ideal: the abundance in which they lived proved the merits of the capitalist democratic system, and it was this way of life the government was dedicated to protecting from the Communist threat.

The fifties family was, of course, built around sharply defined gender roles. Men went to work, and women ran the homes and raised the children. Social historian Elaine Tyler May, who has made extensive study of the domestic dynamics of the Cold War era, says, "Policymakers and the creators of popular culture . . .

pointed to traditional gender roles as the best means for Americans to achieve the happiness and security they desired." Movies and magazines replaced pictures of sexpot stars with stories about how women found fulfillment as mothers. Televisions, one of the fastest-selling consumer durables, filled the airwaves with domestic dramas such as *Father Knows Best,* offering up a daily serving of idyllic family life. A new industry of experts, including Dr. Spock and hundreds of others, told women how they could better raise their children and run their homes.

Women were inundated with messages, both official and those subtly transmitted by popular culture, that they must embrace domesticity in service to the nation in the same spirit that they once staffed the wartime factories. Addressing a national convention of Catholic women in 1956, FBI director J. Edgar Hoover told them that homemakers and mothers had a unique role in fighting "the twin enemies of freedom: crime and communism." He called the women in his audience "career women." "I say 'career' women because I feel there are no careers as important as those of homemaker and mother." Women were instructed to stock their basements with canned goods and bandages in case of a Soviet nuclear strike, and at the same time warned against stifling their sons, producing juvenile delinquents or, worse, homosexuals. (Ironically, the stereotype of the housewife might have played to women's advantage when the air force initially considered candidates for spaceflight: the argument was that housewives, used to all that cooking and cleaning and carpooling, would tolerate isolation and boredom better than men.)

Many women continued to do paid work, of course—for one thing, the crowd Hoover addressed, and the tides moving to the suburbs, were almost entirely white and middle class. Poor women worked to support their families, but most middle-class women working in the fifties did so in part-time jobs intended to supplement their husbands' incomes. Those who did venture into a "career" found the rules sharply defined. Magazines cautioned them about the misery that awaited a woman who earned more—or had more authority—in her job than her husband did. Sarah Gorelick recalls that when she started at the phone company, she was being paid the same amount as her male colleagues. But men, even those less qualified than she, kept getting promoted—after all, they had families to support. "It was just an era where they would give the job to a man," Sarah says. "Some of the men had only a high-school education—and they'd be called Mister So-and-so. And all the women were addressed by their first names."

Like engineering, aviation was a male domain. Despite the presence of a few women, the elite communities around airplanes, rockets and the military—all areas of power and prestige—did not welcome women, explains historian Debbie Douglas, curator of the science and technology collections at the Massachusetts Institute of Technology museum. "You had women who were army nurses. You didn't have women who were army generals," says Douglas.

The small number of women, including most of the Lovelace pilots, who managed to make a living working in nontraditional fields such as aviation accepted certain things. The first step was to set their sights low—as Gene Nora Stumbough did when she decided she could be a flight instructor, but not a corporate pilot, and certainly not a jet test pilot.

Working for a living made a woman suspect, but a woman who worked in a field such as aviation was doubly aberrant. So these women went to great lengths to make sure they did not overtly challenge the prevailing image of women in any other way. They played up all the archetypal images of femininity. The AWTAR contestants raced in full-skirted dresses, heels and hats. Jackie Cochran conspicuously powdered her nose in the cockpit at the end of each record-breaking flight. When Gene Nora applied for a job with Beechcraft in 1961, the savvy vice president of marketing was pleased with the idea of a female pilot—good for headlines—but responded to her query with the caveat that he was interested "if you live up to what your background and résumé indicate—and also, if you are the 'lady' suggested by your photograph." He deemed her sufficiently ladylike and she got the job, a national demonstration tour of a new aircraft. The boss told her to make as many beauty shop trips as she needed to keep her bouffant poofed, but to disguise the bills as "taxi trips" because he didn't want to explain it to the accounting department. Janey Hart rolled her eyes at the bushels of letters from people who told her husband, Phil, that he ought to be controlling his wife better, that Janey shouldn't be flying around by herself and certainly not in Bermuda shorts. Janey was careful, however, to check with both her husband and his campaign staff to make sure she was not seriously jeopardizing his electoral chances.

When Jerrie Cobb went public with her involvement in the astronaut tests, she cooperated on a lengthy profile in *Sports Illustrated.* It was written by a close friend of hers, and it projected a carefully constructed image. Jerrie "resembles nothing so much as a sorority alumna who has lost her way to the annual reunion," the profile reported seriously. "She is a thoughtful girl who reads a lot, especially poetry, and loves all music except rock 'n' roll. At home she likes to wear old shorts, and she likes to go fishing with her dachshund as a companion. . . . Jerrie Cobb, is, in short, a thoroughly feminine being, despite her adventurous background and her awesome masculine ordeal for the man-in-space project."

The third key strategy was for each woman to present herself as one exceptional woman, as opposed to a representative of any larger movement for change. "See, if the word got out that you were really a feminist you couldn't get a job anywhere," Irene Leverton recalls. "So it was a matter of doing the best you could, being quiet and then if it got too bad you told them off and quit.

But if you made big public things all the time, you were dead. You were going to starve."

The women faced a constant assumption that any woman who tried to excel in a male field must have something wrong with her. When Dr. Lovelace first made Jerrie Cobb and her experience with the astronaut tests public, there was one question she faced more than any other. "Why do you want to beat a man into space?" reporters asked her. It left Jerrie startled, almost disbelieving.

"I don't want to *beat* a man into space," she explained, over and over. "I want to go into space for the same reason men want to. Women can do a useful job in space. We aren't in a contest to beat men in anything."

The women ran into doubt and opposition not only from reporters and potential bosses, but also from the men in their own lives. Several of them broke off relationships with men who didn't want them to fly. "It took me a while to find a husband because they all wanted me to stop flying," K Cagle recalls. "I had one sweetheart who wanted to marry me and he said he couldn't bear the thought of me flying. I told him, I was flying long before I ever saw you and I'll be flying long after." Men such as B Steadman's husband, Bob, who thought it just fine his wife was flying, were a definite exception.

Irene Leverton watched in horror as the other women at the airfield, some ex-WASPs with hundreds of hours of flying, met men and quit flying. "They all got married—and some of them not happy, some happy—but they all quit flying." The memory leaves her anguished, more than fifty years later. "Why would you *do* that?" Of course, the other choice came with a price as well. "That's held against you too, if you've never been married. When someone mentions something, I just say I was too smart to ever do that. I said I never learned to cook, I don't clean very well and I don't work for anybody else." But the price of this, she acknowledges, was life on her own.

"Normal" women in this era were married women. Jackie Cochran pointed out to Randy Lovelace, in a November 1960 letter full of advice on how to conduct his women-in-space program, that he should be focusing the tests on married women. If he wanted pilots with thousands of hours of flying time, she said, they were likely to be older, and "when it comes to mental attitudes and emotional stability, you might not find it medically wise to have a group of unmarried oldsters on your hands."

When *Parade* made the Dietrich twins famous in 1961, the news of their astronaut ambitions was received grimly by the men they were dating. "It is an inappropriate goal for a woman," one told Marion somberly. "And I thought maybe he was inappropriate for me," she recalled. Another young suitor cried, "But I was thinking of asking you to marry me!" Marion's reply? "I told him to go right on thinking about it." She didn't have time to coddle boys who disapproved. But at the same time Marion herself had absorbed the idea that involvement in the astronaut program made her somehow abnormal. "I first wondered, who would marry a woman astronaut? The man in the moon?" she wrote, looking back a few years later. "I cannot imagine being completely devoted to a husband and the United States government at the same time. Any thoughts or desires on marriage I temporarily put aside."

Remaining single, however, brought with it a second, and dangerous, image problem. The great unspoken issue in the women's discussion of flying in this era is the almost pathological fear of lesbianism—of being known or being thought to be a lesbian. This was a perilous time to be gay. "It has never been easy to be a lesbian in this country," in the words of an anonymous narrator of *The Fifties: A Women's Oral History*, "but the 1950s was surely the worst decade in which to love your own sex." And to be single (which nine of the thirteen Lovelace pilots were, although all were older than the average age for marriage) at a time when "normal" women were married was to invite questions regardless of one's actual sexual orientation.

In the war years, gay communities quietly flourished in same-sex environments. The American military didn't like it, but the generals discharged few men, and even fewer women, for homosexual activity because they did not want to support the image of the services as a homosexual environment. But if gay men and women suddenly found it easier to make contact with their own communities in barracks and camps, there was nothing resembling public acceptance of homosexuality. When Jackie Cochran began the WASP, she instructed her staff who did the screening interviews to weed out any applicant whom they thought to be a lesbian (although WASPs say that, of course, plenty of gay women passed into the ferry corps undetected). "I looked for clean-cut, stable young women." That was the euphemism Jackie used. She was personally disgusted by homosexuality, and she also intended to be sure that allegations of lesbianism could not be used to criticize her program. In fact, says aviation historian Debbie Douglas, one of the key reasons Jackie hesitated to push for the militarization of the WASP was that she watched and was troubled by the public reaction to the militarization of the Women's Army Corps (Wac). Noisy, hostile opponents of the Wacs leveled two charges against the women: they were either all "whores" or all "lesbians." The charges were equally grave, and Jackie shrank from hearing either label applied to her pilots.

The fear of proliferating lesbianism in all-women environments during the war years became a hostility toward women who did not leave traditionally male jobs after 1945. Historian Molly Merryman says these women were attacked for their sexuality, once again as either "lesbian" or "whore." "Normal women have returned to the home," Merryman explains; "therefore, women who remain are not normal and either want to be men or want to have sex with men outside of culturally sanctioned norms."

Thus began one of the most aggressively homophobic eras in American history. Homosexual activity was actively prosecuted. Police went to great lengths to entrap gay people, men in particular; lesbians and gay men clearly could not report bashings or harassment. A "lavender scare" accompanied the McCarthyite paranoia about Communism. In 1950, the United States Senate prepared a study called "Employment of Homosexuals and Other Sex Perverts in Government" that vowed to purge all those who engaged in "degraded activity" and "immoral acts." In 1953, President Eisenhower signed an executive order that made homosexuality necessary and sufficient reason to fire a federal employee from his or her job. Most defense industries and others with government contracts also adopted the policy. The U.S. Postal Service assisted by tracing the mail of suspected homosexuals, in order to gather enough evidence for dismissal and possibly arrest. (That order stood until 1993.)

Hundreds of government employees were hunted out of their jobs, and the effect spilled over into society at large; anyone with leftist sympathies was suddenly also under suspicion for perversion. There was an almost hysterical level of disgust from "normal" society. If gay young people were not entirely disavowed by their families, they were frequently sent away to mental institutions for electroshock therapy to treat what the American Psychiatric Association pathologized as a grave illness.

"Individuals who chose paths that did not include marriage and parenthood risked being perceived as perverted, immoral, unpatriotic, and pathological," writes Elaine Tyler May. "Neighbors shunned them as if they were dangerous; the government investigated them as security risks. Their chances of living free of stigma or harassment were slim."

How to cope? One obvious solution was to marry, a strategy that many gay men and lesbians in government—and Hollywood—employed. "To escape the status of pariah, many gay men and lesbians locked themselves in the stifling closet of conformity, hiding their sexual identities and passing as hetero-sexuals," says May. Gay and lesbian Americans lived with the crippling knowledge that they could not tell, could not reveal their true identities, not to anybody. Marriage worked for some. Gay women who could manage it tried to emulate the feminine ideal to keep their secret; women who had a stereotypically lesbian, "butch" appearance struggled to find work.

There was a significant population of lesbians in the core of women who made their living as pilots, as there were in many traditionally male-dominated professions at the time. Yet the women did not themselves have to be lesbians to be at risk of suffering for the image. Even the suspicion of homosexuality was sufficient reason to keep a woman out of a job that properly belonged to men. Irene Leverton once left a good job because she was afraid she would be thought to be gay. She was working for a flight school in San Jose owned by a woman, and gradually it dawned on her that the owner was gay, that her "little friend" was her partner. These two women were part of a community of lesbian pilots, and before long a friend of theirs started showing interest in Irene. Soon the guys at the hangar were saying she was "one of them." Irene says that left her no choice; she could not risk earning that label herself: "I had to quit."

None of the Lovelace women faced real antagonism (or at least admits that she did). But they all took steps—in some cases, huge steps—to ensure they would not attract this kind of criticism. When a newspaper reporter asked Jan Dietrich in 1952 what the problems of a "lady pilot" were, she replied, "Counteracting public sentiment that women who fly are tomboyish or mascu-line." The women played the game, emphasizing their femininity, and where necessary playing up stories of broken engagements and boyfriends lost in flying accidents. All but the most stereo-typically lesbian and masculine of female pilots went to great lengths to be judged feminine and heterosexual, flying in pearl chokers and gingham dresses.

Whatever unspoken acceptance there might have been among the community of female pilots, it did not extend to overt tolerance of homosexuality—something that could threaten all of them. "We didn't want anything to do with the ones who were *like that,*" Jerri Sloan says firmly.

Come 1960, however, a faint hint of change was in the air. John F. Kennedy was elected president. Kennedy was in many ways a traditional politician, and he took a hawkish stand against the Soviet nuclear threat and the spread of Communism. At the same time, however, he represented a new generation of Americans. And he promised to tackle the problems that had long bedevilled the country and that were making their way to the top of the national agenda: civil rights and the legions of people who were left out of the American dream.

By 1961, when the women went to the Lovelace Clinic, Rosa Parks had refused to move to the back of the bus. A group of black youths had politely requested service at the Woolworth's lunch counter in Greensboro. The Students for a Democratic Society were organizing out of the New Left. The birthrate had finally begun to drop, after a decade of unprecedentedly high rates; the age at marriage rose that year for the first time since the war. Betty Friedan had begun work on a book about the nameless malaise of white, middle-class housewives, the problem she would come to call "the feminine mystique." Her conclusion— that women needed careers that would give them identities other than wife and mother, and equality before the law— would become something of a manifesto for a fledgling women's liberation movement. On November 1, 1961, fifty thousand American women walked out of their homes and jobs as the "Women Strike for Peace."

That same year, Kennedy established the President's Commission on the Status of Women. After two years of investigation, the commission would recommend equal pay for equal work, paid maternity leave and child care. It would be three more years, however, before it became illegal to keep a woman from a job simply because she was a woman. As the women made their way to Albuquerque, that was still a long way off.

FELLOW
LADY ASTRONAUT TRAINEES

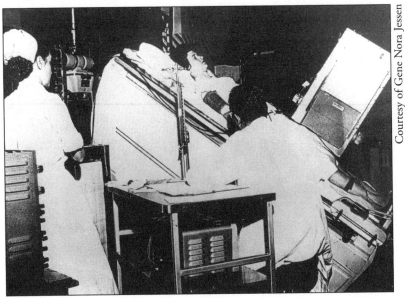

Gene Nora Stumbough on the "tilt table," Lovelace Clinic, 1961.

In the afternoon of January 25, 1961, a short story with a Washington dateline moved on the Associated Press news wire. A few large newspapers picked it up and ran it near the back of their news sections: "12 Women to Take Astronaut Tests," said *The New York Times* headline. "Twelve women have been chosen to undergo a preliminary testing program for Mercury astronauts. The prime purpose is to determine to what extent women may be used in spaceflight research rather than to select space-women. . . . The first of the 12 started the testing program last week at the Lovelace Foundation in Albuquerque, N.M." While the women's names were not being made public, they would take tests "similar to those used in selecting the seven men who were named Mercury astronauts." Jerrie Cobb had already taken them, the article reported. "Miss Cobb is preparing to take more rigorous tests, including rides in the Navy centrifuge at Johnsville, PA. Some of the astronauts have described this as the toughest part of their training program."

But the story attracted little attention: the public focus was on the Mercury men, for an announcement was expected any day on which of them would make the first flight. *Life* was full of glossy pictorials of the men spinning in centrifuges or inspecting the Mercury capsule.

Dr. Lovelace had his list of fourteen initial candidates (including Jan and Marion Dietrich, B Steadman, Jerri Sloan and Wally Funk), and one by one the women on the list received a letter telling them to report to the Bird of Paradise Motel on a Sunday evening and wait for further instructions. The motel was a long, low building across a six-lane road from the Lovelace Clinic. It had a pool and boasted kitchenettes, wall-to-wall carpeting and televisions in every room, but it wasn't a high-class establishment. The sheets were changed every Wednesday. If you checked in on a Sunday night, as the women called for testing did, you slept in someone else's sheets for the first three days. The hotel owner figured out, before very long, what this steady flow of earnest young women was doing at the clinic—and he knew astronaut candidates were forbidden breakfast. He liked to stand near their doors in the morning with a steaming coffee and ask with a sadistic smile if the women would like a cup.

Jerri Sloan and B Steadman arrived on the sidewalk outside the Bird of Paradise at the same time on a Sunday evening in March and soon realized they were there for the same purpose.

They were fast friends by the second day—the petite, flirtatious Texan and the gangly, pragmatic pilot from Michigan didn't have much in common, but they shared a ferocious determination to pass these tests.

That Sunday night, they received their instructions: nothing to drink or eat or smoke. They were to wash their hair and put nothing in it (no pins, no spray) and report to the clinic at 7:00 A.M. the next day. When they did, secretary Vivian Thomas handed them two enema bottles, a brown paper bag brimming with specimen jars and a five-page schedule, then dispatched them down the hall to the lab for their first blood tests.

The days were a blur—sometimes Jerri and B would pass in the hall or meet at the canteen to wolf down some french fries and a soda. When they finally got back to the motel in the late evening, they sat in plastic chairs outside their rooms. "We'd see these cars come in and we'd see them leaving," Jerri recalls. "I'd say, 'Gee, B, this is a ratty-looking place. There are people coming in here, but they don't stay very long.'" B concurred: some folks didn't even stay an hour. "It didn't occur to either one of us," Jerri says, "until finally B goes [she clamps her hand over mouth], and I go [another hand over another mouth, eyes wide], and we go, *Oh!*" Jerri laughs to the point of tears at the memory. "We were so busy with airplanes and babies and husbands and astronaut tests it didn't occur to us there may be a little hanky-panky going on at the Bird of Paradise, the local No-tell Motel."

They sat chatting while they waited for their nightly enema regimen to take effect. "B and I would sit out on the front porch and try to talk and then say 'Excuse me!' and run in and go to the pot and come back out," Jerri recalls. "And then we got to thinking about the guys [the Mercury 7]. We got a mental picture in our minds of your heroes, out there going through all these damn enemas and all this damn Fleet phosphate soda. We got to giggling and laughing about it."

The days, though, were serious work. Jerri tried to bluff her way through the vertigo test. After they shot her eardrum full of ice water, she was to tell the doctors when her vision had returned to normal. "So it had about quit spinning and I said, 'Okay!' And they said, 'No, you haven't!' And I said, 'How do you know that?' And they said, 'Because your eyes are going 'round and around!' And I said, 'That's not fair!'" The worst part, in her opinion, was the blood pressure test, when they plunged her hands into pails of icy water, watched her pressure spike, then waited to see how long it would take to come back to normal. She had no sooner withdrawn one hand from the pail—"My bones just ached"—than they plunged in the other hand.

Midway through the week, Dr. Lovelace summoned Jerri to his office. She wondered if she had failed a test. She never expected his first question.

"Are you having problems at home?" he asked kindly.

Startled, Jerri stammered out an answer. "Yes, sir, I am. But it's just not—my husband is an alcoholic."

"I know that," Lovelace informed her. "I've talked to him many times."

Jerri was stricken. Lou had been calling her at the motel in the evenings, drunken raging phone calls. After every one, B would console her and encourage her to finish the tests, and Jerri was just thankful she had left the kids with her mother. She never dreamed Lou would call Randy Lovelace. "I said, 'Oh, Dr. Lovelace, I am so sorry. I hope this doesn't knock me out of the program.' He said, 'It doesn't, but you better get home and take care of that.'"

She made it through the week, hungry and sore and worried. But she was able to laugh, too—when she and B went for the four-hour-long eye test, Jerri found she could still read after her eyes were medicated, and she picked up the Nero Wolfe novel she had been toting around with her. "B went blind and I didn't. I could feel that she was glancing over at me, so after a minute I looked up and I said, 'Are you okay?' And she says, 'You damn show-off, you know you can't see that book.'" Jerri laughs so hard at the memory she can barely gasp out the story. "I said, 'I sure can, I can read this book.' She said, 'Ha! You know damn well you can't see that book, you're just showing off, you and your damn good eyes.'" They went their separate ways to other tests, and Jerri's eyes were fine—until they met up again to cross the highway back to the motel. When the breeze hit her eyes, Jerri went blind. "I yell, 'B, B—I can't see!' and she says, 'Now you admit you can't see! Well, I can see and you can just get home the best way you can—you've been showing off all afternoon!' I said, 'No fooling, B, I can't see!' So she came back and got me."

B had her first pelvic exam at the hands of Lovelace doctors, (she hadn't even known the test existed before they motioned her into the stirrups). "Do you know how to fly?" she asked the brusque doctor prodding her insides. "No," he replied, without looking up. "Good," she said. "I want to be the one who teaches you."

She shuffled down the hall in an ill-tied gown to the restroom after they pumped her full of barium—the same scene immortalized in Tom Wolfe's *The Right Stuff*, about the male astronauts. "You [could have] no modesty whatsoever." She belted back their cups of radioactive water, and overheard doctors discussing how much better women handled the radiation. The night before the bicycle endurance test, she called Bob, telling him how anxious she was—it had been years since she rode a bike. "Bob said to me, 'Just remember, when you get really exhausted, that's when you get your second wind.' Boy, was that true." At the end of her bicycle ride, with her heart pounding, the doctors told her she had gone further than any of the men they had tested. It wasn't so bad. The only test she really didn't like, in fact, was the one where they drove "a needle like a ten-inch nail" into her hand, then hit it repeatedly with electric shocks to test her ulnar nerve. The pain was horrendous—and then the technician ran out of film, and no one could figure out how to replace it. They were going to take the needle out and start again. "I said, '*No you won't!*'" Using only her left hand, B reloaded the camera, and the technician resumed the shocks.

For the most part, however, the staff were kind and encouraging. "We never complained, we never told them to stop, we never stopped until they told us to stop," Jerri recalls. "We didn't even say ouch and, boy, they hurt us." B says the nurses and doctors frequently remarked on how much more resilient they were than the male candidates who had passed through the clinic. "They were a bunch of gripers," B says they were told. Neither B nor Jerri was going to gripe. "I just knew I was going to pass. I wasn't even worried about it," Jerri says. "You want an astronaut, by God, I'll give you one."

The night before the two were to leave Albuquerque, Dr. Lovelace called the women into his office, a large room on the top floor of the clinic, with pictures of planes all over the walls. Lovelace, wearing his usual white coat and his eyes sparkling, had good news. They had passed. "He told us exactly what he assumed was going to happen," B recalls. "That we collectively had done a good job of showing them what women could do versus what men could do and that there was no reason to exclude us from being accepted by NASA. . . . I left that meeting feeling that Dr. Lovelace wanted women to be a part of this thing and that we had just proven his theory."

The other women's experiences at the clinic unfolded much like B and Jerri's. They all said yes to the strange invitation from Dr. Lovelace—or petitioned him themselves to make the trip. And though it was difficult for some of them to get there, to find someone to run their businesses or take care of their kids, or to persuade the bosses to give them time off, they managed. Lovelace's invitation appealed to a deep-rooted sense of patriotism they all shared. "This was the time of Kennedy, of 'ask not what your country can do for you,'" Sarah Gorelick explains. Not only did the women-in-space program sound exciting, but it sounded very much like something she could do for her country. They made their way to Albuquerque and followed Dr. Lovelace's orders: they didn't tell anybody what they were doing, and they didn't ask questions.

In addition, of course, the testing sparked their own considerable ambitions. Although they were very different personalities, they shared a quiet sense of their own abilities: they were good, and they had a lot to offer. In 1960, when Lovelace mailed out his first batch of letters to female pilots, his name was synonymous with the selection of astronauts. Because NASA had opted not to develop a biomedical department of its own, the Lovelace Foundation had taken on that role and was seen as a de facto arm of the space agency. The crucial and much publicized role that the clinic played in the selection of the Mercury 7 cemented that image. Randy Lovelace was one of only a handful of NASA officials who were present at the huge press conference when the space agency introduced the seven astronauts in April 1959, and he sat up on the dais with the men he had helped to select. A week later, he authored (or at least signed his name to) an article in *Life* that detailed the testing process. In fact, the final choice of the first astronauts was made by three men who reported to Robert Gilruth, but Lovelace's exhaustive medical examination was the public face of the process. In the popular view, and thus in the minds of the women to whom he wrote, he was an integral part of, if not the key person in, the selection of the astronauts: whatever he wanted them for, it was certain to be the kind of opportunity they had never had before. If nothing else, these tests would give the women access to some of the most sophisticated aerospace and medical technology, something that a flight instructor or a Cessna ferry pilot did not get.

Going in, the women knew the tests were going to be difficult, and they all had the sense (as Jerrie Cobb had had, a year earlier) that it was not just their own future that rested on their performance: they felt that they must do well to show not just that they could, but that women could. They felt themselves in competition with the other women, but also (and the staff often mentioned them) the male astronaut candidates who were screened at the clinic. The testing was difficult and painful and mysterious, and they were determined not to complain or balk or even wince.

Jan Dietrich went in January, and each night she added to a letter to Marion, telling her twin what the day had entailed. "You will be up at 5:30 or 6:00 most mornings. You will be running all day long. Come with a little extra weight. You miss one to two meals every day." There was sisterly advice: "a flannel night-gown is nice" and "For heavens' sake bring a travel iron." But she didn't describe the tests themselves—just "try not to have your color portrait taken the day they rub clay all over your head for the electroencephalogram. Or take your exercise test the morning you take three enemas in two hours."

Almost twenty years later, Jan wrote to the clinic to get copies of her records, and a curious doctor asked her what the tests had been like. "In the bicycle ergometer test, my legs were ribbons of extreme pain," she replied. "They stopped me after 11 minutes when my heart rate was 178. At 180 the refilling of the heart is incomplete and one is at the point of collapse. Naturally I never referred to any discomfort, only saying, 'I could have gone another minute,' not the slightest out of breath."

In her letters to Marion, she warned there would be pain. "No matter how much discomfort is involved, just keep smiling," she wrote. "It is appropriate to combine a saint-like discipline with an unholy determination." On her last day, she added one line: "I have passed the tests."

Marion followed her twin to Albuquerque two months later. "Ominously, the motel manager greeted me as I checked in across the street from the testing center," Marion wrote later about her arrival in Albuquerque. "'You're really in for it,' he said. 'It's rough. Rough. Why, the girls today, they were like to quit but I talked them into stayin'. Talked the ones last week into stayin' too. Those doctors should give you girls a pep talk half-way through.' He ended with the obvious. 'But you know, if the girls find these tests hard, I don't see how they can do what they might be preparing for.'"

Marion found the bicycle brutal, swallowing the tube "messy," and the probe of her colon left her "speechless with pain." On her last day, a doctor peering down her throat said, "Uh-oh" and her heart sank. "Everything had gone so well. He just couldn't find something wrong the last afternoon. I felt sick at the possibility." The doctor announced she had adenoid adhesions—bands across the throat that form pockets and collect mucus, and might encourage infections. Not serious, but . . .

"I can break them," the doctor told her. "But it's painful. Lots of blood."

Marion, eyes narrowed with determination, bargained with the doctor. "If you won't put them on my record, go ahead and break them." He led her over to the sink and broke them. Indeed it was painful—but no blood. The doctor was visibly disappointed.

She soldiered through it, determined not to complain. "I felt exhilarated just being there." When she flew to Los Alamos, she sat up front with the pilot in the little twin-engine.

"Isn't that wonderful," he said, obviously aware of why Marion was being screened. "I would give anything to be an astronaut. But I'm too old."

His quiet envy moved her. "I looked at this man who was to me like all pilots combined. This man with thousands and thousands of hours who had flown the Alaska bush and the night mail. Again humbly I felt the responsibility of the chance that had been given me."

Wally Funk received her invitation to take the tests in January and she was there by February. For Wally, the whole experience was a shock. Her mother drove her up to Albuquerque and left her in the dingy room at the Bird of Paradise. A clinic worker delivered waivers for her to sign and the list of instructions, which left her anxious. "I thought a stool was something you sit on. They had to tell me how to do an enema. I'd never been around anything like that." But she threw herself into the tests. In Los Alamos, "I heard the doc say, she's too young [to know any better], she probably won't hit the chicken switch." And indeed she didn't, lying calm in the coffin-like radiation counter. Many of the tests were intensely painful, but she kept her face impassive. "I did not care how badly things hurt. I knew I wanted to be the best." And when they wired her up to the monitors on the infamous bicycle, she had a goal. "Psychologically, I wanted to go for ten minutes. At nine minutes, it was pretty hard. I just gritted my teeth, and I got my second wind and I kept going until eleven—I closed my eyes. They said, 'Wally, you have broken the record, you can stop now.'" She was sure she could get down off the bike herself, but the doctors insisted on helping her—and indeed, she found her legs were like noodles. They had to carry her off.

Jean Hixson flew out to the clinic in August after school let out for the summer, and she kept notes that record, between long lists of tests and appointments, glimpses into how she was feeling. "Missed lunch, had candy bar," she notes between a proctoscopic and six X-rays of her spine. After the eye tests she scrawled "can't see 10 ft." The day didn't get any better: "Bum filled with clog," she writes miserably. "Died of Barium."

But looking back at the experience ten years later, she wrote about it fondly. "In a way, I hated to finish the tests so rapidly. I had not only learned a great deal about myself, but also about many of the new human physical measurement devices—some being the only ones in existence, that were being used on us at the clinic. I will say that as I walked up the steps to my airline as I was leaving Albuquerque—a formal letter in my purse congratulating me on passing the astronaut physical standard tests, I was walking on air. There wasn't a healthier happier person anywhere."

Irene Leverton remembers her week at Lovelace as one humiliating, painful moment after the next. Poked, prodded, then sent to shuffle down a hall with an enema tube in place. Through it all, Irene gritted her teeth. "I just figured it was a test and I was going to beat it. I remember I had in the back of my mind, I'm going to do better than men do." At the end of the week, Irene saw Lovelace in his office. "He said, 'You'll be hearing from me. Lose some weight.'"

Gene Nora Stumbough arrived at the clinic on a Sunday night and met the other woman slated to take the tests that week, Janey Hart. The naive young woman from Oklahoma had no idea who the elegant East Coaster was: Gene Nora asked if she was married, and Janey said yes; Gene Nora asked if she had children, and Janey said yes, eight. Eight! Gene Nora asked what her husband did, and Janey replied calmly that he was a United States senator. Gene Nora was daunted—and even more overwhelmed when Janey threw on a bikini and went out to execute a series of flawless dives into the Bird of Paradise swimming pool.

Gene Nora kept a detailed account of her time at the clinic, writing it all down in a letter to her parents. "All they did was poke tubes up me and down me and take blood out of me!" she began, before filling six pages with close handwriting describing her ordeal. The proctoscopic she described as one of the most painful tests, "but then why not, when they run a Mack truck and 90 feet of fire hose into you?" The doctor who did her pelvic exam told her she was "a nice normal-type girl." She lasted twelve minutes on the bicycle, and was relieved to be told that was in the high range; she worried over low blood pressure but was told it was a good sign that the stress didn't raise it. Her letter was a litany of reports of castor oil and liquid diet, until she jubilantly recorded on Friday, "we could have *anything* we wanted to eat!"

She wrote to her parents about Janey and said her sense of humor had kept the two of them going. Deep underground at Los Alamos, they were listening while a technician explained the radioactivity test, when Janey noticed a picture on the wall behind them. "There's a black-and-white photograph of skeletons—not hanging up, just a pile of bones in a dish. And I said, 'Well, here we are, Gene Nora, this is us now and this is us after we get through this thing.'"

Janey was just short of forty when she went to the clinic, five years past the age limit. B Steadman had suggested her to Lovelace as an excellent pilot, and she had the FAA health certification—the doctor might have been intrigued by the idea of testing a senator's wife, sensing political benefit for the center if she made the cut. Or he might simply have been looking to expand his pool of candidates, for only half the women he tested were passing the medical screening. Regardless, Janey was eager to come.

She remembers feeling bemused by the unending series of enemas. "One morning I had a dress on and I was standing at the curb waiting to cross that highway. A car went by and my skirt went up and I thought, This is certainly never going to give anybody a thrill—it's just like there's nobody *here* I'm so drained out." There was enough of her there to be of particular interest to the clinic's gynecology staff, though—they had never had a candidate who had given birth nine times.

The week went well. The doctors plotted their results against a benchmark set by the male candidates, and consistently, Janey says, their results were as good or better. "We both thought that we were going."

When K Cagle told her husband she had been accepted to take the tests, he was excited and offered to drive her out to Albuquerque. But K didn't like the idea of him driving back alone on all that highway and insisted she would fly commercial, though the price of a plane ticket would badly strain their budget. "And then he looked at me and said, 'You're going to get up there on one of those Redstone rockets to go into space, but you're worried about me on the interstate?'" She giggles a little at the memory. The tests, when she got there (by plane) were exhausting but they didn't faze her much because she had trained as a nurse. And with her goal fixed in her mind, she could cope with anything: "I remember the time when they wired my head up, and then they put me to bed and there were all these bells ringing. I knew this was going to be a test of concentration, so I pretended I was in a space capsule and I had an emergency. I had to go down my checklist very carefully. It must have worked because I passed!"

She saw Dr. Lovelace very briefly at the clinic—she says he told her she was an excellent candidate and that her involvement might require some sacrifice on her part. "He told me I would need to put off having children. I said, 'Fine.'"

Sarah Gorelick arrived at the clinic thirty-six hours after Dr. Lovelace's phone call to the beauty parlor. Sarah, then 130 pounds and five foot six, was told to lose fifteen pounds. "They wanted you to be a *stick*." Her week at the clinic was no more fun than the others'. The doctor who gave her a rectal exam told her brightly, "Don't worry! I'm a married man!"

"Like that makes a difference," Sarah recalls bitterly. "We lost our modesty—we didn't come back sweet and innocent." The clinic wanted to know all about her reproductive functions and insisted she keep an ovulation chart. She was so mortified that a kindly secretary went with her to the drugstore and purchased the hated thermometer. Sarah, too, had a mantra that week: "I've got to get through this, I've got to get through this."

Sarah had two surprising encounters at the clinic. In the first, researchers grilled her about her technical background. "They were already talking about long [space] voyages, with crew members, and what they would need scientists to do." She got the sense, she says, that there weren't too many other female pilots with engineering backgrounds—and that they had plans for her.

Then, midway through her week there, Sarah was invited to Dr. Lovelace's office and was chatting with him about flying and her work when he raised the subject of Jackie Cochran, who was expected soon at the clinic. Sarah says Lovelace mentioned to her that Jackie dearly wanted to go into space herself, and to take his tests, but he had had to tell her she was too old, that with her poor health, she simply wasn't in the shape to do it.

At that moment Jackie herself arrived in the office, and Sarah hastened out of the room, greeting Jackie briefly as they passed. But once she was in the hall, she says, she could hear her. Jackie was furious. And hollering. Sarah had seen Jackie in action before—saw her practically decapitate a photographer at a 99s event who addressed her as "blondie." She knew of her temper. And she had no doubt what this fight was about: if Jackie couldn't go into space, she wanted to run the show, and she was incensed to arrive and find candidates she didn't know being tested.

While Dr. Lovelace made his way through his initial list of candidates that spring, Jerrie Cobb was soldiering through Phase III at the U.S. School of Aviation Medicine at the naval base in Pensacola, Florida.

For the first two days she faced tests that were starting to seem almost routine: back on the tilt-table she went, and into the X-ray room, then more electrocardiograms and electroencephalograms. But the next bit was more exciting: they laced Jerrie into a full pressure suit, an exercise that took an hour and a half. Simply breathing imported oxygen isn't enough at the highest altitudes; without a suit that exerts pressure to keep blood near the vital organs, a pilot will lose consciousness. Jerrie wore the smallest suit the navy had, but even so it bagged and hung on her, and she allowed herself a little daydream about a day in the future when there might be a pressure suit tailor-made for her. Then she climbed into an altitude chamber for a run that would simulate sixty thousand feet. They wanted to see how Jerrie would do flying a craft in this environment. She had no trouble, even with a droopy pressure suit and, when they plunged her down to ten thousand feet, all she did was swallow a few times to clear her head.

Next came physical endurance tests—and here, suddenly, Jerrie didn't stack up to the men. She did okay on the sit-ups. But she couldn't reach the chin-up bar, let alone pull herself up on it. "My biceps, which had never failed me in wrestling airplane controls, or pitching a ball" weren't up to this. She had to scale a six-foot-six-inch wall, and it took three tries, at a dead run, before she made it. As she tumbled over the top, she pictured Jan and Marion Dietrich, four inches shorter, trying to clear it.

The navy scientists shot her up in an ejection seat powered by a fifty-caliber shell—*whoosh* up the track, then *thud* back to the ground. Then came a test to see what happened to her brain at high G-loads. Pilots can feel dizzy or even black out when the normal pull of gravity is augmented by certain kinds of flying; this test was meant to find even tiny changes in her brain waves. Before they ran it, Pensacola doctors wired the Pentagon to get permission—for it meant taking her up in a Douglas Skyraider attack plane. Pensacola explained that the test was being run to establish the difference between male and female astronauts. Washington wired back, "If you don't now the difference already, we refuse to put money into the project." But they approved it, so lucky Jerrie got eighteen needles in her scalp. Then while a movie camera trained on her face recorded her eyeballs bulging out with the accelerated pressure, a navy pilot whipped the plane through racing dives, loops and rolls. The needles sent readings to an airborne EEG, checking her brain-wave patterns as she flew a high G-load stress aerobatic pattern.

A victorious Jackie Cochran is congratulated by Vincent Bendix, Bendix Air Race, 1938.

Jacqueline Cochran, circa 1937.

Jean Hixson, Women Air Force Service Pilot,
at Wright-Patterson Air Force Base in 1944.

Wally Funk catches a ride in a T-33, Ft. Sill army base, 1961.

Irene Leverton in her first aviation job, on the line crew at Elmhurst Airport, Chicago, 1947.

Courtesy of Pat Dal

Jan (left) and Marion Dietrich, Civil Air Patrol lessons, 1945.

Photo by Russ Scott

*B Trimble before her first
victory in the All-Women's
Transcontinental Air Race,
Michigan, 1955.*

Sarah Gorelick and her plane, Kansas City, 1963.

Rhea Hurrle, Texas, circa 1961.

*Jackie Cochran gets ready to break the sound barrier,
assisted by Chuck Yeager, center, 1953.*

Rhea Woltman in 1995.

Gene Nora Jessen in her Beech Bonanza, Idaho, 2001.

Jerri Truhill in 1986.

Janey Hart on her yacht in the Caribbean, 1999.

Wally Funk at a "space camp" in Alabama, 1991.

In an elaborate test for motion sickness, she entered the "slow-rotating room," a deceptively normal-looking apartment built atop a centrifuge. The whole room rotated at up to ten RPM, but it was windowless, so there was no sense of motion and test subjects grew steadily more disoriented. Jerrie felt fine at first, then found she couldn't walk heel-and-toe to the center of the room. She struggled with a series of small tasks—tossing balls in a basket, turning dials as directed. In the end, she held on to her breakfast; her performance "compared favorably" with experienced naval aviators and she was "remarkably less hampered" than a group of male flight students tested just before her, the navy scientists said.

And then she met Dilbert. Affectionately known to navy pilots as the Dilbert Dunker, the test was a round capsule outfitted like a cockpit, on skids that shot into a deep pool at a forty-five-degree angle and then spun over. First Jerrie spent a day with the navy's water survival instructors and was shown the life raft, how the helicopter rescue harness worked, and how to stay alive in and on the water. It reminded her a bit of her ferrying days, when she nearly had to ditch into the Caribbean.

Then the navy men strapped her into the Dunker. A bit like the isolation tank, the primary goal of the test is to see if the subject panics: underwater, upside down, lurching and disoriented, will a pilot keep her head and get out? Or go down with the craft? They packed Jerrie, fully clothed, into a life jacket and a parachute, to give her that "wearing a space suit" feeling. Then they strapped her in, and Dilbert shot down its tracks. She held her breath as it went deeper and deeper and water poured into the cockpit. She undid her seat belt, and moved slowly, telling herself to keep calm, trying not to snare her layers of clothing on anything, and wormed out of the capsule—its top was on the bottom of the tank and she was, indeed, upside down. Turning, she pushed off and glided to the top of the tank, where navy divers were poised to come in after an unsuccessful candidate. She was fine—but the whole experience was chillingly realistic.

Once again, her examiners delivered good news. She had done well. And, Dr. Lovelace told her, the other women who survived the Albuquerque screening would come to Pensacola in July.

Jerrie felt confident at last: "That clinched it, I figured. If the Navy itself was willing to cooperate in astronaut testing of female candidates, then we'd reached the top of the ladder."

Meanwhile, though, Jerrie was puzzled by her relationship with NASA. Sometime after the first women started the testing, she wrote to the new NASA administrator, James Webb, to tell him about it and to ask him to consider formally employing female astronaut candidates in the Mercury program. He sent her a polite but noncommittal response—the space agency was running flat out, up against the ticking clock as the Soviets were poised to launch a man.

On the first of May, she spoke at the Aviation/Space Writers Association general meeting, part of a panel on missiles and space. The meeting's biographical summary lists her as "the first lady astronaut." With her were a Soviet space scientist, a representative of the Air Force Dyno-Soar spaceflight program, and George Low—NASA's director of Spacecraft and Flight Missions. "There are at this time sixteen highly quali-fied and experienced women pilots undergoing the astronaut examinations at the Lovelace Foundation in Albuquerque," Jerrie told the meeting. (Four were yet to be eliminated.) "They are there, as I was a year ago, as part of a research program to determine women's capabilities for spaceflight. These physical tests are identical to the ones given the Mercury astronauts . . . and the results are showing women can withstand the expected stresses of space as well as men—in some instances better." While NASA was not yet involved in the project, the United States could gain a great deal by starting to train a woman—that was Jerrie's message. George Low didn't say anything, but sitting beside Jerrie on the dais he certainly heard about her plans.

So two weeks later, she wrote to James Webb again. "For the past week I have been undergoing 'stress testing' here at the Naval School of Aviation Medicine, which will complete my astronaut testing except for the centrifuge at Johnsville, which is scheduled later this spring. When that is completed I will have passed all the tests given the Mercury Astronauts. I have chosen to do this on my own in the eventuality that you might need a qualified woman in the space program in the future."

Jerrie went on to make an audacious proposal. Alan Shepard had just made his fifteen-minute suborbital flight, and there was mass speculation in the press as to which of the seven men was tapped to make the first orbital shot. But Jerrie warned Webb of rumors that the Soviets were preparing to send up a woman and suggested bumping the Mercury 7 altogether. "If a woman who had been through the astronaut testing program could become familiar with the Mercury capsule systems I'm sure she could accomplish the objective of the MR [Mercury capsule–Redstone rocket] shots you have planned for this spring and summer. I realize this would be unfair to the Mercury Astronauts but wouldn't they sacrifice their chance on one MR shot to see the United States beat Russia in one area of manned space flight?" She closed on a personal note that Webb was going to come to know well. "Didn't mean to 'bend your ear' but as you know this is of utmost importance to me after working 1½ years on astronaut testing—(I would gladly spend 10 or more years if necessary)."

From Pensacola Jerrie went to Paris, for the Salon Aéronautique Internationale, and then home to Oklahoma. In Tulsa that May, NASA was hosting its first conference on the Peaceful Uses of Space. Randy Lovelace was one of the speakers, and in a presentation titled "The Future Problems of Man in Space," he spoke publicly about his *women* in space. He described what had been done to test them so far: "These women are undergoing essentially the same detailed and comprehensive physical examinations, laboratory tests, X-ray examinations and physical competence tests as the male astronauts had." The conference closed with a banquet on May 26, and they wanted Jerrie at the head table; Tom Harris and her mother, beaming with pride, were in the audience. Jerrie was seated beside James Webb, the keynote speaker. When Webb rose to address the room, he introduced Jerrie.

"On one matter of interest to Oklahoma, I have kept silent until now," Webb said jovially. "This relates to the appointment of Jerrie Cobb as a consultant to the National Aeronautics and Space Administration. Recently, at one of our meetings with consultants in Washington, I asked Dr. Randolph Lovelace if he thought Jerrie could contribute to our program. He enthusiastically endorsed the idea. I understand that Jerrie has now finished all of the physiological tests which were basic to the selection of NASA's seven astronauts. So I expect to ask her to serve as a consultant on the role of women in the national space program."

Webb clearly hadn't given this a whole lot of thought, for when pressed for details about the appointment by reporters, he said he just reckoned "she would be a great asset to any part of the program." Did that mean she was going into space? Webb said he wasn't sure. "She's been through all the tests," he pointed out, "and has the judgment and knowledge." In truth, Webb had a simple political strategy behind the appointment: Jerrie was generating plenty of headlines with her speeches about a women's astronaut program, and he felt she could be more effectively controlled if she was at least nominally working for the agency.

Jerrie was shocked by Webb's announcement, but thrilled. She saw this as the biggest boost her space ambitions had yet received. She formally accepted the post with a letter to Webb saying, "It is my heart's desire and serious purpose to see the first woman in space be an American. I assume this consultant position will be concerned with this primary objective. By the end of this summer there will be five women pilots qualified and tested as astronaut trainees and I intend to keep you informed of the progress and results of this research program."

Had Jerrie been watching for them, she might have noticed some ominous signs—no paperwork arrived to make her relationship with the space agency official, and the usual consultant's salary of fifty dollars a day was not paid her. But she never questioned any of that: she was just delighted to be working for NASA.

On May 17, 1961, Dr. Lovelace sent letters to the first round of female candidates he had tested. Some received brief rejections: they were not qualified for the women-in-space program. But B Steadman, Jerri Sloan, Wally Funk and the Dietrichs received exciting news indeed.

> By some time in June, we hope that all of you that passed the examinations here will be able to go in a group to a service laboratory where further tests will be carried out. Just as soon as a definite date is picked, I will let you know immediately. We also hope that funds will be available for your transportation to this service laboratory and your expenses while there.
>
> Meanwhile I would like for you to achieve the best possible physical condition that you can as the forthcoming tests will require considerable physical stamina. I would recommend walking, swimming and bicycle riding as well as calisthenics.
>
> I am happy to say that you are one of those who was successful in completing the examination.

Twelve days later, all the successful candidates found another letter in the mailbox, this one a typed missive from Jerrie Cobb, on letterhead from her Oklahoma office at Aero Commander. It was the first of what would be many such group letters. In this

one, Jerrie brimmed with enthusiasm—although there was also a
hint of what would become her signature paranoia.

Dear F.L.A.T.: (fellow lady astronaut trainee)
　　It is with pleasure that I send my sincere congratulations
to you upon passing the Astronaut examinations at the
Lovelace Foundation.
　　Please forgive this impersonal way of writing you, but I
am attending the Salon Aeronautique Internationale in
Paris this week and must depend on my secretary to send
you this letter, so you may make plans for future astronaut
testing.
　　The U.S. Navy has arranged for us to take a series of
tests at their school of Aviation Medicine in Pensacola,
Florida. These tests consist of physical fitness, endurance,
low pressure chamber, acceleration, clinical examinations,
air-borne E.E.G., etc. I have just completed these tests and
am sure you will find them interesting as well as informative.
　　These tests will require a full two weeks and are scheduled
for July 16–29. Housing will be at the D.O.Q. ($2.00 per
night) and meals at the officer's mess (50¢ to 75¢). Two
copies of the enclosed release must be signed, witnessed
and returned to me. . . .
　　It is of utmost importance that you do NOT mention
this to any press. If there is any publicity on any of you
before these Navy tests, it could seriously jeopardize this
entire research program. The results will be announced
after the tests at Pensacola.
　　I would suggest that you get in as good of physical
condition as possible—especially, running, swimming,
etc. The weather is HOT so bring cool dresses, shorts,
swimming suits and tennis shoes. We will all be there
together (8 of us) and I'm certainly looking forward to
the opportunity to get to know each other. If you have

any questions please contact me after June 3rd in Oklahoma. You will be hearing from Dr. Lovelace shortly.

None of the FLATs but Jerrie knew who the others in the group were, and she didn't reveal their names in that first letter, so each was curious to meet the other women who had made this first cut. But within a few weeks Jerrie wrote again, this time to say that the testing had been postponed until the autumn—it was taking Lovelace longer than he had anticipated to get a large enough group of women together.

Jerrie, meanwhile, had plenty to occupy her. In early June she met with several senior NASA officials to outline her vision of a crash program to launch a woman. And in the middle of the month, she sent a memo to Webb and his deputy, Hugh Dryden, outlining her plans as their consultant on women in space. Webb might have seen her appointment as a way to sideline her and quash discussion of the female astronaut question, but Jerrie had taken her new job as a sign the agency was serious about her goals.

It is possible for the United States to put the first woman in space [she wrote]. Such a scientific feat would receive world acclaim and I propose that we lose no time in assuring that the United States will accomplish this important first.

The public interest in putting a woman in space is overwhelming—no other space achievement at this time would attract more admiration and respect throughout the world. Russia will not delay in their eagerness to reap this acclaim—but let us not wait for their challenge!

The United States can accomplish this as part of Project Mercury—without delaying it since the same purpose of the MR mission would be accomplished. There would be no additional risks involved since the woman would have demonstrated proficiency equal to the men.

Two years ago Russia announced they were researching Mongolian women for space explorations. Six weeks ago the observatory in Germany which monitors all space frequencies announced they had distinguished female voices on the specific frequencies Russia uses for training Cosmonauts. Two weeks ago in Paris I was approached by two Russian scientists inquiring of U.S. plans for putting a woman in space. All this comes as no surprise since the U.S.S.R. has long said they would *also* send the first woman into space.

I am not one to subscribe to the "space race" but I deeply believe the world acclaim such a scientific "first" would receive could greatly enhance our country's space programs.

Women can and will make valuable contributions in future space explorations—not to detract from the true pioneering of men in space—but on a scientific level in missions requiring the unique adaptability of the female sex.

I believe in letting nature take its course—but the natural course of events will probably not include women on space flights for several years. Hence I endorse one exception—that of sending a qualified, tested and capable woman on a Mercury Redstone ballistic mission—thereby earning the world's admiration and respect for the United States by accomplishing this unprecedented scientific feat. (This would also prove the safety, dependability and simplicity of our spacecraft systems. If a woman can do it—it *must* be safe and simple!)

Jerrie was talking in general terms about a woman to be sent up—but in truth, of course, she was sure it should be her, and she said as much to NASA: "Naturally I would love to be the woman selected." She included a biography that highlighted her credentials but pledged to search the country for a woman who would meet whatever specifications they set down.

She had a series of recommendations. To make sure the first woman in space was from the United States, she advised the space agency to get a woman training in the Mercury capsule simulator and if she proved she could fly it as well as the men, slot her in for the next Mercury mission. Meanwhile, to gather the necessary data on women's performance in space, a group of women should be put through all the physical, psychological and stress tests. (These she would have completed by the end of the summer, she noted.) And with those women, NASA should "form a nucleus of potential women astronauts for further research in the determination of how, why and where women can best contribute in future space exploration." And while all that was going on, Jerrie would go back on the speaking circuit, talking to as many audiences as she could (especially young people and women) about the need for space exploration and the importance of relevant education.

She concluded her unsolicited report to NASA with an impassioned plea, the first of many Webb would receive from her. "To each is given the ability to serve. My life's purpose is to find that way in which I can best serve. God has given me the ability to fly—the unrelenting desire to traverse his skies and the Faith to believe. I offer myself—No less can I do."

As James Webb no doubt knew, Jerrie was on target with her speculation about the Soviet space program: the Russians were indeed training women for space. The initial idea to fly a woman was that of Nikolai Kamanin, an air force general who supervised the cosmonauts. His motives were not scientific. "Under no circumstances should an American become the first woman in space," he wrote, explaining his plan. "The first [female] cosmonaut will be as big an active advocate for communism as [Yuri] Gagarin and [second man in space Gherman] Titov turned out to be." Sergei Korolev, the chief designer, initially rejected the idea—but Kamanin took it to the Soviet premier, Nikita Khrushchev, who embraced the plan. The equality of men and women in the Communist system, at least the theoretical equality, was one of Khrushchev's favorite points of comparison with the West. In his famous "kitchen debate" with then Vice President Richard Nixon at the American Exhibition in Moscow in 1959, Khrushchev spoke proudly about the equality of Soviet women and the productive female worker. (Nixon misunderstood the Soviet leader's belief that it was a good thing that women worked and responded by pointing to a model washing machine designed to make life easier for the American housewife.) When Khrushchev approved the plan to train women for space, he designated a committee of the politburo to find them. They looked not in the ranks of the military pilots (of which there were a few women), but of farm and factory workers: Khrushchev wanted his first woman in space to be one who embodied the Soviet ideal—although the committee did seek women with aviation or parachuting experience. After extensive medical screening, including centrifuge and pressure chamber tests, five women reported to a dubious Korolev at the cosmonaut training center in Star City, outside Moscow. They began intensive training, including centrifuge loads as high as ten G's, weightlessness training, water survival techniques, flight training in MiG trainers and study of astronomy and astronautics. It seemed clear that Korolev was going to see this stunt with a woman carried out only once, and so the five women were intensely competitive for that one seat in a Vostok capsule. The leading candidate appeared to be Valentina Ponomareva, a twenty-eight-year-old pilot with 320 hours of flying in heavy planes, a graduate of the Moscow Aviation Institute and a mathematician at the USSR Academy of Sciences. But Ponomareva was disparagingly described by the trainers as independent, self-assured, even a feminist. Those were not the qualities they were looking for in a woman. In addition, Kamanin noted that she was in fact more technically qualified than the male cosmonauts. And so a rival emerged to Ponomareva: a twenty-six-year-old textile factory worker named Valentina Tereshkova. She was reticent and modest, a member of the Young Communist League. She was, Kamanin noted with satisfaction, "Gagarin in a skirt."

Jerrie was right about the Soviet goal of launching a woman, but she badly missed the mark when she wrote to James Webb that American "public interest in putting a woman into space is overwhelming." There was nothing resembling a national agitation to launch women. It was not something that people with a lay interest in the space program were asking about, and the idea had no political backing either. The women's movement was in its infancy, there was little public discourse on equal opportunity, and Americans gave every indication that they felt it entirely fitting that the space program be entrusted to a few brave men. While the Soviet propaganda machine prepared to go to work on the achievements of their female cosmonauts, the American mythmakers had already made seven men—men who embodied all the ideals of American masculinity—into heroes.

Jerrie was wrong on another count as well. While those at work within the agency were constantly aware of their competitors on the other side of the world, NASA said publicly that it would devise its own agenda and would not be influenced by competition. In 1962, when President Kennedy declared the goal of a moon landing, that solidified the position. NASA's engineers worked methodically toward that achievement: the Gemini missions would fly crews of more than one astronaut and then practice the vital maneuver of docking two craft. Then the Apollo missions would journey closer and closer to the moon. George Low said that what the Russians did had "no bearing" on NASA's plan; there was no race. (This was, in the words of space historian William Burrows, "as clever as it was disingenuous": if the Soviets were winning, the Americans could deny they were competing.) But in this context, Jerrie's push to beat the Soviets in flying a woman was directly counter to NASA policy and the optics the agency wanted for its decision-making.

And nobody, not the public and certainly not the space agency, was interested in having female astronauts demonstrate how "safe and simple" spaceflight was—the role women had played in aviation since the days of Amelia Earhart. NASA was working to wring enormous budgets out of Congress, and the mystique of the agency's projects was predicated on their complexity and unprecedented difficulty. In keeping with that image, NASA employed astronauts who were presented as superhuman, courageous and tough, with unequalled technical skills. None of these agendas was served by having a gal with a ponytail lead the way into space.

She didn't know it, but Jerrie had another problem.

Jackie Cochran had read the newspaper articles about Jerrie's new appointment at NASA, and she didn't like this latest turn of events, not at all. She made her first decisive move to get control of the program with the *Parade* article: she flew Jan Dietrich to the clinic for testing herself, and got the twins there for photographs to accompany the text she wrote.

On May 31, 1961, her husband, Floyd Odlum, wrote to Randy Lovelace. It was a long letter, and a stiff one, a letter that belied the close relationship between Jackie, Floyd and the Lovelaces. Jackie was in Paris, Floyd wrote, but there she had heard third-hand that the "girls" were to go on in their testing. This did not jibe with Jackie's understanding that she was leading this program:

> She apparently does not know as much about plans and programs as the girls know who are being medically processed at Albuquerque. . . . Jackie is constantly asked

about this women's program and is so much on the edges
of it that she has to reply in rather vague generalities. She
has the unhappy feeling that you don't really want her to
be a part of the program. This is based on a combination
of circumstances such as the start of the program without
consulting her in any way, the original publicity without
even notice to her of what was coming up, your apparent
lack of full communication with her about the program or
planes while you were at the ranch, the rather "detached"
position she was in while she was in Albuquerque with the
Dietrich twins and what appears to be lack of initiative on
your part in getting her lined up with the NASA or otherwise in connection with the next phases of the program.
In view of the close friendship between the two of you
and her well-established place in aviation, Jackie can't
believe it was pure oversight on your part.

Odlum offered a variety of theories he and Jackie had on why
she had been so unfairly sidelined. Did Lovelace have commitments to *Life* magazine? Did "a certain Air Force General who is
prominent in air and space medicine" (almost certainly a reference
to Flickinger) want Jackie sidelined in favor of his candidate, Jerrie
Cobb? Did Lovelace's clinic staff want Jackie kept out? Regardless,
Odlum scolded Lovelace for having made a serious misstep in
letting Jackie be shunted aside.

Certainly the successful progression of a space program for
women involves much dealing with women and their
psychology, a lot of which does not show up in the charts.
Also certainly a woman who has led the women in aviation for two decades or more and who went through all
these problems in developing the WASP program and who
is not an active competitive candidate herself can
contribute a great deal.

And then Odlum, one of the clinic's principal donors, closed with an implied threat. "Jackie does not want to be around if you don't want her," he wrote. And if Lovelace did want her, he had better start informing her of exactly what was happening with the group. "If you have personal or other problems dealing with the point of this personal letter you should lay them on the table because, as I said above, Jackie is rather unhappy."

This might have been the first time Randy Lovelace ever found himself up against Jackie like this; they had always worked together for joint goals in aerospace, but now he had control of something Jackie had decided was by rights hers. Lovelace replied a week later, with a letter that is a study in diplomacy. He opened on a conciliatory note, advising Floyd that he had just returned from a meeting of the Air Force Association, where he had overseen Floyd's appointment to two important boards of directors. He politely attempted to point out that Jackie had been kept informed ever since he first told her about the program. All the women Jackie herself recommended had been contacted and would be tested in the next few weeks, he said, and he attached a list of those who had already passed; all would be informed that Jackie and her husband were footing the bill. And Lovelace added that he had tried to tell Jackie the latest on the testing, but she was in Paris: the navy would be running further tests in July or August, but if Odlum and his wife wanted, those tests could be delayed. A note of irritation crept into his letter toward the end:

> At the time we initiated this program Jackie was in Europe, so this explains why we did not tell her about it then. While we were at the ranch I told her exactly what the tests were to be on each girl and when she was here with the Dietrich girls we permitted them to have their pictures taken during some of the examination procedures. . . . As far as the NASA is concerned, I had absolutely nothing to

do with Miss Cobb's contacts with them. . . . I was as
much surprised as anyone else when Mr. Webb stated that
Miss Cobb was to be a consultant to him. . . . As far as the
Life commitment is concerned, the Air Force has no
General or any other officer listed in this program and as
you can see by my comments above, subsequent tests are to
be carried out by the Navy at Pensacola. . . . We will
continue to send you copies of all the correspondence in
connection with this program. When we have the names of
the girls that will be coming for tests, we would be happy
to have Jackie write them about smoking and exercise.

He signed the letter "Randy," and softened his tone in a hand-
written note across the bottom: *"I consider Jackie and you the
couple I am closest to of all the couples I know."*

Jackie was placated, temporarily. She answered Lovelace's
letter to Floyd in mid-June and made no reference to her
husband's assertions that she was angry. Jackie wanted the testing
at Pensacola delayed, not only so that all the possible candidates
would be screened, but also, "I would like to be able not to
return from Spain before the middle of September." And once
again, she had a bevy of instructions: Lovelace should be arranging for follow-up medicals. Were the women going to get paid in
Pensacola? Presumably he planned to eliminate some of the
women after Pensacola—had he elicited a commitment from
them that, if selected, they would be able to devote themselves
full-time to whatever came next? "The further stages may be full-
time effort for a year or two or possibly even more. How will
their status and pay be worked out? Will they be on the Navy
payroll or the NASA payroll or some other payroll?"

And at the end of the letter, she returned to what was becoming a growing preoccupation. "It is apparent that one of the girls
has an 'in' and expects to lead the pack," Jackie wrote in a thinly
veiled reference to Jerrie Cobb. "She has stated as much to others

who have reported the conversation to me. Favoritism would make the project smell to high heaven. Furthermore, I think to make it a publicity project for *Life* or anyone else would be a mistake. There has been much unfavorable comment as to this concerning the [male] astronauts. This should be a serious quiet project from now on." It was a mistake to have one participant who had special status with NASA, Jackie wrote. And once again, she reiterated her belief that one woman should be running the show—"a non-competitor."

Floyd put it even more plainly in a letter to Lovelace in July, when he was discussing his donations to fund this program. What, he wanted to know, was "that Cobb woman" doing?

By midsummer, Dr. Lovelace had eleven candidates he considered worthy of the next phase. On July 12, each of those women received a letter from Jackie Cochran, on her signature letterhead—featuring a bold looping J in "Jacqueline" at the top, above her Park Avenue address. She "strongly advised" the women to get to Pensacola, telling them their only expense would be transportation there and two dollars a day for meals, unless they couldn't manage it. "I have agreed to donate to the Lovelace Foundation the needed sum to cover the transportation and meal cost for all of the candidates if and to the extent they need such assistance. If you need and want money for these purposes, please, therefore, write to Dr. Lovelace at Albuquerque and such funds will be provided, in the same way that I handled the costs of the medical checks of a majority of the candidates at the Lovelace Foundation."

She wrote that ten women would be going to Pensacola and that she would not be among them. "As you probably know I am not a participant in these medical checks and tests. They were set up for women under forty years of age. Some of you may therefore wonder why my great interest and my assistance."

And here, Jackie struck her first note of caution. "There is no astronaut program for women as yet. The medical checks at Albuquerque and the further tests to be made at Pensacola are purely experimental and in the nature of research, fostered by some of the doctors and their associates interested in aerospace medicine. No program for women has been officially adopted as yet by any of the governmental agencies. As a result you were under no commitment to carry forward as a result of successfully passing your tests at Albuquerque and you will be under no commitment as to the future if you pass the tests at Pensacola."

Jackie was not, however, ruling anything out. "I think a properly organized astronaut program for women would be a fine thing. I would like to help see it come about. It is possible that my previous experience with group efforts by women in the air can be of some value or help in connection with the possible 'Space Program for Women.'" She warned the women off participating in publicity, saying their best hopes lay in coverage that dealt with the whole group of women, was factual and came from the officials in charge when the tests were done. She said she hoped to be in Pensacola to meet them, and closed with advice that they get plenty of exercise and, if they must smoke, at least cut back. "We are counting on each one of the group to pass with flying colors. That's the best way to make a program for women more probable."

That same week there was a letter from Dr. Lovelace, saying the tests at Pensacola, originally scheduled for July 18, had been delayed. He provided the women with no reason, although with hindsight it appears that he did not think he had a large enough group, since a half dozen women had yet to take the tests. But Lovelace advised the women the program would go ahead in early September.

In August, Dr. Lovelace wrote a second letter, and this one went to twelve women across the country. He told the women who had passed Phase I that they were bound for two weeks of further examination starting September 17. "There is to be no publicity whatsoever about these tests or your trip to Pensacola," he warned. Jackie Cochran would pay the expenses of anyone who needed the help, he wrote. "As Miss Cochran will be in Pensacola for a few days during the tests, you can thank her in person." A week later, he mailed the women who needed the money a check for several hundred dollars to cover their plane tickets and maintenance costs in Pensacola.

That letter left the women with quickened hearts: Lovelace seemed terribly serious about this. "I suggest you study the FAA manual, mathematics, theory of flight, meteorology and things that have to do with design of aircraft and engines. There will be some examinations on all of these subjects." In addition, he wanted to make sure that any woman who passed would be able to continue in the program. And he advised them to meet as a group and to discuss how they intended to handle future publicity, specifically invoking the massive media attention to the Mercury 7. He suggested the women might wish to settle on a deal such as the one the male astronauts made with *Life* to cover their ongoing activities. "As you know, the male astronauts have acted as a group on all matters concerning publicity every [*sic*] since their initial selection and I would like to strongly urge that the results of their group acting in this field be considered very seriously."

Eleven women replied they would be in Pensacola as directed. Irene Leverton, always struggling to hold on to a job, said she could not get time off in early September. She got, she says, a nasty phone call from Jerrie Cobb telling her to find a way: they needed *everyone* to be there. Sarah Gorelick and Gene Nora Jessen had trouble getting time off work, too, but Jerrie wrote their employers a skillful letter that took the bosses into her confidence, telling them "this serious program is being conducted on a highly scientific level and is of utmost importance" and hinting at the benefit they would gain from allowing their employees to participate: "Although it has been necessary to keep this program 'under wraps' as much as possible, after the September tests, the results and names and details will be released. *Life* magazine, among other news media will carry the stories. . . . We know that you, as her employer, must be proud of the contribution she is making to our country's space research."

After more than a year cooling her heels, all the while watching the Mercury men become the nation's heroes, Jerrie Cobb was keen to keep the momentum building. With Pensacola delayed, she asked the women who could spare the time to come to Oklahoma City for the psychological examinations she had undergone a year earlier. This was Phase II of the testing— although Lovelace had decided it did not matter in which order they did the phases. He told Gene Nora Stumbough the psychological tests could be conducted during individual appointments before or after the tests at Pensacola, which all the women were required to do at once. Only two of the women—Wally Funk and Rhea Hurrle—could get away on short notice when Jerrie called, and they came to stay with her while they were examined at the veterans' hospital. A grainy series of pictures shows the three women clowning around in Jerrie's backyard, showing off their push-ups and their jumping jacks, mindful of Lovelace's instructions about being in prime physical shape.

The Albuquerque clinic had found that Wally and Rhea had pretty close to flawless bodies—but astronauts needed to be more than just healthy. The United States had just barely managed to launch a thirty-one-pound satellite, but NASA's brand new Space Task Group was at work on much grander plans. NASA was already planning the Apollo and Gemini missions, and there was talk of astronauts living long-term on a space station. These women might be healthy enough to withstand a launch, but what would happen—to their bodies, and to their minds—once they were up there?

Like Jerrie's, Rhea's and Wally's reactions to extreme isolation were tested in Dr. Jay Shurley's darkened, soundproof tank of water. For two days, his staff constantly monitored Rhea's and Wally's temperatures, then calculated the average. Rhea went first, tucking her hair under the bathing cap, slipping a piece of foam beneath her neck and hips and settling into the water. With typical matter-of-factness, she says her nine hours in the tank were fine. She relaxed, prayed and savored the peace and quiet in the water. "If you kept your wits about you it was fine. But I guess some people couldn't quite handle it. I stayed in until they told me to come out." Wally says she lasted a record ten and a half hours in the isolation tank. It was never difficult, she says, and in fact she dozed off a couple of times. When the women came out, the psychologists were lined up to quiz them—where were they and why? They had to do math problems and drawings to demonstrate their ability to concentrate—it was the same procedure after a series of altitude and pressurization tests. The doctors were looking to see whether the women's faculties or reactions decayed under the different forms of stress, and they were watching for signs of mental weakness or loss of control or will. Sometimes the questions went on for hours, and doctors probed for the thing that would make them crack. They didn't find it. Jay Shurley thought when he first put Jerrie Cobb in his isolation tank and she lasted a record nine hours that she must be some sort of aberration. Now Wally and Rhea had lasted just as long: there was something extraordinary about these Lovelace women.

When Jerri Sloan flew home to Dallas at the end of her week at the Lovelace Clinic, her husband, Lou, met her at the airport with news: he had filed for divorce. Back at the house, she found a terrible mess. "He had all these wonderful pictures of him and his airplane, his crew and his squadron, that were taken by *Life* magazine [during the war]. I had the pictures blown up, and I had them in our living room. He took those pictures and broke them across his knee and said, 'These mean nothing now.' See, I had competed with him. And God knows the kind of flying he did during the war, I had nothing compared to what he had done, and I never felt like I had. . . . It broke my heart."

Looking at her anxious children, who trembled as soon as Daddy came home, Jerri knew she could no longer stay with Lou. She took the kids back to her mother's, and went looking for a house. Then she threw herself into work—building her new company with Joe Truhill. When the letter from Lovelace said she would be sent for more testing at Pensacola, she was quietly elated. Working and taking care of the kids was making her feel worn to a frazzle—but this was something she could do for herself.

And so, on a hot Texas September evening she was packing: she should take shorts, probably, for that jumping-over-the-wall business Jerrie Cobb had told her about, and tennis shoes. Jerri had a plane ticket ready—bought with a check Dr. Lovelace's office sent to cover her expenses. The kids knew Mommy was going away for a few weeks, and they were going to stay with Grandma. Then the doorbell rang, and a delivery boy handed Jerri a telegram. It came from Albuquerque, and across the country, twelve other women were being handed telegrams just like it.

REGRET TO ADVISE ARRANGEMENTS AT PENSACOLA
CANCELED PROBABLY WILL NOT BE POSSIBLE TO CARRY OUT
THIS PART PF [*sic*] PROGRAM YOU MAY RETURN EXPENSE
ADVANCE ALLOTMENT TO LOVELACE FOUNDATION C/O ME
LETTER WILL ADVISE OF ADDITIONAL DEVELOPMENTS WHEN
MATTER CLEARED FURTHER
W RANDOLPH LOVELACE II MD

OUR RIGHTFUL PLACE

Jerrie Cobb poses with the Mercury capsule prototype, 1960.

It was a shock—a sickening shock. For the first few days, the women waited for another telegram, something that would explain, suggest new dates for testing, a new plan. None came.

So Jerri Sloan began another cycle of test flights, and B Steadman went out to the airfield and taught a day of flying classes. Rhea Hurrle delivered an airplane.

But it wasn't that easy for everyone. In early September, Gene Nora Stumbough's boss had been unmoved by Jerrie Cobb's letter—he was, Gene Nora recalls, a petty sort of person—and he told her that if she took the two weeks off, she was fired.

It was a rotten dilemma: Gene Nora had finally finished school, after six years of part-time attendance as she worked to pay for tuition and flying time. She was relishing her first stint of full-time work and the idea that, for the first time in years, she wouldn't be as "poor as a church mouse." But how could she pass up a chance to be part of the space program, even if it was just tests? So she told her boss that she quit.

And now, less than two weeks later, she had no job—and no trip to Pensacola.

Sarah Gorelick was suddenly looking for work, too: AT&T wouldn't give her unpaid time off to do the tests. No letter from Jerrie Cobb, NASA consultant, was going to help that. "In those days men went off to do things like that, not women," Sarah explains. "If I'd been a man, maybe they would have understood." Instead, she had to quit. At her send-off party, the folks in the office had a cake and a model rocket; they gave her a space helmet with her name, *S. Gorelick,* inscribed above the clear plastic visor. No need for that helmet now.

Irene Leverton, too, was left scrabbling. She was already on thin ice at work when the Pensacola invitation came—she had been demoted from charter flying to teaching beginners when she asked for the time to do the first tests. When she told the boss she needed time to go to Pensacola, he told her to forget it: if she went, she was fired. Irene didn't hesitate. "For this, for jet time? Nothing going to keep me from going." But now she too was out of a job.

The news of the cancelation left Jerrie Cobb completely stunned. She was in Pensacola, making preparations for the other women's arrival when the admiral who ran the base informed her that the testing was off. "He said the orders came from the chief of Naval Operations at the Pentagon." She called Dr. Lovelace in disbelief. He told her he didn't know why the decision had been made, but gently advised her that there was little point trying to fight both NASA and the navy. Jerrie said she was going to try anyway. Lovelace wished her luck.

She flew to Washington, found a cheap hotel with a bath down the hall, picked up a map of the D.C. bus system and started knocking on doors at the Pentagon. Pretty soon, she knew who was behind the decision. "When I finally got to see the chief of Naval Operations, he told me the tests were canceled because NASA did not want the tests run on the women."

Dr. Lovelace had taken care to keep his arrangement with the navy quiet. NASA, he knew, wasn't keen on this program he had running with women—in fact, some of the top people at the agency were initially "100% against procedures for girls," he had confided to Floyd Odlum. But Lovelace was a senior figure in the world of "bioastronautics," and there had been no formal protest from the agency when he made Jerrie's test results public in Stockholm, so he wasn't too worried. Arranging for Jerrie to do the tests in Pensacola had taken a bit of finagling, but Lovelace's was a respected name. It was just one woman: everyone turned a blind eye.

Plans to bring thirteen women to Pensacola, however, were a little harder to gloss over. Navy brass let NASA know about it, and James Webb and his colleagues in the administration of the space agency decided that this little experiment of Randy Lovelace's had gone on long enough.

The men who ran NASA didn't want to look as if they were competing with the Soviets, of course, but there was more to it than that. First, and quite practically, the agency did not see any need for more astronauts: there were seven superbly qualified candidates for spaceflight who had been in training for two years.

And once Alan Shepard went up in May 1961, it removed some of the immediate scientific motivation Lovelace had for using women. NASA's rockets had lifted and supported a man, and he had survived the rigors of spaceflight (or at least the rigors of a fifteen-minute suborbital shot: it remained uncertain whether women would prove better able to withstand long-term isolation in space). But for now, the comparative benefits of women were irrelevant.

The agency, in those early days, was staffed heavily with engineers and researchers who had come over from the military—who were used, in other words, to working in all-male environments. On a political level, they had no interest in acting as agents of social change, in putting the agency at the vanguard of equal opportunity with a high-profile infusion of female astronauts. And on a personal level, they gave every appearance of relishing the boys' club: all of Cape Canaveral chuckled when the Mercury 7 started horsing around, faking the sinking of one fellow's sailboat or tossing another man's bed into the motel pool.

And so, late that summer, the agency stepped in to stop Randy Lovelace's women-in-space program. Robert Pirie, the deputy chief of Naval Operations (Air), wrote to ask whether NASA had a "requirement"—an official request—to test women. NASA, of course, said no. So the navy canceled the tests. In October, deputy administrator Hugh Dryden confirmed decisions that had been made orally (between men who knew each other well) with a brief letter. "My dear Admiral Pirie," he wrote. "Reference is made to your letter of August 14, 1961, inquiring as to NASA requirements for certain physiological and psychological tests of a group of twelve women. As you noted, the purpose of these tests was to indicate generally the potential of women as future astronauts. In confirmation of discussions that have already taken place between our staffs, NASA does not at this time have a requirement for such a program."

All of this, of course, was a problem for Randy Lovelace. Thinking like a researcher, absorbed in the problem of how to fly the smallest, toughest pilots, he had happily taken over the women-in-space file when Brig. Gen. Donald Flickinger was hauled off it by the air force in 1959. Protocol at NASA didn't trouble him too much, nor did politics; he was uninterested in how things played for the American public. But in the intervening eighteen months, the space agency's role had formalized—and since Kennedy's man-on-the-moon speech, it was focused very much on one goal. Lovelace had imagined that he could test his women and present his results—and the top candidates—to NASA when he was ready. But in the past few months, operations had tightened up. Space research wasn't going on in a variety of armed forces and private facilities any more; NASA was calling the shots.

Lovelace took considerable satisfaction from his post as chair of NASA's Life Sciences Committee. It gave him access to the most advanced aerospace research projects in the country. But now he was clearly on the wrong side of this issue of testing women, and he had some fences to mend. On September 29, he wrote a conciliatory letter to James Webb—apparently the first time he had ever officially informed the head of NASA about his plans for women.

> I am taking the liberty of writing to give you the latest information on the research program that has been under way here over the past year in connection with the examinations of women pilots. . . . The long-range objective of this program is to ascertain whether or not a particular woman pilot has the capacity to live, observe and do optimal work in the environment of space and return safely to earth. . . . The examinations given these women were practically identical to those given the male astronaut candidates.

Lovelace assured Webb that this wasn't part of any crash program rivaling NASA, and that the women had been made no promises—that they were told it might be years before the space agency needed women. The program was being paid for privately, he wrote, and he tactfully asked whether Webb might not at least let the next phase go ahead: "I would hope to see the subsequent tests not delayed too long." He assured the NASA administrator that he would keep publicity to an absolute minimum (in fact, he said, he had sworn his candidates to secrecy) and, of course, his women's program would not "slow up or interfere in any way with the men's program now under way or even give that appearance publicly." And the government would get all the data, all the results, at no cost.

Lovelace left it at that: he had other projects on the go with NASA, and while this one appealed to his professional curiosity it wasn't worth jeopardizing his standing with Webb.

And so the fight for the women-in-space program fell to Jerrie. She wasn't, by nature, much good at this type of thing—her mother told her how odd it was to see her quiet, shy, younger daughter suddenly a "crusader." But that's exactly what this was for Jerrie: a mission with almost holy implications.

She spoke with anyone in Washington who would agree to see her. She tried repeatedly to get in to see Webb. She cornered any other NASA official she could find; one department head referred her to another. She managed to arrange a meeting with Edward Welsh, the executive secretary of Kennedy's National Aeronautics and Space Council. Welsh, like the other men, was kind and polite, but said he could do little for her. NASA doctors and scientists told her the project was sound, she says, but that it could not go ahead without a "policy decision" from the highest levels. And people at that level avoided her.

Jerrie also took her lobby on the road. She made dozens of speeches such as one to the International Women's Space Symposium in Los Angeles, where she told the crowd NASA could launch a woman—and finally beat the Soviets to a first—the next day, if only the agency was willing. "I wish I could say we were going to do it tomorrow," she said. "But I can't."

All of this irritated James Webb considerably. His strategy of placating Jerrie with a NASA consultancy had obviously had the opposite effect. Webb decided to get rid of her. He wrote to Jerrie in December, telling her NASA's budget and plans were set through 1963, through the Gemini and into the Apollo program. There was no place in there for female astronauts. "Under the circumstances, and since we have not found a productive relationship that could fit you into our program, I am wondering if there is any advantage to continue the consulting relationship that you and I had in mind. Frankly, I am simply unable to get into the details of these programs and those in charge have not come with any assignment that I thought we should ask you to undertake."

But Jerrie was quite sure she had a role—waking Webb up to the importance of launching a woman—so she chose to ignore his ambiguously phrased termination letter. Wernher von Braun, whom she had met in her lobby effort, invited her to Cape Canaveral when John Glenn was finally launched in February on the United States' first orbital flight. Jerrie watched the burst of flame beneath the Saturn rocket and said it gave her "new courage, renewed energy and determination." And, of course, she had just one thought in her brain: I wish it were me.

After an unsuccessful autumn as a solo lobbyist, she enlisted Janey Hart, who knew the mechanics of power in Washington much better than Jerrie did. Janey's keen sense of fair play had been deeply offended by the abrupt cancelation of the Pensacola tests. She was, in these first years of the sixties, drawn to the emerging women's movement, and this seemed increasingly, to her, like a clear-cut case of sexual discrimination. In a letter to her Lovelace pal Gene Nora Stumbough in late January 1962, Janey noted "a serious sag in the esprit de corps" among the FLATs, but then observed that that was to be expected, given that four months had passed with no word on what was to become of their space ambitions. She and Jerrie had lobbied "through all polite and proper channels in Washington," Janey explained, and realized that without NASA approval they were going nowhere. "So far the director, Mr. Webb, has ducked a flat yes or no answer very successfully." The women were going to give him one more try, then go to the president, Janey confided. And they had decided that keeping the female astronaut program quiet had served no purpose, so they were thinking about a new strategy, of going heavy on publicity, in an attempt to shame NASA into dealing with them. Janey was thinking that Lovelace should make their names public, and then all "the girls" could get out there on the speaking circuit.

Janey had also observed that Jerrie was doing a lousy job of keeping in touch with the other women—but then, their self-appointed leader didn't have much to tell them. From Oklahoma, she typed out one of her "Dear FLATs" letters in February 1962.

I truly apologize for not having been in closer contact with each of you but between working with NASA, traveling around the country and my job here, there is little time.

Since the first of the year I have been traveling and working almost entirely for women in space. In Washington, among others, I met with Mr. Webb, Administrator, NASA, and his assistant Dr. Cox. The answers I got were more of the same and typical of bureaucrats—not yes and not no. I am as tired and discouraged about this as I know each of you are—but I will keep fighting for it, 'cause I believe in it. It's an uphill battle but with faith and persistence I still believe it will be done. . . .

Our program has received some support and encouragement from many of our country's space scientists, planners and doctors but those who must make the decision have not been willing to do so. When I press for answers, they give reasons—but none of them are legitimate. . . . I intend to keep hammering and trust that you are all still behind me.

In fact, most of the women had given up. But Jerrie was totally undeterred. She hadn't had a flat-out no, and that, for her, was as good as a yes.

In early March, Janey Hart wrote a letter to each member of both the Senate and the House Space Committees, in which she told them how well women had done in the astronaut tests. "The research on women in space to date has been at the expense of the Lovelace Foundation of New Mexico. Further research would be facilitated by its acceptance by NASA," she wrote. "To date this acceptance has not been forthcoming and the 'arguments' against it have been specious, to say the least. It is my belief that the Russians will have successfully space flown a woman by next September. I sincerely hope that your interest in this matter will serve to help 'get this program off the ground.'" Janey was always frank—blunt, even—and she had a history of giving her husband's press secretary minor heart attacks. But she was deft with a snappy quote, and she made sure her letter to the committee found its way to reporters. Accordingly, there was a flurry of articles about the "Senate wife" who wanted to be first in space. "I certainly don't want my four boys to have to learn Russian so that when they meet some lady on the moon that's the only way they can communicate with her," Janey remarked to a *Washington Star* reporter. She assured a dozen journalists that her children thought the idea was all very exciting and that no, her husband, Phil, wasn't worried. "He doesn't sit there and worry about what would happen if that thing went up with me on the front end of it. I guess he'd be a little tense, just as Mrs. Glenn was."

And then, Janey went through her husband's Senate office and managed to set up a meeting with Vice President Lyndon Johnson. Here was someone who could really help them: he was the head of the president's Space Council, and everyone knew he was the point man on all things to do with space exploration. And Janey tempered her request: she asked only that the vice president help arrange for them to be permitted to finish the canceled testing. It was an easy request, and one that could have been spun to win Johnson favorable press.

But when Jerrie and Janey got in to see him, their half-hour meeting was "torturous," Janey says. Johnson was friendly but visibly uncomfortable whenever she and Jerrie pressed him on what he could do to help; they left with no commitment from him whatsoever. Then Janey knew things looked bad: the vice president was not prepared to use his clout for women in the space program.

Jerrie, however, was determinedly—or willfully—optimistic. A week after the Johnson meeting, she sent the FLATs a more upbeat letter. She and Janey now had "quite a bit of interest stirred up in Washington for women-in-space. I spent a week in Washington during which time I met with Senator Kerr, head of the Senate Space Committee, who said he would help in any way he could. The next day, Janey had arranged for us to have a conference with Vice President Lyndon Johnson, who was very receptive to the idea and said he would check into the matter. . . . However, because of his in-between position on space matters (NASA Space Council, President) he was emphatic about not being quoted." She listed another half-dozen meetings, and men in power she thought were rallying to the cause. But her letter ended with a note of frustration. "Honestly, I have talked with everyone from the janitor to Webb at NASA and the only objection they have (and they keep falling back on it) is that women

do not have the jet test pilot experience which was thought necessary when the 7 Mercury Astronauts were selected three years ago.
Times have changed and I argue that this is unfair discrimination
since women are not allowed to fly jet fighters." She kept asking
NASA just to give them a shot in the simulators, she said—
the darn monkeys weren't test pilots, and they got shot up. "In the
middle of all this I keep hoping and praying that NASA will
wake up and get these important projects started at once."

In truth, of course, the test pilot point was not NASA's objection, but rather their convenient excuse. For all NASA's regretful
assurance that they would take any woman who was qualified, if
only there were any, the real objection had everything to do with
the FLATs' gender.

Jerrie then tried a new angle, going directly to the man who
ran the Mercury program. She sent a careful letter to Robert
Gilruth, the head of manned spaceflight, in early April, telling
him she could guess how he felt about "lady astronauts" but he
had to understand what she was proposing—she wanted to work
with him to win the Americans a space first. "I know that this is
not a simple thing to do, nor an easy decision to make . . . but
you are the *one* who could make it a reality." Gilruth wrote back
a week later:

> Although I can understand and appreciate your interest in
> having women included in our astronaut team I do not
> feel that we can accede to your request at this time. . . .
> The manned space flight program is a serious scientific
> endeavor and we cannot include any but the best-qualified
> personnel in our flight teams. We cannot select women
> just because they are women any more than do other
> exploratory venture groups such as mountain-climbers or
> Antarctic expeditions.
>
> Admittedly, it is possible that Russia may utilize women
> in spaceflight crews before we do but I feel that we are in

competition with the Soviets, not for the accomplishment
of propaganda stunts, but for the acquisition of sound
technical and scientific information on the problems of
human spaceflight. At such a time as the ability of women
to operate effectively in space becomes an important
enough question we will undoubtedly investigate the
problems involved. At present, however, I feel that we
must conserve our efforts and concentrate on problems of
a more pressing nature without introducing additional
variables into our equation from either a scientific or
public-relations standpoint.

Jerrie could not believe that attitude: why were the men at
NASA so blind to the opportunity they were missing? Not just
the propaganda—why didn't they see that research on women
had value of its own? "I agree with the majority of your letter,"
she replied firmly to Gilruth, "and would like to make it clear
that *I do NOT advocate putting a woman in space just because she
is a woman only for any propaganda stunt.* I feel that a woman
should be put in space for the same reasons that men are put in
space and that a woman can be trained to successfully perform
the exacting duties of an astronaut. The fact that she is a woman
is secondary, but would add to our scientific knowledge of the
effects of space flight on human beings. If she were the first
woman in space, it would also add to our country's prestige, but
this is not the main objective."

But Jerrie heard nothing further from the director of the
Manned Space Flight Center. She wrote to Vice President Johnson
again, making the same points she had made to Gilruth. He wrote
back, and this time he made his position official: "The choice
and training for the individuals who will make space flights is
quite appropriately left to the operating agencies in the program."

And then there was Jackie. The two key women in the
women-in-space initiative had met for the first time at an

aviation conference in Texas in January. In February, Jackie attempted to get Jerrie to come to New Mexico to be part of her *Parade* article but Jerrie pleaded other commitments—thanking Jackie, in her telegram, for her "efforts for women in space." Over the next few months, Jackie pushed Jerrie to come out to the ranch, then invited her to cocktail parties in her suite at the Salon in Paris or her apartment in New York. Jackie might have believed she could, in person and on her own opulent turf, persuade Jerrie to step back from the project, yielding to Jackie's vastly greater experience. But it didn't work: Jerrie, as her telegrams always explained, had somewhere to fly to urgently. She says today she was not avoiding Jackie, whom she knew wanted a bigger role in the women-in-space program—but that she had no idea that even as she made the rounds lobbying for the canceled testing in Washington, Jackie was actively working against her.

The two most famous women pilots in the country finally met for dinner in late February in Cocoa Beach, where they were waiting for the launch of John Glenn's orbital flight. Jerrie sensed that Jackie had taken an important role in Lovelace's project, and she used the occasion to try to establish her own position. She pushed Jackie to come out publicly in favor of putting a woman (and that implied, of course, that it would be Jerrie) in space before the Russians did. Jackie was not about to do any such thing.

Two weeks later, Jackie set out her position, in a four-page, single-spaced typewritten letter to Jerrie. It is a letter that clearly shows the political context in which Jackie saw the issue—full of directives colored by her own experience of working within the system:

Women will travel in space just as surely as man. It's only
a question of when. . . . There are quite a lot of women
who would like to be the first woman or the first
American woman to go into space. I feel confident that

this is true with respect to each of the twelve women who passed the medical checks at the Lovelace Foundation in Albuquerque. It's a laudable ambition. I, myself, would like to make that first flight by woman into space. . . . I would like, however, to be helpful to the active aspirants. Because of this detached attitude I can perhaps more objectively consider the factors involved in trying to help get a women's astronaut program by other participants off to a sound start.

I am sure you know from our various conversations that I am in favor of a space program for women. That I put up the money to pay the cost of most of the twenty candidates who took the medical checks at the Lovelace Foundation and then put up the money for most of the ones who passed these checks to enable them to go to Pensacola for the second series of checks should be clear proof of this. . . .

A space program for women is unlike all previous advents of women into various phases of aviation in that space flight for the present is terribly expensive, is an urgent project from the standpoint of national defense, and there is no lack of qualified candidates for the role of astronaut from among our already highly trained flight personnel. In other words, there is no present real national need for women in such a role. When the women pilots (WASP) were organized in World War II there was an urgent need. We were short of manpower and pilot power. I was asked to organize for service the women pilots by General Hap Arnold, Chief of Staff of the Air Force. And the minute the pressure on manpower let up toward the end of the war and pilots were returning from abroad who were available at home for air duty, I recommended that the WASP be deactivated. Otherwise the WASP might have become the subject of resentment by the male pilots.

Many more than twenty women had to be tested, Jackie wrote, in what would become a familiar theme. "These two checks or tests do not constitute a program." Then she took a direct shot at Jerrie's naked ambition: "While each active participant very understandably would like to be the first, there is glory enough for each by being part of an initial group. Within that group each should succeed on her own merits without fear or favor." But most of all, she wrote, there was no point in getting women ready now:

> There is no real present national urgency about putting a woman into space. To attempt to do so in the near future might indeed interfere with the space program now under way which *is* urgent from the national standpoint. I believe you disagree with me about this and on the ground [*sic*] that to put a woman into space before the Russians do would be a victory—at least in the cold war. But at the same time, in arguing for speed, you said to me that there is evidence that Russian women have been training for space flights for a considerable period of time. If so they will be prepared before an American woman. And a hastily prepared flight by a less than completely trained woman could backfire. Such a flight by a woman in the near future might be regarded by a great many as somewhat in the nature of unnecessary drama. And many who would not so regard it might question why the government has gone to great expense to specially prepare the seven astronauts over a three-year period if a woman can do the same thing without long background of experience followed by careful special training.

Finally, Jackie laid out in black and white her view on where women belonged in the new field of space exploration. "Women for one reason or another have always come into each phase of aviation a little behind their brothers. They should, I believe, accept this delay and not get into the hair of the public authorities about it." She closed with one last veiled warning to Jerrie to stop hogging the headlines: "you can be particularly helpful to a program by going out of your way to create the group image publicly."

Jackie made some reasonable arguments: the United States was still behind in the space race, and the existing space program was consuming prodigious amounts of resources and energy. There *was* no national urgency to launching a woman per se, and if a female astronaut were killed in a launch it would certainly damage the agency's reputation. Jackie's letter may have reflected her experience with the WASP, where she let the program get rushed ahead and then could not protect her pilots from a political defeat because she had not taken the initial steps to have them militarized. In addition, Jackie was an insider: she worked toward her goals by manipulating the existing system and taking advantage of a power structure as opposed to confronting or challenging it. From the start, Jackie inculcated her WASPs with the idea that they should never complain, no matter how arduous the conditions they faced, and Jerrie's increasingly public criticisms of NASA were an affront to Jackie's sensibilities.

It took a few weeks for Jackie's letter to catch up with her, but Jerrie immediately wrote back, restating her position. Of course she didn't want to disrupt the existing program. "I really think that we agree on the important points. I don't think it is important who is the First woman in space but I do feel that it's important to our country that she be an American."

But Jerrie had no idea what she was up against in Jackie. Jerrie had never been the intended target of the letter addressed to her.

Jackie copied that long, stern letter to Jerrie Cobb to each of the twelve FLATs—and to every important man in the space business. She sent it to James Webb, the head of NASA, and to Hugh Dryden, his deputy. She sent it to Robert Gilruth, the head of spaceflight, and to Gen. Curtis Le May, chief of the Air Force. She even sent it to the vice president, telling him it would take only eight minutes to read but was "of great national importance." With each copy of the letter she sent out, she included a brief cover letter that made clear she thought Jerrie pushy and unreasonable—and that Jackie herself was toeing the NASA line. Some women might be pushing to be astronauts, her letter implied, but not Jackie—she was, as always, on their side.

In a letter of markedly different tone from the one Jerrie had recently received from Lyndon Johnson, Jackie received a friendly reply to her letter to the vice president. Johnson thanked her for her copy of the Cobb letter and confided, "I had a good time telling Jerrie Cobb and Mrs. Philip Hart of our friendship when they came to see me about lady astronauts. I told them you made me in favor of lady fliers a long time ago." Unbeknownst to Jerrie, Jackie held special favor with the vice president. They didn't agree on politics—Jackie had become a Republican when Floyd changed parties in the 1930s. But when Johnson was campaigning for a Senate seat in Texas in 1948, he developed a vicious case of kidney stones. A botched operation to remove them left him violently ill. But Johnson was afraid to publicly admit his incapacitation so close to the election. One of his campaign workers knew Jackie was in Dallas for an air force meeting, and he arranged for Jackie secretly to fly the would-be senator to the Mayo Clinic just after dawn in her Electra. On the way, Johnson developed pneumonia. The way she later told the story, Jackie put the plane on automatic pilot while she stripped him down, wrapped him in blankets and held a pan while he vomited. She got him to the clinic, and he was treated and back in Dallas in time to narrowly win the seat. Thereafter, Jackie said, he called her the "pretty gal" who saved his life—and his career.

The rest of the men who received copies of the letter to Jerrie wrote back praising Jackie's reasonable assessment of the situation and her good sense. Lovelace himself thought she made a reasonable proposal. Dryden wrote, "I wish to compliment you on the excellent analysis you have made of the role of women in space," while Gilruth—the man who had just summarily rejected Jerrie and her ideas—told Jackie she had "an excellent understanding of the problems facing us" and that he greatly appreciated "your quite evident understanding of the situation."

In fact, NASA saw in Jackie Cochran the perfect person to do its public dirty work on this pesky issue of female astronauts. "I am in complete agreement," Walter Williams, the associate director of the Manned Spacecraft Center, wrote to tell her. "In fact I wish that I or other people in NASA could state the situation in the same lucid manner. . . . I think since you state the case so very well and in view of your leadership in aviation, it would be highly desirable if your position could be made public. It would be of great help to our program if your views could be published in at least the trade journals in the form of either your comments or feelings in that regard." Jackie replied that, of course, she would do whatever the space agency needed her to. Williams's letter, like many of the others, began with a familiar "Dear Jackie" and concluded with an apology that he had not made it out to the ranch to visit Jackie and Floyd; many of the other men thanked her for recent dinner party invitations and congratulated her on her latest records. Jackie had personal relationships with the power brokers that Jerrie could not hope to approximate.

Jackie was careful to assure everyone she addressed on this subject of her impartiality, but in truth this was a very personal battle for her, and her emotional involvement would come to color both the nature and the degree of the action she took toward getting women into the space program. NASA's history archives contain a small folder of papers that are a remarkable example of her hostility to Jerrie. Right about this time, in May 1961, Jackie sent Dryden a formal note stating she thought it important, at a time when so much history was being made, for the record to be kept as accurate as possible. She attached a photocopy from the most recent edition of *Current Biography*. The pages were the entry for Jerrie Cobb. Jackie had made heavy pencil marks by the areas that irked her. "*Current Biography* say this was originally written by and prior to publication approved by the person being talked about," she wrote on the first page. She objected to the article's claim that Jerrie was "the first woman to satisfy the criteria for space flight," that she "might be the first woman in space" and the assessment that Jerrie had proved women were as or in some cases better qualified than men. Dryden agreed they had best get someone to look into the matter.

By now, James Webb was getting as many letters from Jackie on this subject as he was from Jerrie (Jackie apparently did not believe her advice to "stay out of his hair" applied to herself). In June, Jackie made her move. "I believe, with more than 13,000 hours of flying time as command pilot and much high speed precision flying, several hundred hours of which have been in jets, I may be and probably am the only woman meeting the qualifications [to lead the program]," she began, establishing once again her credentials to address the issue. Nonetheless, she said, she had removed herself from the competition, but she certainly had advice: if the NASA chief didn't come right out and ban women, she said, he was asking for trouble. "I think you are likely to let yourself in for a lot of continuing harassment if you continue to take the position that even now women with such experience will, if they apply, be considered along with all other applicants. This position stated by you may be looked upon by some as a slightly cracked door to be opened with a push."

No surprise, Jackie had a solution. "I have a general plan in mind that might solve your problem in this connection, with satisfaction to most of the feminine contingent, without getting any women actively into the astronaut training program for the present or short-term future." And she would be in Washington next week if Webb wanted to discuss her plan, which involved turning the whole mess over to Jackie, who would run a nice big research program with dozens of women, without any one record-setting pilot making headlines.

But within days, Jerrie was back in the papers again: she and Janey had succeeded in arranging for a special hearing of a subcommittee of the House Committee on Science and Astronautics (popularly known as the Space Committee), a hearing charged with determining the qualifications for the "selection of astronauts." Finally, Jerrie's lobbying had paid off. She met Space Committee chair George Miller at a convention and gave him her usual impassioned speech, explaining about the abruptly canceled tests. Miller decided the matter might bear looking into (and the fact that the wife of one of the most highly regarded members of the Senate was involved in the program was likely not incidental in that decision). He turned the question over to committee member Victor Anfuso, a Democrat from New York. Jerrie believed that the committee, having been alerted to the female astronaut situation, was concerned about a real instance of discrimination. (This was two years before the Civil Rights Act would be passed, however, and so discrimination on the basis of sex was, in fact, perfectly legal.) Janey, the Washington insider, was privately cynical: she wondered whether Anfuso, who was facing an election against a tough opponent, was using the sensational topic of girls in space to win some headlines. But she said she would testify.

The hearing convened on July 17, 1962, a hot day with an endless blue sky. Jerrie and Janey met up outside the hearing room. Janey was calm, but Jerrie was visibly uneasy. Anfuso told them how the day would proceed, and Jerrie, pale beneath her freckles, tried to calm her nerves. The two took their seats at the witness table, facing the row of representatives, a crowd of the curious behind them. Ten of the twelve were men, wearing dark suits; they were split between the two parties and were from all over the country, but all but one of them was a war veteran. There were two women on the committee, both of them much older.

Anfuso called on Jerrie almost immediately. Feeling her stomach knot, she reminded herself of just how important this was—this might be her only chance—and just how *angry* she was. She took a deep breath.

She began by explaining how she came to be sitting before them. "Almost three years ago, Dr. Randolph Lovelace II and Air Force Brig. Gen. Donald Flickinger asked me to be the first woman to undergo the Mercury Astronaut tests at the Lovelace Foundation in Albuquerque, New Mexico." She passed, she told them. "As a result it was decided to test a whole group of woman pilots. . . . In 1960 and 1961 I passed two additional phases of testing as a candidate for spaceflight, to qualify myself and to prove the feasibility of having a group of women in a space research program." She told them how she had been a NASA consultant since the previous summer. "After a group of 12 other women had passed the Mercury Astronaut tests, I was sort of drafted to be spokesman for all 13 of us." The unease was audible in Jerrie's husky contralto. "As you can tell, it certainly wasn't because of my speaking ability."

But the combination of ponytail and gravity had the committee charmed. No taxpayers' money, she assured them, had been used to select the thirteen. Then she revealed that the reason they had never spoken out as a group was that the eleven women not present did not even know one anothers' names. For the first time, she then made them public, detailing each woman's credentials for the congressional record.

"Jan Dietrich: Single; California native; age 35; 5 feet 3 inches tall, weight 103 pounds; college graduate; pilot for large company; airline transport pilot's license—multiengine, single-engine, seaplane; flight instructor ratings; 8,000 flying hours . . . Sarah Lee Gorelick: Single; Kansas native; age 28; 5 feet 5 inches tall; weight 130; university graduate with degree in mathematics, physics and chemistry; commercial pilot's license—glider, multi-engine, single engine, seaplane, flight instructor, instrument instructor ratings; 1,800-plus flying hours." Jerrie ran on through the list.

Then she struck a conciliatory note: the women were "not trying to join a battle of the sexes. As pilots, we fly and share mutual respect with male pilots in the primarily man's world of aviation. We very well know how to live together in our profession!"

Jerrie's campaign to NASA had been couched in language of scientific and public relations achievement, but here, to the lawmakers, she took a different tack. With Congress, she raised the issue of justice.

"We seek only a place in our nation's space future without discrimination. We ask as citizens of this nation to be allowed to participate with seriousness and sincerity in the making of history now, as women have in the past. There were women on the *Mayflower* and on the first wagon trains west, working alongside the men to forge new trails to new vistas. We ask that opportunity in the pioneering of space."

She outlined the medical and scientific reasons why it made sense to use women. And then she appealed to national pride: "We have seen the reflected pride of the entire free world in the accomplishments of U.S. Astronauts [Alan] Shepard, [Gus] Grissom, [John] Glenn and [Scott] Carpenter. All Americans, and certainly all pilots, salute them. Now we who aspire to be women astronauts ask for the opportunity to bring glory to our nation by an American woman becoming first in all the world to make a spaceflight. No nation has yet sent a human female into space. We offer you 13 woman pilot volunteers."

Jerrie sat back, her stomach still in knots, having said all she could. The chairman thanked her with a wisecrack that had the whole room chuckling. "I think that we can safely say at this time that the whole purpose of space exploration is to someday colonize these other planets, and I don't see how we can do that without women."

He next introduced Janey—"Mrs. Philip Hart, an excellent wife and mother as well as a pilot"—who was much more comfortable in this formal atmosphere than Jerrie. Poised and calm, Janey spoke lightly but with great seriousness.

> It is inconceivable to me that the world of outer space should be restricted to men only, like some sort of stag club. . . . I am not arguing that women be admitted to space merely so that they won't feel discriminated against. I am arguing that they be admitted because they have a very real contribution to make. Now, no woman can get up and seriously discuss a subject like this without being painfully aware that her talk is going to inspire a lot of condescending little smiles and mildly humorous winks.
>
> But happily for the nation, there have always been men, men like the members of this committee, who have helped women succeed in roles that they were previously thought incapable of handling. . . . Let's face it: for many women the PTA is just not enough. Now I think women should be allowed to go into space without delay. But even the extreme view that women will have no place in outer space for many years does not justify the cancelation of a research program that had already begun and that would doubtlessly supply information useful right now as well as in the future.

Whatever Janey thought privately, she knew it was not enough simply to argue this case based on discrimination. That idea wasn't going to persuade anybody in this room. Janey knew how to play politics, and she was careful to hit all the right notes. "Above all, I don't want to downgrade the feminine role of wife, mother and homemaker. It is a tremendously fulfilling role. But

I don't think, either, that it is unwomanly to be intelligent, to be courageous, to be energetic, to be anxious to contribute to human knowledge. I just think we would be making a serious mistake if we assumed that women just have no contribution to make to space exploration."

The floor was then given back to Jerrie, who asked that the lights be dimmed. She ran through a series of slides of the tests: here she was on more comfortable ground, and made a joke of her own. She told them about the wire from the Pentagon to Pensacola—"If you don't know the difference already, we refuse to put money into the project." She described her nine and a half hours in the isolation tank, then noted by way of contrast, "The Mercury astronauts spent three hours in an air-filled room." Then she made her most serious point: "The qualifications that the authorities of NASA have set down have made it impossible for women to qualify as astronauts or even demonstrate their capabilities for spaceflight, as I am sure you know."

But, it soon became clear, the committee did not know. Anfuso asked if this was because the astronauts had to be engineers. No, Jerrie said, there were plenty of female engineers. Then Anfuso asked if any of the thirteen were test pilots.

"Some of us have worked as test pilots, but it is impossible for a woman in this country to be a jet test pilot because there are no women pilots in the military services and the test pilots schools are operated solely by the military services," Jerrie said patiently. "There are no other test pilot schools except those of the navy and the air force, and since there are no woman pilots in the services they do not have the opportunity to go to these schools to learn to be a jet test pilots or to fly in the latest supersonic jet fighter equipment, either, since they all belong to the military, and civilians are not allowed to fly them."

The light began to dawn on the committee. "In other words, one of the requirements laid down is that astronauts be test pilots; is that correct?" Anfuso asked.

Jerrie ran through it again. "That is the requirement that NASA has laid down, which automatically eliminates all women because jet pilot experience is not available to them in this country." France and the Soviet Union, she noted, had women doing jet flying in their armed forces.

Joseph Karth, a representative from Minnesota, homed in on the crucial question. First he asked Jerrie if she felt it was essential that astronauts be test pilots.

"I personally do not feel it is essential at all," she replied. "It is a means to an end, but it is certainly not the end itself. An astronaut must pilot a spacecraft—not test jet fighters. If you total the flying hours of this group of women pilots you will find the women averaged 4,500 hours each, which is much more than the men astronauts have. Some of the women in this group have over three times the amount of flying hours that the male astronauts have."

But Karth had a serious question: "There is considerable difference between straight flying—commercial or private—and test piloting; isn't there?"

Then, to Congress, Jerrie made the argument she would make for the next forty years:

I suggest there is an "equivalent experience" in flying that may be even more important in piloting a spacecraft. Pilots with thousands of hours flying time would not have lived so long without coping with emergencies calling for microsecond reactions. What counts is flawless judgment, fast reaction, and the ability to transmit that to the proper control of the craft. We would not have flown all these years, accumulating thousands and thousands of hours in all types of aircraft without accumulating this experience. This experience is the same as acquired in jet test piloting. I think you might acquire it faster as a jet test pilot but it is by no means the only way to acquire it. Some have 8,000

to 10,000 hours—have flown a million miles in all types
of airplanes. This is the hard way to acquire that experience,
but it is the same experience. [Aircraft design researcher]
E. E. Clark reported women usually came along on the first
and second try, executing the maneuver more quickly and
efficiently than the male test pilots. We women who want to
be astronauts offer our flying experience, we offer thousands
of flying hours over millions of miles and literally dozens of
years, and experience in all types of aircraft, in lieu of the
few hours of jet test pilot experience required by NASA.

When Anfuso again had the floor, he wanted to know if it was
worth the risk. "Do you believe that the recognized hazards in
such a feat and the possible worldwide repercussions to our
prestige are worth the risk and expense for us to achieve that
objective of trying to put the first woman in space?"

Jerrie did not hesitate. "I very definitely do—very strongly do."

So her complaint was with the military, asked Jim Fulton (a
Pennsylvania Republican who was a veteran of the navy's campaign
in the South Pacific in World War II)—since they were the ones
who would not let her fly with them. No, Jerrie said, there was
no need for women in active service in the air force; she recognized that. But NASA was asking for things that no woman
could get, something an astronaut didn't necessarily need—"and
if it is, it could be proved easily enough by letting some pilots
without the jet test pilot experience go through the simulators
and see how well they do—compare the results." With a small
note of frustration creeping into her voice, she noted that NASA
had a whole "chimp college" where it trained chimpanzees for
experimental spaceflights. She volunteered to replace the chimps
for a couple of days. "I think it would be at least as important to
let the women undergo this training for spaceflight."

Jerrie by now had slipped off her black pumps, one stocking
foot resting on the other, the way she often did when she was

engrossed in something. The chairman gave the floor to the Republicans, and Edward Roush of Indiana took the microphone. "Miss Cobb, I couldn't help but overhear a conversation between you and Mr. Anfuso prior to and during the course of that conversation you said . . . 'I am scared to death.' How do you reconcile this emotional statement with the fact that an astronaut must be fearless and courageous and emotionally stable?"

Jerrie was not fazed. "Going up into space couldn't be near as frightening as sitting here." Her frank response caused the politicians to chuckle.

Now Ken Hechler, a Democrat from West Virginia, wanted to probe the central mystery of the women's testimony. "I notice, Mrs. Hart, you used the phrase 'Somehow the program was canceled.' Could you explain this a little bit. What were you informed about the program?"

"As to why it was canceled?"

"Yes."

"I have no idea, sir," Janey said. "That is one of the mysteries of the past year."

"The phrase you use is a rather mysterious one," Hechler admonished.

"I don't know why we couldn't continue, put the rest of the 12 through the other 2 [or] 3 phases, which they had not done," Janey replied.

Jerrie joined the conversation, saying she knew at least a bit about why Pensacola was canceled.

I went down there and took these tests, which took two weeks. All the arrangements were made with the School of Aviation Medicine there and through the Lovelace Foundation; Dr. Lovelace was working closely with the group at Pensacola. I was to be the first woman subject to go through these tests so they could see how many changes they would have to make to test women. They had never had a group of women there. That is the reason I went through the tests first. I passed and the arrangements were all set for about two months later for the group of 12 women to come down for the tests. Miss Cochran offered to pay their expenses, the girls arranged with their employers to take off from work, and two days before the tests were to start I got word that they had been canceled.

I immediately notified all the girls. Two of them had already quit their jobs to participate in these tests. It is hard for a woman pilot to find a job in the man's field of aviation. They had quit good jobs to take part in the tests. This is how serious they all are about space testing. About two days before the tests were to begin they were canceled. I wanted to find out why. I came to Washington and talked with NASA and Navy people here. I first contacted Pensacola and they said, 'We are set, still want to do the tests. We have got everything all set up down there.' They said, 'We got word from the Pentagon that the tests for the girls would have to be canceled.' I talked to people with the Navy Department. It all got thrown back on NASA. I went to NASA and all the way up and down—it took me two days—I finally found out that NASA would not say to the Navy, 'We [have] a requirement for this.' The Navy tests were canceled for the lack of a piece of paper from NASA. It was not for funds. The Navy wanted to do the testing.

Anfuso broke in here, seeking to head Jerrie off before she became any more impassioned.

"Will you permit me to say this to you, Miss Cobb and Mrs. Hart," he said unctuously, "that this committee has the assurances that NASA wishes to cooperate and is cooperating. I indicated in my earlier statement that these hearings are indeed helpful. And I know that you don't criticize any branch of the government. You just want answers."

There was a bit more debate before Fulton, seeking to lighten the mood, broke in with a joke: "Did it strike the women that the reason the tests were canceled was because the men thought the women were too successful?" The committee laughed again. Jerrie and Janey did not reply.

Now Joe Waggonner, a Louisiana Democrat who was a veteran of both World War II and Korea, turned the conversation serious. "NASA has said to us on occasion that they had the requirement for the astronauts to be jet test pilots as well as engineers for a specific reason. That reason was that they felt it was not, as you said, just important that the astronauts be able to pilot the spacecraft, but more important than that, to be able to bring back certain scientific information. I realize there are comparable degrees of being able to do this, as you have mentioned, but would either you or Mrs. Hart care to comment on this requirement in light of that statement, that to bring back the information NASA feels at this point the experiment in space is probably even more important in their eyes than just being able to pilot spacecraft and therefore maybe there is some justification for these qualifications?"

Jerrie was ready for this. "I think this is true that the astronaut has more duties to perform in space than just to operate the spacecraft," she acknowledged. "But the primary function is still that of flying the spacecraft. That is why it is easier to take a pilot and teach him the other jobs which need to be done in space than to take an engineer or a geologist, or some other scientist and teach them to be a pilot."

Waggonner wasn't finished. "Do you think that we ought to sacrifice anything in the way of accomplishment in time with regard to our lunar landings and other space activities, or to go into this program to the extent that we would put a woman in space at the expense of slowing down another program?"

"No, sir, I do not," Jerrie replied.

"Would you think that it would be a reasonable thing to assume that maybe after this next orbit flight, which will go as many as six orbits, that we continue our present program toward a lunar landing, and then as soon thereafter as practical, in one of the perhaps three-orbit flights, there would be one that we could train a woman astronaut for?" Waggoner was being conciliatory now. "Would that be something along the lines that you ladies have in mind?"

Jerrie steeled herself. "No, sir: I think that we do not have to wait for the landing on the moon before women can go into space." At least let the other twelve candidates do the rest of the tests, she said, and then if a woman does as well in the space simulators as the men, "insert her into the next orbital flight plan."

Once again, Anfuso struggled to keep the message palatable. "I think, in conclusion, I might say, Miss Cobb, that what you would like to accomplish is a parallel program, but not to interfere with any existing program; is that correct?"

Jerrie acceded to the political line. "I think it need not be a separate program, nor interfere with the current program."

Jerrie's discussion of qualifications had been interrupted midway through by the chairman, who noted for the record the entry of Jackie Cochran to the chamber. She wore a well-cut suit and was, as always, flawlessly made up beneath her bright blond curls. Jackie made her way to her seat, nodding at those she knew, not the slightest bit bothered about her late entrance.

Now the chairman called on Jackie herself to address the committee, introducing her as "the foremost woman pilot in the world, and who holds more national and international speed, distance and altitude records than any other living person." Jackie arranged her papers in front of her and began to read. Jerrie was anxious: there was no love lost between her and Jackie, but she knew Jackie had the political connections that could help them. And she was the only woman in the country who had jet experience: she was the one who could make clear that women were up to this. Jackie could make this happen.

Jackie began with a bald statement of her credentials: "I received my airplane pilot's license in 1932. Since then I have flown more than 13,000 hours as command pilot in many different kinds of planes and have had several hundred hours of solo time in jet aircraft. This flying has involved much high-speed precision flying. I hold more national and international speed, distance and altitude records than any other living person." She mentioned the WASP, and the Distinguished Service Medal she earned for the program.

And then she bluntly made her point: "I do not believe there has been any intentional or actual discrimination against women in the astronaut program to date. As one who has had much experience in high-speed precision flying and over the years has passed many of the tests that were given to select the seven first astronauts and also as one who would like exceedingly to go into space, I do not feel that I have been the subject of any discrimination."

This was a telling illustration of the way Jackie's much more conservative politics differed from Jerrie's. Human spaceflight was expensive and a matter of urgent national interest, she said, so it was "natural and proper" to select astronauts from male pilots who had proven themselves testing high-speed aircraft. "The determination whether women should be included at this time in the program of training and use of astronauts should not depend on the question of sex but on whether such inclusion will speed up, slow down, make more expensive or complicate the schedule of exploratory space flights our country has undertaken."

NASA, she said, was quite capable of making the decision about who should be involved, and since there was no pressing need for more astronauts, "and there is no shortage of well-trained and long-experienced male pilots to serve as astronauts," there was no need for women.

Furthermore, she said, there was not sufficient research to conclude women would compare favorably to men in the environment of space. Jerrie's jaw dropped, but Jackie went right on: "I believe, based on my experience with women in the WASP program, that women will prove to be as fit as men, physically and psychologically, for space flying. But such proof is presently lacking. It should not be searched for by injecting women into the middle of an important and expensive astronaut program." Rather, Jackie said, "a large group of women of various ages and experience" should be recruited and tested. She outlined an elaborate aerospace medicine research program, involving two hundred women: before Congress, she saw her chance to oversee a new program of which she would truly have control. "Such a program would take considerable time to complete because the 'lead time' for research having to do with people is quite long," she said. "It might well develop a well-selected group of a dozen or more qualified women . . . to start an astronaut trainee program for women." At the next table, the women who believed that there was already such a group, all ready to go, listened in horror. And no need to limit the tests to pilots, either, Jackie said. Why not include women from the armed services?

And then, in a moment of terrible irony, Jackie showed just how determined she was to win this debate. She invoked exactly the same argument she had once fought against at a committee hearing like this one, when men were trying to shut down her WASP program. She said training women would be an extravagance, because a large percentage would take their new skills and leave to get married before they could ever serve their country. "You are going to have to, of necessity, waste a great deal of money when you take a large group of women in, because you lose them through marriage."

A few of the committee members bridled at that line of argument, noting that if extended, it would bar women from *all* the professions—and that all the male astronauts were married with children. "They didn't have [the babies]," Jackie snapped back.

The committee was preparing to break up for the day, and Jackie leaned forward to make one last comment. "Even if we are second in getting a woman into the new environment, it's better than to take a chance on having women fall flat on their faces," the greatest female pilot in the country told the members of Congress.

Her testimony stunned Jerrie—but it came as no surprise to Janey. She had not been optimistic about Jackie's testimony at the hearing. Two weeks earlier, Jackie had summoned Janey to her home in New York and outlined her position. Janey didn't trust Jackie, and she hadn't thought they would get much help from this quarter.

Nor did Jackie's speech surprise anyone at NASA, for Jackie had had it approved by Webb, Dryden, Gilruth and Le May days after she agreed to testify. They all deemed it "excellent"; Webb asked only that Jackie add a few of the points she had made in her letter to Jerrie Cobb in March. Jackie also sent her draft to Randy Lovelace, and he did want changes: he emphasized the skills, the determination and the tolerance of altitude that pilots brought to the job. He suggested Jackie stress the urgency of the need to resume the tests, and that they could be integrated without distracting from the men's program. Jackie didn't make those changes—and Lovelace himself had not come to testify. So Jackie, officially representing the position of the female pilots, had delivered NASA's line.

When Jackie was done, Janey and Jerrie walked out of the chamber. Janey watched Jerrie with dismay: she looked stricken. And then at the door they faced a gauntlet of reporters, and once again it was all the same questions: Why do you want to beat men into space? You're not married, are you? Aren't you scared? Why do you need to compete with the men? Jerrie gamely stopped and answered the men with the microphones; Janey leaned on a pillar and watched with disgust.

The next morning, the women came back to the room, to the gallery now, because three new witnesses, three men this time, had the committee floor. And the room was electric with excitement at their arrival: in came George Low, director of Spacecraft and Flight Missions in the Office of Manned Space Flight, with two of America's golden boys.

"There is no question that the witnesses who appear before us today have demonstrated by their background as engineering test pilots and as products of NASA's astronaut training, that the criteria for choosing space pilots at this point in our national space program were wisely selected," Anfuso said, opening the hearing—and effectively answering the question it was meant to be investigating. "Today we have with us two Americans of heroic stature, of whom nothing further need be said. They are Col. John H. Glenn and Comdr. M. Scott Carpenter." Glenn reigned supreme in the American pantheon of heroes, five months after that first orbital flight. Carpenter had made a three-orbit Mercury flight just eight weeks earlier. On that trip, he had struggled with his experiments, been distracted by the view, overshot his landing target and caused the engineers in Houston untold consternation. NASA had privately blacklisted him from future flights. But for Americans, he was still a hero, one of just three of their own men, and six in the world, to have flown in space. Anfuso also noted that George Miller, head of the House Space Committee, was present—Miller hadn't bothered to attend the previous day, but he came out to hear the astronauts.

Low was given the floor first, and he began his presentation by submitting his own biography, and those of the Mercury 7. These were impressive lists—of wars in which the men had flown and medals they had won. But there were a few telling details buried in the litany of achievements: neither Carpenter nor Glenn had a university degree when he was selected for the Mercury program. Both were awarded honorary degrees after their spaceflights, having "earned" them through equivalent experience, their bios said. Neither was a graduate engineer.

Low outlined the qualifications for astronauts as they then stood: U.S. citizen, under age thirty-five, less than six feet tall, a degree in the physical sciences or engineering. In his fifth point, on the subject of experience, he explained why jet test pilots were the best people for the job:

> . . . of all existing occupations, the testing of jet aircraft most nearly approximates the piloting of spacecraft. All jet test pilots are selected and trained to make rapid decisions and take immediate action based upon their own evaluation of the situation in the presence of high personal risk. In many ways, manned spacecraft can be considered as a next generation of very high performance jet aircraft. Their velocity and altitude capabilities are very great. A spacecraft has life-support systems, and many other similarities with high performance jet aircraft. Thus, there is a logical reason for selecting jet test pilots—who have the training and best directly applicable occupation—for the piloting of spacecraft. In order to limit the selection to those applications [sic] who have demonstrated their capabilities, the further qualification that the applications be experienced jet test pilots was established. . . . Each spacecraft differs slightly from previous ones. Procedures are modified and improved from flight to flight. Test pilots are trained and experienced in just this type of work. Thus the requirement that the candidates must have attained experimental flight test status through the military services, the aircraft industry of NASA, or must have graduated from a military test pilot school was established. This . . . provides a preliminary screening of candidates since only the better pilots are selected for test pilot duties.

Low ran through the rest of the qualifications, and concluded, "NASA finds that the average applicant meeting all qualifications is 33 years old, is married, and has three children, has a total of 2,500 hours of flying time of which 1,500 hours is in jet aircraft and has been in test flying for 2½ years." The Manned Space Flight Office director didn't say it, but it was implicit in his words. The qualified applicant was male.

Anfuso then began the questions. "In your experience, and from the experience of Mr. Shepard and Mr. Carpenter and Colonel Glenn and other astronauts, is it necessary that he be a test pilot?"

Low deferred to the man beside him, and Col. John Glenn took the floor for the first time. "First, let me preface my remarks by one statement. I am not 'anti' any particular group. I am just pro space. . . . Anything I say is toward the purpose of getting the best qualified people, of whatever sex, color, creed or anything else they might happen to be."

Anfuso quite took his point. "You are not against women. You are a married man, you have children."

Exactly, Glenn agreed. Then he resumed his explanation. "I think there are several requirements for the program. There are technical requirements certainly that everyone is aware of. The demands of just understanding the space vehicle systems requires a good technical background. It is an experimental program, also. In that regard, you use your judgment of past events, and past experience, of course, in applying this judgment to this new experimental area. . . . We felt that the person who can best perform all these functions is still represented most nearly by the test pilot background. That is the cadre of people we have available in this country now without a lot of special training, and are available immediately for selection for a program of this type more than any other single source we know of."

Then the chair of the House Space Committee weighed in. George Miller had a point to make. He asked Glenn how long it took to train a test pilot, and Glenn explained that it was really a two-year process. Miller noted that a non–test pilot astronaut would need those two years of training, plus the astronaut training: he furnished the committee with his opinion. "While I, like the Colonel, have no prejudices, and I feel that eventually women will come into this field, I think perhaps at present it is a little premature to introduce them into our manned space program unless we could find the extraordinary one who is qualified as a test pilot."

Suddenly, though, the women got support from an unexpected quarter: astronaut Scott Carpenter spoke for the first time. "I would like to add one thought," he said. "I believe that there is nothing magic about a test pilot, although they have had the benefit of training and experience. The best reason for selecting test pilots for this job, I believe, is that they have had the opportunity to demonstrate that they have the capabilities required of the job by reason of the fact that they have been employed in the past in the profession that most nearly approximates spaceflight."

Low quickly ended that line of discussion. He went on to make the point that NASA was now accepting civilians in its applications for the second group of astronauts—although they still needed to be test pilots. Anfuso seized on this: "And women can become test pilots, they can be trained as test pilots. Miss Cochran, for example, is a test pilot?"

"Yes," Low replied, "Miss Cochran is an outstanding example."

So, Anfuso said, how about the others?

"Miss Cochran is the only woman test pilot that I know of," Low replied disingenuously. Jackie was, of course, the only female pilot in the country to be hired to test new aircraft. (In the war years, however, the WASPs test flew reconditioned planes—Jerrie had worked briefly testing war surplus aircraft.) Jackie was an extraordinarily good pilot—and she'd had some extraordinary opportunities to acquire those skills, by virtue of her husband's prominent role in the aerospace industry and their extreme wealth. There was not another woman in the country who had opportunities that were even remotely comparable.

The NASA director had another point to make to the committee. "We don't foresee in the near future—talking about the next 5 or 10 years now—the need, at any given time, for more than perhaps 40 or 50 space pilots in the NASA program. We see, therefore, at this time, no need to broaden out the available pool of people that we could use as test pilots."

Anfuso hit him with a tough question: "Would the fact that the Russians are training women alter your opinion in this regard?"

"I don't think it would at this time, Mr. Chairman," Low replied, "because we do have this large pool of qualified people that we can draw on for our present piloting needs." And, he added, NASA flight-training equipment, centrifuges and vacuum chambers were "very much loaded up at the present time."

This was the political solution Anfuso was looking for. "That is the best point you have made. In other words, you are not objecting to women, but at the present time, to let them use the things that you are using now for the astronauts would be interfering with that program."

"We would be interfering with the current program," Low agreed.

"All right," Anfuso said. "That I can see. In the future, when that relaxes, and when more equipment becomes available, you think you will give consideration to it?"

"Then I think we should certainly look into this problem," Low replied.

"We do not want to leave out the women," Anfuso chided, mindful of Jerrie's eyes on him.

"No, sir," Low replied. "I certainly don't."

Now the other members joined the questioning. Joseph Karth (the Democrat from Minnesota) wanted to get back to this question of test piloting. "Pursuing qualification No. 5, which is the one involving experience of test pilot training, yesterday two of the witnesses spoke very strongly about this qualification.

They felt, quite frankly, that an extensive number of logged hours in actual flight compensated for all of the variable and invariables and the emergencies that one might meet as a test pilot. Therefore the test pilot requirement was not a fair one, because it ruled out too many people who normally get this training if they had logged a great number of training hours. Would you care to address yourselves to that?"

Low took the floor and disagreed. "The type of emergency situation that test pilots get into daily in their own flying experience is not matched by the piloting community as a whole. It is true that other pilots also get into stressful situations, but not as often as frequently as these men do—as the experimental test pilots do."

Then astronaut Carpenter put the point in terms everyone would understand. "A person can't enter a backward swimming race and by swimming twice the distance in a [front] crawl qualify as a backstroker."

Jim Fulton, though, was still in the women's corner. "On the basis of the requirements that Mr. Low has stated, obviously Colonel Glenn would have been eliminated. You wouldn't have passed, because you don't have an engineering degree—do you?"

"I have one now," Glenn replied. "I did not at the time of selection."

"You would not have been selected," Fulton repeated.

He went, then, on a bit of a tirade. Women were not allowed into the military test pilot schools, they weren't allowed to fly jets—why couldn't their experience be factored with the same sort of "equivalency" used for Glenn's engineering experience? Jackie Cochran had shown women could be test pilots, he said, while Jerrie and the twelve other women had shown they could pass the tests. Jerrie was a NASA consultant but not allowed to do any serious work. "Since this group of women has passed these tests successfully, NASA should outline a training program that does not interfere with the current programs but will let women participate. . . . It is the same old thing cropping up, where men want to protect women and keep them out of the field so that it is kept for men." Fired up by his own rhetoric, he delivered an eloquent if somewhat irrelevant monologue on the contributions of women through history, from Sacajawea to Elizabeth I.

John Glenn elegantly shot him down. "I would like to point out too that, with all due respect to the women that you mentioned in all these historic events, where they performed so fine, they rose to the occasion and demonstrated that at the time they had better qualifications than the men around them, and if we can find any women that demonstrate that they have better qualifications for going into a program than we have going into that program, we would welcome them with open arms."

Committee members dissolved in laughter, and Glenn played it up.

"For the purpose of my going home this afternoon, I think that should be stricken from the record."

The wind was quite gone from Fulton's sails. Conceding the floor, he concluded, "May I compliment Col. John Glenn and Commander Carpenter. We as Americans are very proud of you and the wonderful job you have done, as well as the other astronauts. And I want to tell you, Col. John Glenn is a stellar witness before a congressional committee."

Anfuso had the floor again. "Gentlemen, I believe it is necessary to set this testimony straight, for the record, as far as it has gone. According to your new regulations there is absolutely no discrimination against women."

Correct, Low said.

"If women can meet those conditions you have set out, they will qualify," Anfuso pressed.

"Yes, sir," Low said.

"And you have set up these regulations, I gather, first of all to achieve success in this program, because you want the best?"

"Yes, sir."

"As Colonel Glenn said, whether they be women or men is immaterial, but you want the best."

"Yes, sir."

"So that we can advance this program?"

"Yes, sir."

"Now, of course, I assume also that you are taking into consideration the question of safety," Anfuso said. "Now, there is a lot of talk about women astronauts. I am in favor of women. I am certainly in favor of giving them every opportunity—and they are getting it at this hearing. I will push and fight to see that the opportunity in spaceflight will be given to them. But I am sure that if we had lower standards than those that you have outlined, it might be dangerous. I think the loss of prestige in losing a woman in space would certainly be something that we would hear about. So let us not be too hasty in changing those regulations."

He advised that NASA should, without interfering with its existing work, "carry on some kind of parallel program, to give these women a chance to someday become test pilots."

"Yes, sir," said Low.

"You say, perhaps, in your next regulations you will come up with something which will include women; is that correct?" he pressed.

"We will certainly consider all possible qualifications and reconsider them," said the spaceflight director.

Fulton was back with his pet idea. "Why not have a 'first woman in space' project and get started on it right away?" Anfuso thought the idea was reasonable, but others on the committee did not.

"Mr. Low, wouldn't the establishment of a national goal at this time to be the first nation to put a woman in space interfere with our present program?" asked Edward Roush.

It was just the opening Low was looking for. "Yes, sir," he said, "absolutely. . . . It would slow it down in that all of the resources that we have available—and I can only speak for the manned spaceflight program now—are required for projects Gemini and Apollo. If we diverted some of these resources, both financial and personnel, to another program, we would necessarily have to slow down our national goal of landing a man on the moon before the end of this decade."

In the gallery, Janey and Jerrie looked at each other and rolled their eyes. NASA was saying they weren't qualified to operate an electric drill, and yet at the same time a small group of female pilots apparently had the power to derail the national push to get to the moon. But the committee was convinced.

Now Rep. Walter Riehlman turned to a subject that still wasn't clear to the members. Why was the testing canceled, he asked Low. And the NASA man said he had no idea, for it was never NASA's affair: the military was going to do the tests, and eventually they got around to asking NASA if it needed them. NASA, of course, didn't. "That was the only time we were asked about this program. We were asked only that one question, and our answer was that we had no requirement."

Glenn chimed in to address a point that had been particularly irritating him: just because the thirteen women passed the tests in Albuquerque didn't mean they were qualified for spaceflight—it just proved that they were each "a good healthy person."

"A real crude analogy might be: We have the Washington Redskins football team," Glenn explained. "My mother could probably pass the physical exam that they give preseason for the Redskins, but I doubt if she could play too many games for them." Once again, the astronaut had everyone chuckling.

Now Jessica Weiss, a New York Republican who was one of the two women on the committee, had a few questions on the issue of discrimination. Perhaps it wasn't intentional, she said to Low, but he had to admit there was a built-in barrier to women getting those jobs, since they weren't allowed to fly for the military. "Is there anything, in your opinion, that can be done to enable women to be accepted as test pilots?"

Low blandly agreed that women could be test pilots, playing on Weiss's failure to specify the elite military world of *jet* testing. "I see no reason why women should not enter into the test piloting field. I don't think that in the civilian test pilot area there are any roadblocks now. It is just that none of them have seen fit to get into this area, in large areas at least."

Weiss, puzzled, glanced at her copy of Jerrie's testimony. "My feeling was there was a definite roadblock against them in that the field was relatively closed to women."

Low deferred to the astronauts, and Glenn had an answer ready.

"I think this gets back to the way our social order is organized, really. It is just a fact. The men go off and fight the wars and fly the airplanes and come back and help design and build and test them. The fact that women are not in this field is a fact of our social order. It may be undesirable." He corrected himself, and continued. "It obviously is, but we are only looking, as I said before, to people with certain qualifications. If anybody can meet them I am all for them."

Waggonner spoke up now, rejecting Fulton's idea of a national program "to land a woman on the moon," saying it would be "to the detriment" of the existing program. "The idea is, among some, that we should do this because the Russians do it. I do not think the women of America want to do all the things that Russian women have to do, in the first place, nor do I believe that we Americans should do something simply because the Russians do it, or that we as neighbors ought to do something that the Joneses do." And to clear matters up, he asked the astronauts to describe their days so everyone would know about the sort of sophisticated work they were doing. Carpenter spoke first and, most unhelpfully, said he thought women could hack the program and probably also stand up in space. Waggonner snapped that that wasn't his question, and Glenn stepped in, describing in great detail what he said was his itinerary from the past few days: he had tested a mock-up of the Gemini craft, modifying the ejection seat and simulating takeoffs, then met with the medical team to talk about just how long the astronauts might be able to push their time in orbit on the next mission. This was the kind of stuff the committee wanted to hear from astronauts.

Now another guest spoke up, Walter Moeller of Ohio—a member of the House Space Committee who had not been appointed to this subcommittee but was sitting in. He returned to the problems that including women would create, leading Low with a series of questions.

"If you got a directive today that women astronauts are to be trained, and our priority program today is to get somebody on the moon, would your program be in any way impeded by this directive?"

"Very much so," Low replied.

"People in industry today say that it costs them more in many, many instances to use women in their employ than men," Moeller continued, "and it is for this reason that ofttimes women take lesser pay than men take. Would it cost the government more money to train women astronauts and use women astronauts than it would men?"

Low, of course, agreed that it would.

"So that if today our priority program is getting a man on the moon, maybe we should ask the good ladies to be patient and let us get this thing accomplished first and then go after training women astronauts." Moeller sat back, satisfied.

Fulton made one last try: the trip to the moon was going to take a decade—was NASA telling Jerrie and the others they had to wait at least ten years to have a part in America's space program? "To me that is the same thing that has been said to women when they were interested in suffrage, or when they were interested in planes. . . . Of course, nobody wants to retard the Lunar program. You have adequate facilities. You are being given $2 billion more this year, and it is not all programmed. You have been changing your programs. You could very well make a small test program for these women and get them started." (And, of course, the canceled test program was being paid for privately and wasn't going to cost NASA anything.)

Once again, the floor went back to John Glenn. "We have not seen the idea of women in space put forward with the idea that they are better qualified, which is what we are looking for. The only thing we have seen thus far is women coming in space just by the very fact they are women . . . to spend many millions of dollars to additionally qualify other people, whom we don't particularly need, regardless of sex, creed or color, doesn't seem right, when we already have these qualified people."

And with that, Anfuso announced that they would adjourn, and the hearings were ended.

In the gallery, Jerrie and Janey were once again caught totally off guard. Jerrie had planned to speak again, to rebut Glenn and Low. But now the third day was canceled. Their audience was over; they would have no further chance to make their case for justice. Slowly they got up and headed down the stairs. Once again, a crowd of reporters was waiting. As the two women moved out of the hearing chamber, they turned and looked back. The members of Congress were crowded around Glenn and Carpenter, eager to get the autographs of the day's star witnesses.

ABANDONED

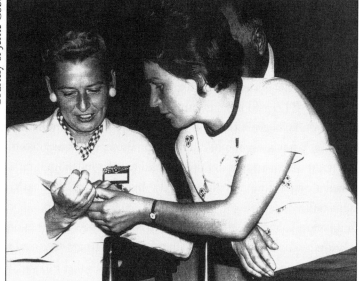

Jerrie Cobb with Valentina Tereshkova, the first woman in space, Mexico City, 1963.

BREAK LOOSE NOW THE DOOR IS OPEN NOW YOU CAN HELP FURTHER OUR CAUSE. SUGGEST YOU CONTACT EVERYONE YOU CAN REQUESTING THEY WIRE PRESIDENT KENNEDY AT WHITE HOUSE, URGING IMMEDIATE PROGRAM FOR WOMEN IN SPACE. GOOD LUCK AND WE ARE ON OUR WAY, SITUATION LOOKS GOOD.

Jerrie sent this optimistic telegram to each one of the FLATs hours after the congressional hearing was adjourned. But not even Jerrie, with her relentless dedication to her "crusade," could have believed the words she wired. The situation looked anything but good.

The hearing made great fodder for the evening news—what editor could resist a story that combined a guest appearance by America's heroes with entreaties from a couple of good-looking women in heels who claimed to want to go into space? Much of the coverage was sympathetic. A headline in *The Washington Post* said, "2 Would-be 'Astronettes' Plead: Let Us Beat Reds." Janey's lines, that space "shouldn't be a stag club" and "for some women, the PTA just isn't enough," got big play. She and Jerrie were called "two dauntless blondes"; their many qualifications (including Janey's eight children) were listed and the tests they passed were breathlessly detailed. Dozens of newspapers ran an AP photo of Jerrie listening intently, her shoes off beneath the witness table.

But Jackie Cochran got plenty of coverage, too: "The world's best-known woman pilot noted that girls tend to get married and have babies—and if women get into spacework this kind of thing could play hob with the countdown," began a UPI wire story carried all over the country. The article went on to misrepresent a 40 percent washout rate of WASPs (parallel with that of male cadets) as a 40 percent dropout of women who ran off to get married and have babies. And John Glenn's solemn declaration that they were just looking to get the best people for the job was widely reported. "Hero Dodges Women's Ire," said one headline, while another cracked that Glenn "Would Welcome Woman 'With Open Arms.'" The *Chicago Tribune* said, "2 Astronauts 'Scrub' Bid of Women Pilots," in a story that began, "Gently but firmly, a couple of America's space heroes today drained the fuel from the proposal to train women astronauts." The *Tribune* reporter said George Low "was chivalry itself as he skated delicately around questions as to why women aren't allowed in the program" by explaining it would inevitably slow the drive to get to the moon.

Deprived of a chance to rebut the NASA testimony by the hearing's abrupt adjournment, Jerrie sent a supplemental statement to the committee members. In it, she pointed out that no expert witness had ever testified on whether women were as or better qualified for the stresses of spaceflight, that John Glenn cited only opinion. And she reiterated what she and the other women wanted: NASA had the money to train women; the committee members themselves had said so. "Understandably this would be a parallel program which would not interfere with work on the current programs. I do not think 1 woman of the 13 of us wants to interfere with the national goal of putting the first man on the moon. We only ask that we be tested and trained in order to be part of, not ahead of, the manned space flight program of our country." The argument that they would hold things up was absurd, she said; of the thirty-two candidates in the second group of men NASA was screening, only five would be chosen, and the testing and training facilities were scattered over eight locations, which "must have some free time to schedule a small group of 13 or fewer women among the males." The women wanted simply to complete the tests they had been scheduled for, she wrote, and for those who passed to go on for more rigorous tests and training. "All we need is the opportunity to prove that we are 'capable,' 'qualified' and 'required.'"

Jerrie followed the appeal with a list of her test results, including the doctors' conclusions that she had "much to recommend her" for spaceflight and would "qualify for special missions." But in the congressional records, Jerrie's addendum is followed by another—from Jackie Cochran. Six days after the hearing, Jackie wrote to Richard Hines, the Space Committee's chief staffer. She explained unapologetically that she missed the first morning of testimony because she was chairing a meeting of the National

Aeronautic Association, of which she was president. Thus she missed Jerrie's speech and the chance to "correct" her on many key points. Jackie wanted these points inserted into the record as if she had spoken them that morning—and if the committee wouldn't do that, she wanted them appended at the end. Thus the record of the hearing ends with a forceful statement of Jackie's position: "There is not now and to date has not been any women in space or women astronaut program. No woman to date has passed the Mercury astronaut tests." Jackie entered a totally revisionist version of events into the record: Dr. Lovelace, she said, wanted to test a lot of women and asked the 99s for names, but "only one, Miss Jerrie Cobb, showed up." So Jackie was brought in to find more women. And, Jackie insisted at the end, Jerrie had no right to speak for the others.

As far as Jerrie was concerned, she was leader of the group, and she was waging a campaign on their behalf. On August 15, she wrote to the FLATs: "The Congressional hearings are over, and all in all the results were encouraging. The subcommittee recommendation has been written and will go before the full House Space Committee sometime this week or next—then straight to NASA." Since she had read the names of the women into the congressional record, their astronaut ambitions were now public, and each of them was deluged with calls from local newspapers and radio stations. "I have seen some of the publicity on some of you and generally I think you did a fine job in fielding the reporters' questions," Jerrie wrote. "I'm real pleased the way we have all stuck together and expressed similar, serious views— please continue to do so, in the interest of unity for our cause. As you are well aware, Mrs. Hart and I presented this program to the subcommittee on a sound, serious and harmonious basis— the differing testimony by the other woman pilot present was certainly no help, and was resented by most of the subcommittee members and some of the press." And Jerrie said they should be hopeful: "I'll continue to do everything I can for this program and will appreciate your moral support and help. The more letters and wires coming into the White House urging an immediate program for women in space the better, so keep working on that angle. Letters to your Senators and Representatives will also help. After all, this country IS still run BY the people!"

A week later Jerrie wrote to the FLATs again, to say that the House was in recess but that they should be doing all they could for publicity. Janey was going to write a piece for *Town and Country* and Jerrie asked the women to send in pictures. "Candid and glamorous, NOT in pants," she added emphatically. And now Jerrie attempted to formalize her position as leader of the female astronaut candidates: "So that we can stick together as a group there should be a central contact for all publicity on a national level. I will handle it from here if you want me to; or if any of you think you could better take care of it, let me know. Also, there should be one spokesman for the group and I would appreciate your views on that. As my prepared statement before the subcommittee pointed out, I assumed that role more or less by default, and because I have worked three years getting this program started."

Jackie Cochran, meanwhile, was sending out letters of her own. She sent a memo to James Webb and Hugh Dryden, reiterating the points of her House testimony. "I could not agree more with the testimony of Mr. Low of NASA and Astronauts Glenn and Carpenter before the House Committee," she began. "I would not like any of my own sex to do or say anything that would lower, here or abroad, the prestige and dignity of our American women." Then she outlined a nine-point plan for the kind of multiyear research testing of two hundred women she was proposing—and concluded with an offer to come in and discuss it with them. In her original draft of the memo, she included one additional paragraph: "A woman responsible to NASA, and working closely with the Armed Services, to the extent they are involved, should have direction of certain non-scientific or medical aspects of the program such as discipline among the candidates and the problems of women as such in a group activity of this nature." But that, she decided, was a little too obvious, and she dropped that point from the final copy. She would let the NASA chiefs make their own decision about appointing the best-qualified woman to run this show.

Hugh Dryden wrote her back, a polite brush-off—this time.

The same day, Jackie sent out another letter. Each of the FLATs but Jerrie received a copy. Jackie enclosed an offprint of her testimony to the committee, and then she gave the first overt sign of the conflict she and Jerrie were having behind the scenes. "I spoke only for myself without claim to represent any of the women who passed the Lovelace tests. Miss Cobb stated that she was the spokesman for all of the [eleven] not present. I am satisfied that this is not true as to some who had already expressed their views to me. Was she authorized to act as spokesman as to you? I'll be glad to hear from you."

Inevitably, there were divisions between the Lovelace women: they were thirteen big personalities, thirteen women used to achieving things in the face of considerable opposition and, for the most part, to getting what they wanted. None of them was close to Jerrie before this business started, and a few were openly dissatisfied with her leadership: they felt that she wasn't keeping them informed, that they should all have gone to Washington to testify, that Jerrie was too interested in making sure she was first. In June, after receiving her copy of Jackie's long letter to Jerrie refuting the need for a women's astronaut program, Gene Nora Stumbough had written to Jackie to tell her benefactor where she stood. "I agree with your thoughts expressed to Jerrie wholeheartedly and 100%. Women *will* travel in space, but there is no need to train women right now. And to frantically send up a woman immediately just to beat the Russians, is, in my thinking, totally invalid. . . . It is my hope that Washington will one day soon recognize a need for further research on women in the

aviation and space vein; but I am not under the delusion that one
of us next week or even next year will be shot off to the moon. I
am only afraid that by nagging those who make the decisions,
we are hurting ourselves." (Jackie held on to this letter and
submitted it to the House subcommittee as proof that Jerrie
didn't speak for the others.)

The twins, too, disavowed Jerrie. They used the sudden media
attention to parrot Jackie Cochran's position. On July 19, 1962, a
day after the congressional hearings, an article under their joint
byline went out on the UPI wire. "American women will go into
space too, when scientists decide they are needed. But at present
no American woman is in training and none has completed
testing," they wrote. "We believe the testing of women astronaut
candidates should be continued immediately. Then if scientists
determine women are needed for space work, qualified candidates
will be ready." But they said women would have to be slotted into
the space program eventually—maybe as passengers. And in
subsequent interviews, the twins hotly denied any discrimination.
"Miss [Jan] Dietrich does not advocate training of women as
astronauts until scientists decide they are needed," said an article
in the *Santa Monica Evening Outlook.* "She explained that she does
not feel women have been unfairly kept out of the astronaut
program since there are no female jet test pilots in this country. All
the astronauts chosen so far have been jet test pilots. 'They have
simply used the people who are qualified. There is no shortage of
astronauts.'" Marion herself wrote, "There is no point in sending
a woman just for a ride." All of the reports noted that the twins'
view was "considerably different" from that presented by Jerrie and
Janey in Congress. The *Los Angeles Times* quoted Jan: "Those who
asked [for the inclusion of women in the space program] certainly
didn't speak for the group," the petite, blue-eyed brunette told
us, "and I for one am not in accord with their ideas."

Jan responded obediently to Jackie's query about whether
Jerrie spoke for them. "Jerrie did not ask permission to represent

me at the hearings," Jan Dietrich wrote to her champion. "I would like to see the testing of women continued, but I am concerned that the antagonism necessarily engendered by the hearings will preclude this for some time." Marion echoed her twin sister.

The twins, of course, had their star hitched to Jackie. Most of the other women recognized that Jerrie had been through the tests first, had got furthest and had the most contacts at NASA— she was, after all, its consultant. Their hopes for reviving the program lay with her. Now, however, Jackie succeeded in taking the natural differences of opinion between the women and split-ting the group up into camps—divisions that would widen over the coming years. B Steadman, who had always admired Jackie Cochran, answered her query about Jerrie's leadership by saying that she had spoken to Janey, though not to Jerrie; she implied in her letter that energy might be better used in organizing than in fighting over who spoke for whom. "For Heaven's sake, Miss Cochran, if this Space Program has a meaning, why don't you grab the reins and get it going," B asked. "It needs one leader with wisdom, understanding and the ability to get people to work together. We are without this type of leadership now. If the program is not necessary then I'd like to forget it and get back to my own business."

K Cagle was even more emphatic: "This is the way I stand. Miss Jacqueline Cochran (you!) paid my expenses at the Lovelace Clinic. . . . I consider you my sponsor and spokesman. I believe in you, I trust your judgement in any situation. You have had a great deal of experience in dealing with government officials and important business people. I am sure I can't even visualize the forest of important people you have influenced to your side. I like your seasoned judgement, your soft, feminine approach. You know what we can get, so why ask for the impossible and make enemies? You are asking for what we CAN get. Jerrie Cobb is asking for the impossible, I think. I wish I could orbit tomorrow, and I know you do, too. . . . I am on *your* team. I know we can get from 'the men' what we want, not by pushing, but by winning. You've got the know-how. S-o-o Take the reins, we are YOUR girls."

And Irene Leverton now repudiated Jerrie, blaming her for not getting the other women involved in the hearing, although she admitted she had meant to send Jerrie her views and not got around to it. "To beat Russia with a female astronaut was very poor thinking on Jerrie's part. I'm afraid the idea hurt us all a lot," Irene wrote to Jackie. "Sure, I think the U.S. should be first—we must always strive to do things better and first. But to rush a sub-orbital flight is not wise. I'm sorry that a statement by each of us wasn't read at the hearings. We might all have differing opinions but an overall picture would have been available to Congress." But Irene was not enamored of Jackie's position either. "I admit that I don't agree with all that you were quoted as saying about marriage and our possible attrition rate . . . after weathering 18 years of ignorant prejudice against women in aviation, I wasn't about to let domesticity keep me from a chance to enter such a program. . . . Perhaps sometime in the future we women will start pulling together."

This certainly wasn't that time. By lining up the opposing views, Jackie exacerbated tension between the women. They identified one another as the problem, and one anothers' campaigns or lack thereof as the thing keeping them out of space. Jerrie knew what was going on. "I agree with you on the clipping you sent by the Dietrichs and I resent it also, but I really have no control over it," she wrote in a frustrated letter to Jean Hixson after Jan and Marion publicly backed Jackie in their UPI wire story. "Either the group must work together supporting my efforts to get women included in the space program or Cochran will turn it into a debacle . . . as you know she is trying to do so. I really feel sorry for her as she must be a pretty unhappy person."

None of the correspondence between the women in these months mentions the testimony by the astronauts or George Low, or the attitude of NASA or the congressmen.

When the House subcommittee came back with its report a few weeks later, NASA was vindicated. "The requirements laid down by NASA, which all astronaut applicants must meet, are based on . . . sound scientific rationale and upon a wealth of knowledge gained in ultra-high-speed, high-altitude piloting experience. The astronaut criteria in no way were formulated with the intent to exclude automatically possible applicants because of race, creed, color or gender." There was merit, the committee said, in "considering the possibility of establishing a scientific program of medical research upon which to base the training eventually of highly qualified women as astronauts. . . ." But "the present urgency of our manned space flight program, the high costs involved, the limited and continuously used training facilities, and the foreseeable need for only a relatively few astronauts, preclude at this time the establishment of a woman astronaut training program in spite of the fact that it would establish a new space 'first' for the United States."

The congressional hearing had not accomplished what Jerrie hoped it would—in fact, it hadn't yielded anything except a few news stories. With that in mind, Jerrie took her campaign back on the road, and now she had nothing good to say about NASA. In October 1962, she went to the Air Force Association convention (the same meeting where she had met Randy Lovelace and Donald Flickinger three years earlier), and this time she gave a speech about "Project WISE"—Woman in Space Earliest. She was openly critical of the space agency:

The fulfillment of Project WISE was easily within our capability—did not require any additional funding— could be accomplished quickly and easily—and would shock the world! . . . By now, Russia had put the first man into orbit and American prestige was at a *new* low. President Kennedy asked for any effort that could put the United States first in any new space endeavor. . . . [But] Project WISE died. It was just too simple and too spectacular to put the first woman in space. Administrator James E. Webb appointed me a consultant to the civilian space agency, NASA. Since I'm not a Ph.D. with three different science degrees, I assumed my appointment had something to do with women in space. That was over a year ago and—believe me—I'm the most unconsulted consultant in any government agency today. . . . It didn't take long to find out that the subject of women astronauts was taboo—and not even to be discussed by those who wished to stay in the good graces of NASA.

Jerrie's unhappy speech attracted some sympathetic publicity. In *The Christian Science Monitor,* for example, Neal Stanford wrote, "It can't be said that Miss Cobb hasn't knocked at the right doors to win the distinction of being America's first woman astronaut. She is a one-woman lobbyist known to every space-minded official in Washington. It is not that she is hiding her ambition under a bushel. It is the space agency, it seems, that refuses to let her ride atop an Atlas." There may have been more truth than he knew when Stanford observed that a space trip was not just Jerrie's ambition, but an "obsession."

In November, Jerrie spoke to the Women's Advertising Club in Washington. "We're bypassing the one scientific space feat we could accomplish now—putting the first woman in orbit. It would be comparable to Russia putting the first man in orbit. But NASA says it has no need for women astronauts. It says it has enough astronauts already. With that kind of attitude, it's no wonder we're second in the space race." This time the headlines were even closer to home. "NASA Program Winged by Aviatrix," said *The Washington Post.*

Eventually, her media campaign provoked James Webb to the point of a formal rebuke. On December 17, 1962, he summoned Jerrie to his office in Washington. After reiterating that NASA had no intention of changing its qualifications for astronauts, he reminded her that her consultant appointment had not been renewed—she was no longer affiliated with the space agency, and frankly she was nearing the limit of what NASA would tolerate silently. In minutes taken of the meeting, Webb's assistant R. P. Young noted,

> [Webb] pointed out, however, that the government has a very great stake in the success of the space program and he wondered what her motives could be in pursuing this further. Miss Cobb replied that she was only doing what she thought was right and what she believed in. Mr. Webb then suggested that by pursuing it in an irrational manner, she could harm herself more than help her cause. Mr. Webb explained this to her by saying he has been asked several times to comment on her speeches and if he continues to be pressed for a substantive comment as a result of her speeches, sooner or later he would have to state that he had not consulted Miss Cobb because he had not found the occasion on which he felt her judgment would be of any assistance in solving the problem at hand.

Still Jerrie pressed on. She made more speeches, and she petitioned both President Kennedy and Vice President Johnson. In April 1963, Webb wrote to her again, bluntly advising that none of this was going to change his position—and again reminding Jerrie that her relationship with the space agency had been severed. "It is certainly fine with everyone in NASA for you to work toward any goal that you believe in. The only point of my conversation previously was that your association with NASA had come to an end, that I did not think it would help you work toward your goal to criticize this relationship under which you had been asked to serve as a NASA consultant, and that this relationship had not proved of the value I had hoped it would."

In fact, Webb had a new consultant on the issue of women in space: he swore Jackie Cochran into the job in early June. It was a reward for her own public campaign—while Jerrie was talking up the need for an American first, Jackie had toured ladies' clubs and symposiums pointing out that she had funded the research into women's qualifications for space and thus that she was well placed to say there was no need to start training them. Her payoff appointment gave Webb a convenient new public face for the issue, someone to point to when pressed by reporters on the subject of female astronauts.

And suddenly, this was a very hot topic indeed.

On June 16, 1963, the Soviets launched *Vostok 6*. The capsule carried a cosmonaut wearing dozens of sensors, a seamless knitted sweater and culottes, paper socks, a blue pressure suit and a bright orange flight suit. Her name was Valentina Vladimirovna Tereshkova, and her call sign was "Chaika"—Seagull.

Tereshkova's worker credentials had, in the end, beaten out the better-qualified Valentina Ponomareva, and she was Sergei Korolev's choice for the first woman in space. Valya, as she was known, had a model Soviet biography: her peasant father was killed fighting the Germans in World War II, and Valya was raised in suitably humble circumstances by her mother in Yaroslavl on the Upper Volga. After high school she went to work at Red Perekop Factory No. 2, a fabric plant where her mother and sister also worked, but she continued to study at night school. In 1959, at age twenty-two, she made her first parachute jump with a local aviation club and then organized the Textile Mill Workers Parachute Club. She made dozens of jumps of increasing difficulty, performing with the team at public fairs.

After Yuri Gagarin's flight, Tereshkova was one of thousands of Soviet citizens who wrote to the Central Committee and volunteered for future space missions. Those letters were stored away in boxes—until the politburo approved the plan for a female cosmonaut. A committee plowed through the letters and drew up a short list of women. Tereshkova passed the medicals and the interview, and a few weeks later she was sent to the cosmonaut training center in Star City, outside Moscow. She was instructed to tell her mother and her collective that it was part of training for the national parachute team.

Tereshkova had some instruction in how to fly a plane during her year of training, but it was her skill as a parachute jumper that was most important for the Vostok flight. Unlike the Mercury astronauts, whose capsule landed in the sea, the Soviet cosmonauts bailed out at ten thousand feet and came down by parachute on their own (for they had to reenter over land within the Soviet Union, and the cosmonaut would not survive the capsule crash). At Star City, she and the other four female candidates rode the centrifuge repeatedly, and each spent a full week in isolation rooms, a closed-circuit camera trained on them the whole time. According to Tereshkova's official biography, the male and female cosmonauts got along well together and joined in informal games of ice hockey. Male reporters with the news agency TASS would later say that the men did not take their female counterparts seriously, and indeed Tereshkova herself quoted Korolev as greeting the arrival of the women with "I ask for cosmonauts and they send me a bunch of girl parachutists."

Regardless, a bit more than a year later he deemed her well-enough qualified to entrust a Vostok capsule to her. Cosmonaut Valeri Bykovsky went up on *Vostok 5* on June 14, and Tereshkova joined him in orbit two days later. Shortly after she launched, her voice was broadcast to millions of Russians on Moscow Radio: "Here is Seagull. Everything is fine. I see the horizon; it's a sky blue with a dark strip. I see the earth. Everything is in order. I'm feeling fine. The machine is working well." Television pictures were broadcast back of Valentina laughing and smiling in her helmet. In her logbook, she wrote of just the kind of pictures Jerrie Cobb so longed to see. "On the sixth orbit, I saw a storm over the Indian Ocean. The sky was lightened by bright flashes. The nocturnal horizon was rather uniform even before sunrise. Before each sunrise there is a unique sight. The clouds over the ocean have the form of ridges and more often, of streets with small breaks in them."

Khrushchev made much of her flight. Shortly after Korolev confirmed that Tereshkova had been successfully launched, the premier sent a telegram, read to her by mission control.

DEAR VALENTINA VLADIMIROVNA, MY HEARTIEST CONGRATU-
LATIONS TO YOU, THE FIRST WOMAN COSMONAUT IN THE
WORLD, FOR A REMARKABLE FLIGHT IN OUTER SPACE.
THE SOVIET PEOPLE ARE PROUD OF YOUR TRIUMPH. WE
ALL FOLLOW YOUR HEROIC FLIGHT WITH GREAT ATTENTION
AND FROM THE BOTTOM OF OUR HEARTS WISH YOU GOOD
HEALTH AND GOOD LUCK AND A SUCCESSFUL COMPLETION
OF THE FLIGHT. WE WILL MEET YOU WITH GREAT PLEASURE
ON OUR SOVIET HOMELAND.

Then, on her fourth orbit around the earth, Khrushchev was patched through to Tereshkova's radio. "I hear you very well," he boomed happily. "Your call sign is Seagull, I believe. Permit me to call you Valya, Valentina. I am very happy, and it gives me fatherly pride that our girl, a Soviet girl, is the very first in the world to be in outer space and to be the master of a very advanced technology." The cosmonaut (at least in the version released to TASS) thanked "Nikita Sergeyevich" for his kind words and pledged to see him soon again on earth.

There was speculation that Tereshkova's craft and *Vostok 5* might actually dock, a maneuver vital to the success of a future moon landing. They came to within three kilometers (two miles) of each other, so that Tereshkova caught sight of Bykovsky's craft, but they did not attempt to dock—neither Vostok ship had rocket thrusters that would allow the pilots to alter the trajectory of their orbits. Tereshkova and Bykovsky took a series of photographs of the sun and of its transitional spectrums; made astronomical observations of constellations; measured ion fluxes in fields of radiation and made observations of the earth. In addition, of course, Soviet scientists closely charted the impact of the spaceflight on their different (or, as it turned out, not so different) male and female physiologies.

After Valya's forty-eighth orbit, the capsule was realigned and she was pulled back down toward earth—by a force nine times that of than gravity, which flattened her into the seat of the capsule. She ejected right on target and landed in a field in the Kazakh highlands, in fine condition but for a cut on her nose caused by flying capsule debris as she was parachuting away from it. Farmers working nearby ran to greet her with the traditional Russian welcome of bread and salt.

Tereshkova was in the air for two days, twenty-two hours and fifty minutes—more flight time than the six male Mercury astronauts combined.

How did she do, this first female astronaut? The accounts vary wildly. There were rumors—seized upon in the United States— that she suffered terrible space sickness (intense nausea and disorientation caused by weightlessness), that she could not carry out her mission as intended and that Korolev ordered that the machine be controlled entirely from the ground. There were reports that her mission was canceled early (Bykovsky stayed in space almost five days) and also that it was extended from the one day initially planned to almost three, when it was discovered that she was coping well in space. In an event reported in great detail in *The New York Times* on June 18, she could not be reached by ground control for some time during her first night in orbit, later telling Korolev, "I fell asleep for some time contrary to schedule. I shall do better. I feel fine." Space historian Asif Siddiqi, however, has made an extensive study of the once-secret records of the early Soviet space program and says that while Tereshkova had a few problems, none was critical. Tereshkova's brief space sickness passed, and she completed the planned duration of her mission, Siddiqi says.

The Soviets always said publicly that she had made a perfect flight. Just as Jerrie Cobb had predicted, the first woman in space was a hero. Thousands of people turned out when she and Bykovsky were paraded in Red Square, and the premier gave them the country's highest honor, the Order of Lenin. "Bourgeois society always emphasizes that woman is the weaker sex," Khrushchev thundered to the crowd. "That is not so. Our Russian woman showed the American astronauts a thing or two. Her mission was longer than that of all the Americans put together!" He pointed one thick finger at Tereshkova. "There is your weaker sex!" Then the feared Soviet leader pulled her into a bear hug and planted a big smacking kiss on her cheek. Tereshkova was dispatched on a global tour; she met the Queen of England and was honored at the United Nations. Rapturous crowds greeted her in India, Nepal, Sri Lanka and Burma.

The primary reaction in America was shock—and an almost titillated fascination. "Russian Blonde Spins Around Earth Toward Possible Rendezvous," screamed a headline across the front of *The Dallas Morning News* that Jerri Sloan picked off her front step on June 17. A headline in the *Berkshire Eagle* of Massachusetts demanded, "Why Valentina And Not Our Gal?" And in *Life,* Clare Boothe Luce, wife of the magazine's founder, Henry Luce, wrote a stunning article. She was a former Republican Congresswoman and a virulent critic of Communism, but this time, she said, the Reds had it right. The article—headlined "But Some People Simply Never Get the Message"—is a telling sign that NASA had failed to keep pace with the changing attitudes to women's role in society: one of the most powerful conservative voices in the United States was left praising the Russians for their female cosmonaut. "Why did the Soviet Union launch a woman cosmonaut into space? Failure of American men to give the right answer to this question may yet prove to be their costliest Cold War blunder. But already they are giving the wrong answers," Boothe Luce wrote. U.S. space experts "hold—to a man—the view that Valentina Tereshkova was fired from the launching pad as a Soviet space program female guinea pig, and that the experiment is useless, at least for the foreseeable future. The right answer is that Soviet Russia put a woman into space because Communism preaches and, since the Revolution of 1917, has tried to practice the inherent equality of men and women." The progress of women in the U.S.S.R. was "spectacular," she wrote, and rattled off the statistics to prove it—74 percent of Russian doctors were women. In 1917, the country had only six hundred female engineers; by 1961 there were 379,000. "The astronaut of today is the world's most prestigious popular idol. Once launched into space he holds in his hands something far more costly and precious than the millions of dollars' worth of equipment in his capsule; he holds the prestige and the honor of his country." An astronaut is "the symbol of the way of life of his nation. In entrusting a 26-year-old girl with a cosmonaut mission, the Soviet Union has given its women unmistakable proof that it believes them to possess these same virtues. The flight of Valentina Tereshkova is, consequently, symbolic of the emancipation of the Communist woman. It symbolizes to Russian women that they actively share (not passively bask, like American women) in the glory of conquering space."

In the same issue of *Life*, America met its female "astro-nots." Under the headline "The U.S. Team Is Still Warming Up the Bench," there they were, the thirteen abandoned candidates from the Lovelace experiment. There was a photo and a brief biography of each of them. "The U.S. could have been first to put a woman up in space merely by deciding to do so," the introduction said. "All of [these women] were experienced pilots with qualifications far more impressive than Valentina Tereshkova's. To a woman, they were eager to go into orbit."

No doubt many *Life* readers thought Clare Boothe Luce had lost her marbles. If the Soviets were crazy enough to put a woman in a spaceship, well, thank heavens NASA had more sense. At a time when only 25 percent of women in the United States had paid jobs, the thirteen women presented in *Life,* pilots and would-be astronauts, appeared unusual in the extreme. And yet, at the same time, few Americans were oblivious to the way the country was changing, to the new debates about discrimination and what fields should be open to women. A few politicians saw the situation the way Jerrie did—on June 27, 1962, Ernest Gruening, senator for Alaska, entered the *Life* article into the Congressional Record. He bemoaned another Russian space first, when this was one the Americans could have won "but for the narrow exclusiveness of our space agency." Sputnik was bad, he said. "But the sending of a woman into space—and as it happens, she was not even a flier—is, in my judgement, a far greater defeat for us, because its implications are far wider." But for most Americans, the launch of Tereshkova only served to reinforce the merits of their own society, with its clear-cut gender roles. The NASA position—that this was a job for men—was still the predominant one.

A few days after Tereshkova's mission, a couple of reporters from the Soviet daily *Izvestia* were allowed into the area where she and Bykovsky were being held in quarantine. They brought a book with them to show Valentina. She couldn't, of course, read the English title—but she puzzled over the picture of a woman's face in a space helmet on the cover.

The woman was Jerrie Cobb. Her close friend Jane Rieker had ghostwritten Jerrie's story, from her first flying lessons at twelve to her crusade in Washington. *Woman into Space* was published by Prentice Hall weeks before Tereshkova's flight, and it ended with the hope that the United States might yet be first with a woman in space.

Well, now the first woman in space held the American's book in her hands. Tereshkova had heard of Jerrie (at least, a Soviet journalist was willing to report that she had). "I sincerely sympathize with her," Tereshkova said. "I think of her as a courageous and daring woman. It is really too bad that the American leaders have disgraced her so. They shout on all the street corners about their democracy and at the same time announce they will not let a woman into space. This is obvious inequality." At this, according to *Izvestia*, "the commander of the ship *Vostok 6* became excited. Fires of indignation burned in her eyes."

She also offered a condescending sympathy to her American rival. "Yes, I have sincere pity for Jerrie Cobb. She is an excellent pilot and a brave woman. It is not easy to fly a jet plane; it requires a great willpower, good training and lightning reflexes. When I think about Jerrie Cobb's failure, I see not just a personal failure. We and Jerrie Cobb have different wings. That's the main thing."

K Cagle put her faith in her hero. At home in Macon, Georgia, K read the news about the congressional hearing, she read Jackie's statement and she prepared to bide her time. If this was as far as Jackie thought things could go now, well, she would just wait. "Jackie had presented her case, and it wasn't over," K says. "We just weren't going to be used now—that was the thing." K waited, but there were no more letters from Jackie. And no call from Jerrie, or Dr. Lovelace. A year or two went by, and she realized with a start one day that no one had mentioned women in space for quite some time. Maybe it was over, after all. K decided, at least, that she no longer needed to honor her promise to Dr. Lovelace to put off having children, and she and Walt had a daughter, Joy.

Many of the other women knew from the day of the hearing that their dreams of space travel were finished. "I did not believe that Jerrie was going to be powerful enough to change things," B Steadman says. One by one, the women went back to their lives. Some were left scrabbling: Gene Nora Stumbough, Sarah Gorelick and Irene Leverton had all quit jobs to go to Pensacola. And Jerri Sloan had a divorce on her hands. They scrambled, but they managed. They pasted the telegram from Dr. Lovelace into their scrapbooks, beside clippings about Valentina Tereshkova's flight, and the first Gemini missions—already yellowing. Some saw the space episode as a good tale to tell at 99s meetings—and some didn't speak of it at all. "That was past," Rhea Hurrle says simply.

But it wasn't over for Jerrie Cobb.

Her updates to the FLATs trickled off after the hearings but her one-woman campaign in Washington continued. She tried repeatedly to see President Kennedy, and sent him a wistful appeal shortly before Tereshkova's flight. "It is difficult to write this letter knowing it will be read by your secretaries and assistants and the chances are slim that it will get through to you. I feel compelled to do so anyway, in the faith that the matter will in some way be brought to your attention. . . . I have worked, studied and prayed for this over three years now and could not give up without one last, final plea to the commander-in-chief."

But the president's office, as she had expected, shunted her to Webb. In August, she sent the NASA administrator a letter with a newly desperate note of appeal:

> If I went back to college and got an engineering degree
> and managed some way to get some jet test pilot experience,
> could you tell me if I'd be acceptable as an astronaut
> candidate then? I would do this, or whatever is in my
> power, to qualify myself but it would take several years
> and Russia would beat us again. If you would just give me

a chance to work out on the simulators when they are not busy, then we would know if I needed to go back and get the degree and jet test time. I beg of you, just for the opportunity to prove myself.

It sometimes seems ironical to have to fight so long and hard for something that would accomplish so much for the United States and for which I would willingly give my life.

A month later, Webb addressed her appeal in just two lines: "I am sorry but I just am not able to give you the kind of commitment that your letter of August 7th requests."

Thus Jerrie decided to try a new route: if she couldn't go up with NASA, could she fly the X-15, the astonishing aircraft that air force pilots were now taking up as high as fifty miles? That would give the Americans a woman technically "in space" even if it wasn't a rocket ride. In some ways, in truth, it would be better—for no one disputed that the X-15 pilots had full control of their ships.

But Raymond L. Bisplinghoff, the man who ran the X-15 schedule, was directed to write her back and turn her down for, as he himself pointed out, the same reasons she could not be an astronaut. "The number of X-15 flights which we can undertake is limited, and the costs incidental to each flight are substantial. As a consequence, participation in the program has been restricted to engineering test pilots with extensive experience in jet aircraft, and even these must undergo months of training before piloting an X-15 flight. If we are to continue to extract the maximum benefit from public funds invested in this program, we believe that it is essential that the existing standards of training and experience be maintained."

No matter whom she asked or what she asked for, nobody in the American space program wanted anything to do with Jerrie Cobb.

After Tereshkova's flight, Jerrie's frustration began to deepen into bitterness. Much of the publicity in the United States featured her, and she made no effort to temper her scorn for NASA. "Exactly two years and one day after I recommended that NASA begin training women for space flight, Valentine [*sic*] was sent into space by the Russians," she snapped to reporters. "That's kind of ironic." And the space agency had only itself to blame, she said. "Mr. Webb appointed me two years ago and I haven't heard a thing from them since then."

When astronaut Gordon Cooper, asked about matching the latest Russian first, said that the number of American women qualified for spaceflight was "absolute zero," Jerrie responded, "That's the same old NASA line he's using."

Still, she told the *Houston Post* on July 1, she had hope. "If they think a woman ought to be a parachute jumper, I will become a parachute jumper. If they think it is necessary to be a jet test pilot, I would be happy to become one if I could. . . . I am disappointed and frustrated that they were able to have the first woman in space. It seemed to me that this was one area in space where we could have beaten the Russians if NASA hadn't been so prejudiced against women. . . . I don't have any more hope, I have the same hope, which is all the hope there is. It means more to me than anything else, and I am not going to give up."

But her letters grew more desperate. On February 10, 1964, she wrote to Lyndon Johnson, now the president, reminding him of their conversation two years earlier about the urgency of putting a woman in space.

> As you know, no action was ever taken on this important subject (not even after a special congressional subcommittee recommended it) and Russia did indeed put the first woman in space.
>
> I urge again your consideration to giving women an active part in our country's space program. The longer we

wait the further behind we will be in this important aspect of space travel. I'm sure you are aware of all the reasons why women should be given an equal opportunity in astronaut training.

During the past three years I have done everything within my power (including passing three phases of astronaut testing) for the inclusion of women astronauts in our country's space program. I have resigned my executive position in the aviation industry so that I might devote myself wholeheartedly to the service of my God and my country. If there is no possible way of utilizing my services in the astronaut program, would you please advise me if I might be of assistance in the U.S. AID or Peace Corps programs? I am quite serious about this and offer 20 years of varied aeronautical experiences as a pilot and administrator.

But the president likely never saw the letter. A memo from an aide in Johnson's office directed it to NASA to draft a reply, and while the letter Jerrie eventually received conveyed the president's folksy pleasure in hearing from her, the missive came on a multicarboned form from the space administration.

You are aware, I am certain, of the contribution women can make to the overall well-being and progress of the United States of America in almost every field of endeavor. Today, fewer restrictions based solely on sex are in effect than ever before. Fortunately for our country and for the world women are gaining their proper share of responsibility in many challenging jobs. The number of jobs open to women is increasing each year. It is my hope that all restrictions against hiring or promoting qualified women workers will be ended as soon as possible. You are aware, probably, of my personal efforts to expedite the implementation of this concept among the Federal civil service.

But his position of two years earlier, that it was up to NASA to pick its astronauts, remained unchanged, Johnson wrote—and the space agency's list of qualifications had not changed either. The same went for the X-15—its pilots had to be the best in the field, and the president wasn't going to tell the air force who should get that job.

At the same time, Jerrie also wrote to Sen. Clinton Anderson, then chair of the House Space Committee, asking that he try to get her a chance to fly the X-15. Her goal at this point seems to have been a trip into space by any possible means. Anderson apparently checked this request with NASA, because Hugh Dryden, the deputy administrator, wrote him back in March, giving the stock answer—only test pilots. Anderson informed Jerrie that that route wasn't going to work either.

She had indeed resigned her job at Aero, perhaps out of exhaustion. In late 1964 she moved to Florida and took almost a year trying to figure out what to do. Aviation consulting, she decided—and her first gig was delivering film and copy to *Life* headquarters in Chicago after a Gemini space launch. *Life* arranged for her to fly a jet for the job.

Jerrie was, at this point, resigned. "I have no doubt that women will go into space someday—probably as scientists—but I'll be too old by that time," she told *The Miami Herald* in April 1965. "I worked so hard to get through those tests and in my heart I very much want to participate in the space program. But my head tells me the chances are slim."

A few months earlier she had volunteered to test a STOL (short takeoff-and-landing) plane in Peru and while she was there, had become interested in the work of Wycliffe Bible translators, missionary linguists. Now she thought about a way to move down to South America—she had applied to a missionary organization in the late 1950s but been rejected because they only employed men; maybe this would be a way into the job. "I hope this consultant thing works out," she told the *Herald*. "Instead of always worrying about making a buck, I'd like to earn just enough to live and have time to devote to these people in the jungle. I have a great love for Latin America and the people there."

That year, Jerrie ran away.

"The fact that women are not in this field is a fact of our social order." With those words, John Glenn helped to seal the fate of the FLATs. The social order, however, was starting to change. In 1963, John F. Kennedy announced the findings of the presidential commission on the status of women, which reached the conclusion that women were in vastly unequal positions in the workforce. That same year, the Equal Pay Act became law— mandating that a woman must receive the same salary for doing the same job as a man. In 1964, the Civil Rights Act outlawed discrimination in employment based on race—and gender. In 1965, President Lyndon Johnson signed an executive order that prohibited discrimination in government contracting and established guidelines for affirmative action programs.

The laws reflected the transformation that swept the country in those years: the civil rights movement, women's liberation and growing protests against the Vietnam War demanded changes to the traditional systems and hierarchies. The pace of change was such that the same nation that looked at *Life* in 1963 and shook its head at the women who were would-be astronauts did not, five years later, find the idea nearly so strange.

NASA, through this period, made changes in its recruitment procedures. Mere months after arguing to Congress that it was vital that astronauts be military test pilots, the agency accepted two civilian test pilots. A year later, NASA dropped the test pilot restriction and said regular jet pilots would be fine. This removed the official barrier to the participation of women, who were still prohibited from flying in the military and could not attend jet test pilot schools. And in 1963, NASA opened up the recruitment not only to pilots but also to scientists, who were taught to fly after they signed on. Sixty new astronauts joined the space agency in that period. All were men.

But now, the idea of female astronauts was without a champion. Randy Lovelace had stayed in the background of the congressional hearing and kept out of the women's political fight—in fact, he essentially dissociated himself from the women from the moment NASA's displeasure became evident with the cancelation of testing in Pensacola. Lovelace had initiated the program, but he had an important position with NASA, one that provided his foundation with both income-generating contracts and prestige. At the time of the hearings, for example, his clinic was secretly doing the physical certifications for U2 pilots from all over the world (including the Greek, Turkish, Swedish, English and Canadian air forces) for the CIA. Lovelace did not intend to jeopardize any of that.

"He could read the handwriting on the wall," says his friend and then employee Donald Kilgore. "He was a good poker player and he knew when to fold." Lovelace's strategy of ducking the initial fight seems to have served him, for he was not penalized for his key role in the women astronaut affair. In fact, in 1964 he was promoted to the post of chief medical adviser to the space agency.

Dr. Lovelace's research on the women was used only for a short article by two foundation doctors in *The American Journal of Obstetrics and Gynecology* in February 1964. In it, Johnnie Betson and Robert Secrest seized on menstruation, saying it made women unfit to be astronauts—because they would have to do flight tests at several different points in their cycles and would have trouble functioning "in an environment of time tables and rigid schedules." The doctors revived an argument that had been used since the start of the century to keep women from flying while they were menstruating; they cited studies that had found women's coordination and peripheral vision changed over the course of their cycle.

The short academic article, emphasizing women's physical differences, was much in keeping with the thinking in NASA, still very much a male-dominated institution. Randy Lovelace, however, did not lend his name to it. He might well have continued to consider the idea of testing women, of perhaps incorporating women into the astronaut corps, waiting for tensions to ease before he introduced it again. But Lovelace, with his wife, Mary, was killed in a plane crash on December 12, 1965. Almost two thousand people attended their funeral in Albuquerque. Astronaut Scott Carpenter headed the dignitaries; Drs. Charles Mayo I and II were there and so was Sen. Clinton Anderson, head of the Senate Space Committee. Jackie Cochran, of course, was there, grief-stricken and trying to comfort the Lovelaces' suddenly orphaned daughters. Randy Lovelace died the day after the successful in-space rendezvous of *Gemini 6* and *7*. President Lyndon Johnson addressed the event, saying, "A day of great achievement in space was marred by news of the death of Dr. William Randolph Lovelace II. His life was too short, although his legacy to space medicine will endure and will be a resource of assurance to future astronauts whose names and deeds are yet unknown."

Even though Lovelace's death and Jerrie's departure for South America relieved NASA of the two previous champions of women in space, this sticky issue of female astronauts kept popping up in the media. In fact, in November 1967, a pair of female would-be astronauts once again made the cover of *Parade* magazine, this time with the headline "No space for them." The article interviewed a half-dozen women—including a mountain climber who had written eleven scientific papers on orbital flight and a woman with a Ph.D. in biology doing research on the poisoning effect of high concentrations of oxygen for astronauts—none of whom had made the grade in the latest round of applications. Successive waves of astronaut candidates were being taken into the agency to train for Apollo, candidates who were both scientists and pilots, but none were women.

Dogged by the female astronaut issue, NASA went on a public relations campaign to highlight some of the other roles women were filling with the agency. They made chief astronomer Nancy Roman, the first woman to hold an executive position at NASA, their showpiece. She gave dozens of speeches and wrote numerous magazine articles about the handful of female engineers and physicists at the space agency. The tone of NASA's campaign, however, remained one of marveling at a few extraordinary women. "Apollo Project Engineer Is a Pretty Grandmother," said a headline in the Philadelphia *Evening Bulletin* in 1964, describing Catherine Hock, a reliability engineer on the moon project.

Despite the public relations campaign and the new laws, NASA's thinking about who could be an astronaut was not changing. In 1972, the Equal Opportunity Act was extended specifically to include government agencies. That same year, NASA administrator Chuck Berry told a space medicine conference in Nice, France, "For long-duration space flights such as Mars, the crews would be confined inside their spacecrafts for nearly a year. With so much time on their hands, they'd react like . . . other normal human beings, they'd want sexual diversion. It is therefore unrealistic to plan future flights without coming to grips with the problem of women. Naturally the women would be fully operational crew members . . . not only there for sex."

But pressure on the agency mounted steadily. In 1972, the executive director of the National Association for the Advancement of Colored People publicly called it "shocking" that there were no black astronauts. Ruth Bates Harris, director of NASA's new Equal Opportunity Office, advised the director of spaceflight that she faced "constant" questions about the all-white, all-male composition of the astronaut corps. The Civil Rights Commission asked NASA to investigate the issue; the agency said that was the commission's job. By 1975, the political haggling resulted in another congressional hearing on diversity in the space program. This one produced no more conclusive or binding results than that of 1962—but the public heat was so intense that NASA's deputy director of public affairs, Ken Donnelly, sent his superiors a memo advising that "it may be time for us to go out and get ourselves a black astronaut from the Air Force or Navy (assuming these branches have qualified pilot candidates)."

In 1976, NASA finally acted in response to the pressure and took steps to make its astronaut corps reflect the country it served. The agency launched a campaign targeting historically black colleges and drew up lists of qualified women to be wooed. In 1978, from 8,037 applicants, of whom 1,142 were women, NASA chose its first six female astronauts. (There were also three non-white men in the group of thirty-five candidates selected.)

One of the women in that group was Shannon Lucid, who had a doctorate in chemistry and would go on to international fame in 1996 when she spent 188 days on the Russian space station *Mir*. Lucid vividly remembers the introduction of the Mercury 7 in 1959, when she was a college chemistry student. "I couldn't believe it when they selected the first seven. It was incredible, the feeling of anger, because there were no females included in the selection. Even though they were all military people, that didn't justify anything. There was absolutely no reason not to have any females."

Lucid and the other five women began astronaut training in 1978, but as NASA rotated through its astronauts (including those who had been in the agency before their recruitment) it was five years before NASA finally employed one of them on a space mission. Astrophysicist Sally Ride was launched on the space shuttle *Challenger* on June 18, 1983. There was massive public interest in her flight; NASA had never before faced anything like the volume of requests for media accreditation for her launch. Ride tried in vain to keep the discussion to her mission, not her gender. She insisted she was just one of the crew, and indeed she performed exactly as the other astronauts did on the mission. But when she landed, NASA had a protocol officer on hand to present Ride (and only Ride) with a bouquet of roses and carnations as she stepped out of the shuttle. An angry Ride refused to accept the flowers, and then was criticized for her surliness in the press.

NASA's subsequent rounds of new astronaut candidates always included at least one woman and one visible minority. Slowly the astronaut corps began to diversify, and there was rarely a shuttle mission without either a woman or a nonwhite man on the crew. In 1992, Mae Jemison (a medical doctor who is also a chemical engineer) became the first woman of color in space. But Jemison, and all the American women who went into space before her, were "mission specialists": scientists and researchers. They flew on the shuttle. But they didn't fly it.

Then in 1994, there was big news indeed: NASA announced that a United States Air Force flier decorated for service in Grenada and elsewhere would pilot a mission the next year. Her name was Eileen Collins, and she was the first woman to take the controls of an American spacecraft. The FLATs heard about her assignment on the evening news and thought, *finally*.

"LET'S STOP THIS NOW!"

*President John F. Kennedy and Vice President
Lyndon B. Johnson meet in the Oval Office.*

NASA did not state publicly that it required astronauts to be experimental jet test pilots until the women came pressing for admission in 1961. But the choice was difficult to dispute.

NASA got seven excellent pilots in its first astronauts, and the Mercury flights provided no end of tests for the men's lightning reactions and their icy calm in the face of crises. When John Glenn's automatic control system failed two orbits into his trip, he used the manual controls to realign the capsule. Then, as the world held its breath and ground control tried desperately to figure out the problem with the lost heat shield, which seemed to have dislodged, Glenn negotiated a series of last-minute changes to procedure. Totally unrattled, he made a rough reentry, which might at any moment have seen him incinerated and landed nearly on target. In his Mercury mission in May 1963, Gordon Cooper was dogged with problems—he lost use of the key instruments, lost oxygen in the cabin, lost his automatic control and stabilization. But Cooper lined himself up perfectly for reentry; even flying manually, he managed to splash down closer than any of the other astronauts to the target of the aircraft carrier sent to pick them up. Both flights were stunning testimony to the peerless skills and the nerves of steel the two men had acquired in their years as experimental test pilots.

Their years of test piloting gave them an inside advantage, as well: men such as Bob Gilruth in the brand-new NASA office in Langley in 1958 wanted test fliers because they already spoke the language of engineering. Test pilots knew the specifications and the technical terms. They knew the designers and engineers, they were all used to working together and they integrated quickly into the Mercury project.

And, of course, these men were military pilots. There is an argument that military aviators have a set of skills that even civilian jet test pilots cannot match. "Combat flying requires an intensity and skill far beyond anything in peacetime aviation," astronaut Buzz Aldrin wrote in his memoir. "Years later those of us who'd served in Korea were prepared for the hazards and uncertainty of space flight because we had already come to terms with fear." Military test pilots had also provided the largest body of data then extant on how the human body functioned in the outer reaches of the atmosphere. They had shown they could work in secret and under discipline. History had accidentally prepared this small group of fliers—they had been winnowed to an elite band by the military selection process and had already made clear that they accepted the attendant risks in the service of their country. It is not hard to understand why President Dwight Eisenhower saw them as a quick solution, as the easiest pool from which to draw America's astronauts.

None of the Mercury women had anything like that kind of flying experience. The only woman in the United States who did was Jackie Cochran, and she had never flown in combat.

Wally Schirra, pilot of the fifth Mercury mission, is still irritated today by the assertion that a group of female civilian pilots could have done as well. "I had over four carrier deployments [in] combat in Korea. [I was a] graduate of the U.S. Navy Test Pilot School, [I had] over three thousand hours in jet fighters," he says. "And some of those women have the gall to say they were not given a chance to be part of the Mercury program!"

No, the women did not have military jet time. They countered that what they did have was thousands and thousands of hours in the air—in some cases, four times as many hours as the men. And in those thousands of hours, they had developed an intuitive understanding of the functioning of an aircraft, a sixth sense for problems and the unflappable calm a pilot needs to bring an ailing craft of any size safely back to ground. It was the same essential skill set in a single-engine prop plane or an F-86, the women said, and they could have learned to apply those skills to the more complicated aircraft.

This is the key point: the Mercury astronauts were taught. This was all new, this business of flying a spaceship, and whoever did it had to be taught. The Mercury men trained almost seven days a week for two straight years before their first flight. They were taught, among other things, propulsion, astrophysics, trajectory calculations, astronomy and desert survival. And they spent hundreds of hours in simulators designed to mimic spaceflight. Even so, the systems in the Mercury capsule were fully automated. There was some basis to the jibes of test pilots such as Chuck Yeager that the astronauts were "Spam in a can." Robert Voas, the astronaut training officer, constructed his curriculum around the idea that the astronaut would in fact be involved only if the regular system failed. Voas's primary goal in training was to desensitize the astronauts to stress induced by the immense G-forces or weightlessness.

Could female civilian pilots have learned to fly the capsule? Would they have needed more training than jet test pilots? Would their simulator tests have stacked up as well as the men's? There is no way of knowing, for despite Jerrie Cobb's years of requests, no female pilot ever got to make even one simulator run.

When the House hearings were over, after Jackie Cochran had delivered her damning testimony and all the snide headlines about "Astro-nettes" were written, it was easy to forget that there was ever any serious reason to include women in the United States astronaut program.

Randy Lovelace and Donald Flickinger began the project for sound scientific reasons in 1959. And yet the letters collected in the NASA archives, in Jackie Cochran's vast trove of papers, in Lyndon B. Johnson's files all make it clear: the Fellow Lady Astronaut Trainees were never going into space—not on an American rocket. Early on, the men who ran the space agency made their decision. They wanted no women involved. And they let the whole drama play out over several years in the public theater without ever reevaluating that decision.

So what grounded them, these thirteen dedicated women in prime physical shape, with thousands of hours flying all kinds of aircraft in all types of conditions? What really kept them out of the space program? Why couldn't they change NASA's mind? Sexism, certainly—but also the lethal combination of the personalities involved.

Jerrie Cobb was not a natural leader of women. She was shy, never comfortable in public and very much a loner. She saw herself as leader of the group, but she did the tests ahead of and apart from them, and after the congressional hearing she narrowed the focus of her campaign to her own spaceflight. In truth, she believed that she was best qualified. And while there can be no doubt that her desire to see the United States have this space first was rooted in entirely genuine patriotism, she also wanted desperately to be that woman herself. To make that flight, to see the curve of the earth and the black daytime sky, just as she had dreamed since her first flight as a child. While she tolerated reporters and their inane questions, Jerrie had by her early thirties developed an addiction to her public profile, to achievements and to recognition. She wanted this one for herself. Had she been willing to keep the terms framed around a research project on a large group of women, had she even been able to bring herself to work with Jackie Cochran (accepting, initially, more circumscribed terms for the project than she herself thought best), the rest of the women might have got much further.

Jerrie's naiveté and her intensely personal response to the denial also helped to ensure that the idea of female astronauts was increasingly marginalized by the political figures who might, when the initial uproar died away, have been willing to entertain the possibility. Jerrie's correspondence with James Webb, Hugh Dryden and Lyndon Johnson through her years of lobbying is almost painful to read. She was deaf to, or chose to ignore, the all-but-overt dismissals from the men. Her letters grew more and more obsessive and desperate—until there was an almost audible "not again" tone in Webb's replies as he was obliged, once more, to tell Jerrie she still could not be an astronaut. Aides in Kennedy's and Johnson's offices immediately shunted her letters to the space agency for handling; Webb eventually started passing them to flunkies in the public relations office. The miracle, in fact, is that after the first year anyone was answering her at all. She was relentlessly persistent, and her pleas were impassioned, colored with an emotion and a religious fervor quite out of step with NASA's formal scientific tone. "I hope you don't mind if I keep trying, 'cause this means more to me than life itself," she wrote to Webb in October 1962, a letter with a sort of sweet innocence to it that was entirely alien from the rest of the brisk, professional correspondence that crossed his desk.

Even had NASA been willing to concede that Jerrie had a point about including women in the astronaut program for scientific purposes, it is doubtful the agency would have handed the controls of a Mercury capsule to someone with her monomaniacal ardor. Her relentless faith-fueled campaign reinforced the men's preconceived ideas about women's reactions and their place in a serious scientific endeavor. While the Mercury men's practical jokes and prodigious drinking were seen as confirmation that they had the character for this kind of job, Jerrie's emotions played right into the then-popular idea of female "hysteria" and lack of control.

Jerrie was further discredited by her miscalculations of the politics involved. Her constant emphasis on the idea that the United States needed the "first" launching a woman—which seemed to her more politically palatable than anything based on charges of "discrimination" or even the need for scientific assessment of female response to space travel—simply served to underscore her distance from NASA. The space agency, of course, was emphatically denying that it was in a race. NASA's historian, Roger Launius, explains that while the intention of the Soviet space program was constantly to one-up the Americans (as, for example, in 1965, when the Russians sent cosmonaut Aleksei Leonov on the first space walk just weeks before a long-planned, publicly announced space walk by American Ed White), the United States eschewed any such game. "They said this from the top right down to the bottom, over and over and over and over again," Launius says. "Everybody in a management position said this: we are not trying to match one for one what the Soviets are doing. We have a program, it's well established, it looks out several years, it's got missions associated with it, it's got different spacecraft, and we're going to systematically pursue that program. And whatever the Soviets do, they do." Jerrie no doubt thought she was arguing on NASA's terms, with her earnest talk of propaganda value, but in fact she was only emphasizing her own remove from the agency's thinking.

Jerrie's personality was one part of the equation that kept the women grounded. Another was the character of the man who first got her involved. In his letters to Jackie Cochran, Randy Lovelace placed more emphasis on the research nature of his undertaking, and to James Webb at NASA, he deliberately downplayed its seriousness. But to the thirteen women directly involved, he talked about "women astronauts." Almost certainly, Lovelace was not intentionally misleading; he likely did not realize the impact of his words on the women to whom he wrote. The idea of testing and training women had sound scientific underpinnings and seemed reasonable to him, certainly worth pursuing, so he did. Working from his fiefdom in Albuquerque, Lovelace had little patience for the bureaucracy and departmental rivalries that consumed Washington. At a time when NASA was plagued by politicos (and some flight surgeons) who questioned the wisdom of launching even one person, Lovelace was talking to his staff about a near future when large crews of men and women would live for extended periods of time in space and carry out all manner of scientific experiments. He was thinking big.

In a tribute to Randy Lovelace six months after his death, Brig. Gen. Ernest Pinson said the space doctor "had a rare talent for visualizing the significant actions required to be done now— for future needs." University of New Mexico historian Jake Spidle, who has written a history of Lovelace and his foundation, says Randy had "a sure grasp of the structure and workings of the nation's military establishment" and "was able to move swiftly and easily through (and sometimes around) the government bureaucracy, relying on his knowledge of the system as well as the assistance of his personal acquaintances." It might have been those qualities that prompted Lovelace to gather a group of the country's top female pilots for testing in 1960. He was also a man with a keen appreciation for his own sense of vision, and so he began almost immediately to talk to those women about his "women-in-space program," detailing future plans without any confirmation he could in fact deliver on them. But Lovelace was no social revolutionary: when the issue heated up, he ducked out of the fight, intent on preserving his personal interests. And he was killed before he ever had a chance to show if he would resume his plans for women in space.

And of course it was Lovelace who brought the incendiary element of Jackie Cochran into the mix. As intensely patriotic as Jerrie Cobb, Jackie wanted to see the United States victorious in the space race. She genuinely believed it was right that men should go first, and women follow, and that to insert women, simply because they were women, into the space program might damage the national interest. Jackie might also have been concerned, as she was with the WASP, that a rush program to put women into space would not really open doors, but rather only be, in her words, a "flash in the pan." Jackie was both politically astute and intensely conservative. She saw only negative repercussions from a public fight over an obviously doomed issue, and she saw no point in pushing a program that had opposition at the highest levels.

But Jackie also had more personal motives for the way she handled the women-in-space issue. She wanted her status as the country's top female aviator to go unchallenged. When Sarah Gorelick heard Jackie yelling at Dr. Lovelace at the clinic, she certainly sensed the depth of Jackie's frustration at not being part of the program herself, and her intention to keep control of it.

Jerrie Cobb says today that she felt it, too, in her rare face-to-face meetings with Jackie. "I knew her help could be beneficial to the program. But she considered me a stumbling block since she really wanted to be the first woman in space and be in charge of the whole program. . . . Her whole attitude was, I'm going to be in charge, and if I don't get to go, no woman will, for a long, long time." Jackie's scheming on behalf of the Dietrich twins, and her campaign against Jerrie, suggest a relentless determination to manage the program if she could not herself be the first female astronaut. Jackie had been a generous and devoted friend to Randy Lovelace, and had done much to engineer the advancement of his career. But as he discovered on the subject of women in space, there were some things on which Jackie brooked no opposition. For all that she was warm and protective of Lovelace, she was also jealous and spiteful.

And powerful. She pushed all the right buttons, setting herself up in contrast to Jerrie when she was troublesome and making sure all the men in power knew Jackie was on their side. In her lobby against allowing women into the astronaut program, she carefully chose palatable language, then exploited her personal connections to make her views known. She had her positions vetted by NASA and the air force before she made them public, and she went over Lovelace's head to take control of the issue, putting herself forward as an alternative to Jerrie Cobb as NASA's public face on the issue. Her letters to the space insiders from that era are masterful, making casual reference to her connections and her positions of influence, combining powerful arguments with invitations to vacation at her ranch.

Jackie cherished her membership in the boys' club. Women had less power, and so she eschewed their company. She didn't race women, she didn't fly with them and she didn't like spending time with them. She wrote candidly in her autobiography that she "preferred the company of men. Men liked me. I liked being with them." Glennis Yeager, the wife of pilot Chuck Yeager, and one of Jackie's few female friends, said "[Jackie] couldn't stand women . . . [she] would get annoyed if any women's groups invited her to give a talk. 'What do I have in common with a bunch of damned housewives?' she would complain."

Certainly Jackie saw herself as unique in the field of female pilots. "The chances were that if a woman had been selected for [training as a professional pilot], before she had returned any profit on the heavy investment in such training, she would have converted herself into a wife and mother and stopped working." She chose, she said, to be one of the rare women who dedicated herself entirely to flying—a statement that disregards the vast personal fortune that allowed Jackie to maintain her role as Floyd Odlum's wife and her business obligations and still keep flying.

Jackie's performance in the hearing on qualifications for astronauts was not unique. She worked against her fellow women in aviation in 1950 in a report on women in the air force, saying that she didn't think they belonged there at all, but if they did, then they had to be "attractive" women (in the same way that she screened her WASPs, lest anyone get "the wrong idea" about them). And in 1975, Jackie went to Congress once more, to lobby against the opening of the military academies to female students. This, too, was a position supported by her male friends in the military brass—although it put her in direct opposition to Jeanne Holm, director of the Women in the Air Force. Jackie told the hearing that the proper role for women in American society was "mother and housewife" and, invoking her experience with the WASP, said that women had no role in the military in peacetime. (On this issue, Congress didn't listen to her.) Jackie later spoke out repeatedly and forcefully against women serving in combat roles in the armed forces—while she stated at different times that women could fly as well as men, she constantly emphasized gender differences. "If for no other reason than because women are the bearers of children, they should not be in combat," she said in 1978. "Imagine your daughter as a ground soldier, sleeping in the fields and expected to do all the things that soldiers have to do. It presents to me an absolute horror."

Jackie's own identity was built on her rare admission to the power brokers' inner circle. Presidents consulted her, generals were afraid of her and everybody saw the advantage of having her on their side in a fight. That power, calculated on the most traditional of scales, gave her a great sense of gratification. She clearly relished the attention that came with her public persona: her entries in *Who's Who* and *Current Biography* grew year by year to cover several columns, listing every award and every record. In her collected papers, housed today in the Eisenhower Presidential Library in Abilene, Kansas, she has saved what appears to be every single article that ever mentioned her name, including copies of the same wire service story from hundreds of different newspapers. Wielding the influence she did came with a price, and it was one Jackie was willing to pay. In the hearing on qualifications for astronauts, she belittled her WASPs as prone to running off and getting married just as soon as she was finished training them—she sold out the project that had been one of her great accomplishments, in defense of NASA. To continue to be in the club, to fly the big air force planes and to be able to get the president on the line when she wanted him, she had to toe their line. It is doubtful that Jackie herself recognized, or allowed herself to recognize, any distinction between her own position and that mandated by the Washington power brokers. She certainly never saw herself as a pawn.

The idea that the FLATs were stabbed in the back by one of their own plays conveniently into the popular notion of a "cat fight," of the stereotype of conflict between powerful women. But in many ways Jackie was as much a pawn as any of the thirteen: she had to play by the rules if she wanted to stay in the boys' club. Could she have done more? If she had been able to see past her own emotional response, and her need to defend her insider status, she might well have made some difference to the twenty years it took to get an American woman into space. Jackie had, as she made very clear, peerless political connections. She had repeatedly demonstrated in the past (as one of the first women in the Bendix, with the WASPs, with her flight through the sound barrier) that she could make extraordinary things happen when she wanted to.

If Jerrie Cobb had been more politically astute, if Jackie Cochran had been less conservative and more generous, if Randy Lovelace had lived—the drama of the women-in-space program might have played out differently. But it is nonetheless unlikely that the women would have realized their dream of spaceflight. In the larger picture, the women were grounded for one simple reason: they stepped outside the boundaries of the accepted roles for women in their time.

In the Cold War era, foreign policy was based on a masculine warrior ideology. President Kennedy spoke to his advisers about the "virility" of American engagement and the "emasculation" of the Soviets. He advocated aggressive action—as, for example, in his showdown with the Russians in the Cuban missile crisis. The political elite that drafted the policy, and the military and intelligence services that carried it out, were led by and almost entirely staffed by men. Women's patriotic duty, in this context, was to stay home and run comfortable homes, visibly demonstrating the merits of the capitalist system that brought them washing machines and dishwashers.

The aerospace industry, the pinnacle of scientific achievement in both civilian and military life in the early 1960s, was maintained as a male preserve—and, implicitly, as a field of the highest status. NASA wanted not just test pilots, but experimental jet test pilots from the military, the elite of fliers, to reinforce the new space agency's own cutting-edge image. Astronauts, too, were from the moment of their invention essentially and incontrovertibly male. They were the new warriors in the Cold War fight. In their book *Moon Shot*, two of the Mercury 7, Deke Slayton and Alan Shepard, conclude a lengthy discussion of the necessary qualities for astronauts with the single line, "And, of course, no women, thank you." The job and its requirements were hypermasculine—astronauts were portrayed as having almost mythic amounts of courage and extraordinary skill, an elusive package immortalized by Tom Wolfe in his 1979 best-seller as "the right stuff."

Where Jerrie Cobb and the FLATs saw an opportunity for their country to show off the strength of its women, Kennedy and the NASA chiefs flatly rejected the idea of sending a woman to do a job that had been institutionalized very much as a man's. They saw any such move as completely counterproductive in terms of the image they were trying to foster. CIA records show NASA had solid information about the Soviet intention to launch a female cosmonaut months before Valentina Tereshkova's flight, but this did not alter American plans at all. Her flight was the first Soviet space "first" that the Americans did not push to match—unlike Sputnik or the Yuri Gagarin launch or the multiday missions, they let this one go. This wasn't an achievement. "NASA thought the Russians were wusses," historian Debbie Douglas says succinctly.

And it wasn't just NASA that opposed flying women: many American citizens did too. James Webb got plenty of letters advising him to, in the words of one Miss Irma Reynolds of Alabama, "keep the women out of the space flight—damn crazy thing." Many people thought the women who were petitioning to be allowed into the space program were unnatural and making highly inappropriate demands. When her involvement in the women-in-space program was made public, Jean Hixson, for one, suddenly found herself at odds with one of her closest friends, Betty Gillies, a founder of the 99s with whom Jean had flown as a WASP. In September 1962, Betty wrote Jean a long, heartfelt letter discouraging her from publicly pushing for the program, saying the whole idea was in fact dangerous to American national interest. "John Glenn, by his spectacular orbital flight and by his outstanding personality, has given the young men of our country a new world to enter and opened up a new field in which this generation can strive to become heroes," Betty wrote. "To reach the top of accomplishment—to be able to wear with great pride the NASA wings—to be a part of a great expedition into the unknown—to be respected and admired for one's courage and ability—this is what our young men *need.* Somehow I feel that a great deal of the inspiration, the inspiration to be brave and strong, would be killed by the mere existence of women space pilots!!!! . . . Now we have a whole new generation of young men to work with and I can't help but feel that the field of space should be theirs and theirs alone for a while—it should not be 'belittled' by the intrusion of women."

Betty's stab at psychoanalysis may not have been far off: the men who ran NASA didn't like the idea of including women, and their public comments suggest that the Mercury 7 didn't care much for it either. The astronauts were men with big egos made even more arrogant by the wave of adulation that greeted their achievements. Even the suggestion rankled, that women, a group of female civilian pilots, might be able to equal their achievements.

The FLATs were trying to break into the tightest of the boys' clubs. The Mercury 7 had pinups taped in the ready room and centerfold girls in their flight plans. They raced Corvettes, drank fiendishly and were wildly promiscuous. When Alan Shepard finally made it to the moon, he smuggled a golf club and some balls aboard the *Apollo 14* and did a few unplanned putts in zero gravity—provoking much hilarity and head shaking back in Houston. Wernher von Braun, then at the Marshall Space Flight Center, cracked up an audience at Mississippi State College in 1962 with this line: "Another question that I am frequently asked is this: 'Do you ever plan to use women astronauts in your space program?' Well, all I can say is that the male astronauts are all for it. And as my friend Bob Gilruth says, 'We're reserving 110 pounds of payload for recreational equipment.'"

Chief astronomer Nancy Roman, the only woman in an executive job at NASA in 1961, says that the people on her side of the shop were "open-minded and cooperative." But in astronaut territory, almost everyone had come over from the military: "It was a boys' club, it was a testosterone-fueled culture." While she says the decision that military test pilots were best qualified was probably quite a sound one, Roman also says it would not likely have occurred to anyone in the Manned Space Flight department to consider flying women.

Once the successful launches of the men removed the need to fly a lighter woman, the idea was never raised again. Once a few men had survived the trip, the department of Manned Space Flight did not say, Now we should fly some women and see how they hold up, or, Now we need comparative data on female bodies. Debbie Douglas notes that while Gilruth and his colleagues made a logical decision that they wanted test pilots, there is inherent sexism in the fact that they never noticed they were stipulating qualifications that automatically excluded women. "It never occurred to them that women would *want* to be astronauts."

Except, perhaps, for humor value. NASA's astronaut training officer Robert Voas gave a speech to a YMCA gathering in February 1963 in which he derided the rumored Russian intention to fly a woman, then made a string of jokes about female astronauts. "If you made a woman leave her purse behind, you would achieve some weight-saving over using a man," he cracked, then noted that telling a female astronaut she looked fat would probably also help to cut back the payload. Voas championed the role of secretaries in keeping NASA functioning, and concluded, "I think we all look forward to the time when women will be a part of our space flight team, for when this times arrives, it will mean that man will really have found a home in space—for the woman is the personification of the home." As historian Margaret Weitekamp explains it, NASA saw women's place in space coming only when it had been "domesticated—rendered safe and routine," not while it was still a Cold War frontier.

Neither side in the Cold War battle was really prepared to see women succeed in this environment. When Valentina Tereshkova made her historic spaceflight, she was widely reported (in 1963 and for years afterward) to have been incompetent, to have been crippled by space sickness or to have "gone to pieces" in the air, to have been unable to complete her mission. But in reexamining of the Soviet space program in recent years, historians now concede the reports of her mission were "hypercritical." She was nauseated for a time, had some trouble with an initial attempt to steer the capsule and disobeyed a few minor orders. But she experienced no truly significant problems. Space historian Asif Siddiqi writes that "part of this hostility toward Tereshkova was clearly because she was a woman. The standards by which all the engineers, physicians and military officers judged her performance were completely different than for the men. [Second man in space Gherman] Titov, who had suffered severe motion sickness and was unable to do many of the tasks assigned to him during his mission, was never considered a pariah after his flight."

Roger Launius, NASA's historian, does not dispute that there was gender bias within the agency in the early years. But he can also see the perspective that Robert Gilruth and other decision-makers likely brought to the discussion about women in space. "To be kind, they're doing something that's never been done. This is really unprecedented. And they've got a whole lot of stuff on their plate. And they are saturated. They are growing very quickly. They are being asked to do tasks that are unprecedented both from a technical perspective and every other way you can think of." They did not know if they could get a man into space and then whether that man could survive there, and the clock was ticking. And after May 25, 1961, when John Kennedy pledged the country to a moon mission, NASA became streamlined and entirely focused on that goal. "And their response would be, okay, let's deal with what we've got on our plate and we'll worry about anything else down the road." Launius cautions against evaluating the decision-making entirely on modern standards. "It was a different time and a different place and these people were doing a specific job and this [using women] probably didn't necessarily enter into their thinking at the time. . . . They probably didn't consider themselves social revolutionaries. That might be enough of a reason." But as Launius himself points out, the only people who could answer those questions with certainty have died, and it is not the sort of discussion or idea that is preserved in the official record.

Additionally, of course, there was this whole question of losing a woman. The country might have been behind NASA in the space race, but the administrators never lost the sense that the public support and the federal funding were precarious. Losing an astronaut would be bad—but losing a female astronaut would be a complete disaster. Jerrie Cobb argued it would be no different than losing John Glenn or any of the men (just as Amelia Earhart had to argue, in the first Powder Puff Derby in 1929, that the death of a female pilot was no different from the death of a male one). But Jerrie had even less success with that argument than Amelia did: many people felt that a dead female astronaut would be very different indeed in the eyes of the American public. Military test pilots went to work every day with, to some degree, an expectation that they might not come home. There were periods in the early 1950s when almost a pilot a week was killed at Edwards Air Force Base. These were men expected to take risks, men who were in fact paid to risk their lives each day.

Scott Carpenter said in the 1960s, when asked about female astronauts, "we're protecting the space program" by not risking women. Mercury 7 Flight Director Christopher Kraft elaborated forty years later. "What we wanted were people who were used to putting their lives on the line daily and making in-flight decisions that would not be tainted by fear. Had we lost a woman back then because we decided to fly a woman rather than a man, we would have been castrated." Launius, drawing on the reaction to the 1967 fire in *Apollo 1* that killed three astronauts and even on the reaction to the space shuttle *Challenger* deaths in 1987 (which heavily emphasized the loss of teacher Christa McAuliffe), says it is genuinely questionable whether the space agency would have survived the loss of a female astronaut in the climate of the early 1960s.

And there may be another clue in the fate of John Glenn. After his first successful orbital flight, Glenn repeatedly pushed to fly another mission. "But a flight assignment didn't come," Glenn wrote in his own autobiography. "I began to get frustrated sitting at a desk, so I asked Bob Gilruth when I might expect to get another flight. Bob said headquarters didn't want me to go up again, at least not yet. Later, author Richard Reeves wrote that President Kennedy had decreed that I was too much of a national asset to risk on a second flight, but I had no inkling of that at the time, and have never known whether it was true." Launius says there is no paper trail to support this, but that it is something Glenn might well have been told. The same president who would not risk losing a hero might have been equally reluctant to risk a dimpled pilot with a long, blond ponytail. Certainly the Soviets grounded Yuri Gagarin after his historic first mission, and made no secret of the fact that they were not going to risk losing an international symbol. His experience, and Glenn's, suggest that the political decision-makers considered the composition of astronaut crews with the same gravity as did the technical planners in the Office of Manned Space Flight.

In the end, the decision that the FLATs would never get a chance to fly was made by James Webb, NASA's administrator, and his deputy, Hugh Dryden. It was Dryden who penned the letter to the navy in October 1961 that canceled the testing at Pensacola: "the purpose of these tests was to indicate generally the potential of women as future astronauts. In confirmation of discussions that have already taken place between our staffs, NASA does not at this time have a requirement for such a program." It is a telling phrase, that "in conversations between our staffs": although there is almost no paper record of NASA's role, the men in the most senior posts at the space agency had clearly talked about this issue.

NASA took the line that the agency knew nothing about the women-in-space program until suddenly its administrators were called to account for it in front of Congress in 1962. Chris Kraft articulated this stock position forty years later in his autobiography *Flight*. "Lovelace . . . allowed some female volunteers to go through his tests without our concurrence. One of them was the wife of a U.S. Senator, and before long we were being dragged through the 'Why no woman astronauts?' controversy. Nobody seemed to understand that President Eisenhower had ordered us to pick astronauts from active-duty military test pilots, and none of them were women. We had our orders, and the subject of including women never came up until it was raised by outsiders."

In truth, NASA knew much earlier. Lovelace had made the results of his tests on Jerrie Cobb public in August 1960. That made headlines—and in fact a month later NASA was moved to issue an official denial that it was actively training women. In addition, Lovelace almost certainly discussed his plans with his colleagues on the Life Sciences Committee. In April 1960, Jerrie Cobb was tested on the MASTIF at a NASA facility. In May 1961, Jerrie herself wrote to Webb to update him on the progress of the tests. A month later, NASA's own public relations department had received enough questions about women and their acceptance into the space program that the staff wanted to know the official position. G. Dale Smith, assistant director for program planning in the Office of Life Sciences, appealed to George Low, the director of Spacecraft and Flight Missions, explaining his problem: "women fall within the physically qualified; therefore, there must be other valid reasons why or why not we are to use women in our space flight program." Low directed him to explain that women were not de facto excluded but that no women who were test pilots had applied. Finally, Lovelace provided Webb with an exhaustive description of his program and its purposes in a letter in September 1961. By then, of course, the space agency had already acted to stop the program, but it is clear that NASA knew all about it long before the subject ever got to Congress in 1962.

Neither Webb nor Dryden is still alive and they left no record of their thoughts on this subject, other than their letters in reply to Jerrie Cobb's petitions. And so one must take the explanation in those letters at face value—that NASA had all the astronauts it needed and saw no reason to bring women, whose qualifications were considered inferior, into a program already under great pressure. But the thinking of the space agency czars was right in line with that of their own bosses: neither Kennedy nor Johnson wanted to see this happen. Jerrie Cobb might have come away from her meeting with the then vice president optimistic about his support. But in truth, Johnson was deeply offended by this campaign by a couple of pushy women who thought they should get into the space program.

While he would later move forward a number of pieces of legislation aimed at combating discrimination against women, the idea of female pilots in the space program did not sit well with LBJ's vision of what women ought to be doing. He was raised in the rural South, and he once wrote an editorial that said the highest form of emotion was the love a man should give his mother. He was an inveterate philanderer, who regularly seduced his young aides and secretaries. He liked women who were pretty and stylish—but his world of politics and power was entirely male. Jerri Sloan saw LBJ at a Democratic party function her mother dragged her to shortly after the congressional hearing. "I braved the chauvinist pig in his den, I walked up to him and I said, 'Sir, I'm Prissy Springer's daughter.'" Here she does rather a good imitation of the former president. "'Well, how-dee do, you're as purty a little thing as your mother.' I said, 'You know, sir, that I was one of the women that passed the astronaut tests. You were head of the space bureau as vice president—I'm surprised that you didn't back the program to include us. I was very disappointed, sir, in you.' And so he said, 'Well, well,' in his way, 'cause he was a typical man of his generation, patted me on the back and looked down at me smiled and said, 'Well, honey, I know yo' daddy didn't want you doing anything that dangerous—why, little lady, you could *swoon*!' and I said, 'Sir, with all due respect, and I think your daughters will bear me out, women haven't swooned since they took off those damn corsets!' And he just chuckled and walked off."

Jerri didn't know it, but Johnson had indeed once held in his hands an opportunity to give them crucial support—he might well have totally changed the course of the women-in-space program. On March 14, 1962, two days before Jerrie Cobb and Janey Hart were scheduled to meet with him, Johnson's assistant Liz Carpenter prepared some background notes for him, explaining the women's position: "They claim: 1) women have as much sense as Enos the monkey; 2) outer space is not for men only; 3) Russia is planning to put a woman in outer space and the U.S. should get there first."

A dozen women had passed the grueling astronaut tests, Carpenter wrote. "But they cannot get additional training from Lovelace, the Navy or the Air Force, until NASA says it is okay to proceed with them. Jerrie Cobb saw Jim Webb and Mrs. Hart describes him as 'sympathetic but not willing to say yes or no at this time.' She thinks a word from you would help."

Carpenter had done her homework; she got a former Johnson aide who had gone over to work for the space agency to sound out Hugh Dryden on the subject. The aide reported that Dryden said orbital flight was still too dangerous for any but military test pilots who had the engineering background to allow them to take over the controls if they had to. Dryden sent word they would consider a woman who had those qualifications—and left the door open. "As orbital flight becomes more routine we can relax these rules."

Carpenter had assessed this situation, given the growing tide of support for the women's movement, and she thought it was clear what Johnson ought to do. "I think you could get a good press out of this if you can tell Mrs. Hart and Miss Cobb something affirmative. The story about women astronauts is getting a big play and I hate for them to come here and not go away with some encouragement."

She had drafted a letter from Johnson to James Webb, and she recommended the vice president show it to Jerrie and Janey and then sign it and send it off. "Dear Jim," the letter began:

> I have conferred with Mrs. Philip Hart and Miss Jerrie Cobb concerning their effort to get women utilized as astronauts. I'm sure you agree that sex should not be a reason for disqualifying a candidate for orbital flight.
>
> Could you advise me whether NASA has disqualified anyone because of being a woman?
>
> As I understand it, two principal requirements for orbital flight at this stage are: 1) that the individual be experienced at high speed military test flying; and 2) that the individual have an engineering background enabling him to take over controls in the event it became necessary.
>
> Would you advise me whether there are any women who meet these qualifications?

If not, could you estimate for me the time when orbital flight will have become sufficiently safe that these two requirements are no longer necessary and larger numbers of individuals may qualify?

I know we both are grateful for the desire to serve on the part of these women, and look forward to the time when they can.

Sincerely,
Lyndon B. Johnson

But Johnson did not show the letter to Jerrie and Janey. Nor did he sign it. In fact, Carpenter's mild missive seems to have infuriated him. In heavy one-inch handwriting, he wrote *"Let's stop this now!"* across the bottom of the letter, and then beneath that, the preemptory instruction, *"File."* The letter was diligently filed, and thus the one record that inadvertently shows the strength of opposition at the highest levels to the idea of women in space was preserved in Johnson's archives.

This was a time of great political change, and Johnson saw himself as a champion of equality for women. But what these women wanted fell far outside the bounds of what was acceptable. Space was the domain of astronauts, and astronauts were men.

There is an irony in this—for Lyndon Johnson was one of the first champions of the idea of affirmative action. If there is one lingering lesson from the FLATs' story, it is that a talented individual, even an extraordinarily skilled individual, can get only so far if the system is stacked against her. These women achieved things few other women in their society did, often in the face of considerable obstacles. But at a certain point, they could go no further: they could not overcome the systemic discrimination. They could not, for example, qualify as jet test pilots when women were barred from the air force. Without recourse to legal action, they could not change those rules. Without the lawsuits and the legislated changes that opened most of these fields to women (some, such as active ground combat, are still off limits today), it might have taken much longer than twenty years for the doors to space to be opened to women.

Astronaut Eileen Collins says kindly that she believes the women's fight in the 1960s made the road a little smoother for her generation of astronaut candidates. "The Mercury women—they wouldn't call it a success, but I would say there was some success in there," she says. "Their success had a direct bearing on our generation of astronauts. They didn't succeed in the end in getting selected as astronauts, but they showed that they could compete as well as the men." But in the end it was not the women's superior performance on the tests, or their fight in Congress, that opened those doors. It was the efforts of the larger women's movement that eventually succeeded in making it illegal to keep women out of a job purely on the basis of their gender.

Janey Hart, an early feminist, saw this clearly in the sixties. But few of the other women did. Jackie Cochran preferred to manipulate the existing system, and keep herself defined as the one woman to whom the rules did not apply. Jerrie Cobb believed she could achieve her goal of spaceflight based purely on her own extraordinary qualifications and her force of will. Neither she nor the other Lovelace women seemed to realize, then, that they would not get the opportunities they wanted so badly until society, the whole system, changed—not just one office at NASA.

As one might expect of twelve different people, the FLATs hold a variety of views about what kept them grounded. Some blame the individual actors, and some blame the era. Most of all, they feel that in this, as in so many things in their lives, they were ahead of their time. They were pushing to get into a club that was not ready to open its doors to women.

Irene Leverton believes it was sexism, pure and simple. "That's why they kept us out of Pensacola: if we could have gone there and got a few hours of jet time and shown that we could do that just as well, that would have shown them up." K Cagle blames Jerrie Cobb for irritating the powers that were; Jerrie was obsessed with the idea that NASA owed her a ride, K says, and alienated the space agency to the point that none of the others had a chance to get in the door later. Today she still believes that if the program had been turned over to Jackie Cochran, they might have got their chance.

B Steadman is one of the few women who knew Jackie personally; Jackie and Floyd used to travel in their mobile home (to accommodate Floyd's arthritis) to visit B and Bob in Michigan. B had immense respect for Jackie and her accomplishments, and while she acknowledges that Jackie could be harsh, B always believed that was a "shell," a cover for the insecure person inside. It still saddens B that Jackie did not come to their defense in Congress. "I was really disappointed with Cochran. I thought, Damn, you know, of all the times for her to act so stupidly, this was just not it. We needed her help, but she just backed away from it totally." B believes Jackie was too accomplished to be jealous, that she must have acted on information she was hearing in Washington, that she really believed that incorporating women would somehow have jeopardized the space agency. And B thinks that Jackie was mimicking the prevailing attitude of the men, who did not want women involved. "In the testimony that Glenn gave, he gave NASA every reason to simply say no, and then when Cochran came in and said what she did, she just buoyed him up, and I think at that point they just said, well, okay, if the women don't want it enough to fight for it, we don't have to make that decision." Glenn's testimony, B says, reflected the predominant sentiment of the time. "Most of the men were very much in favor of 'men only,' and they said that it was because they didn't want to kill women, but I think it was simply they didn't want to share anything, at that time anyway. They were deities, practically."

Jerri Sloan blames Jackie Cochran, for one. With typical frankness, Jerri calls Jackie "a self-serving, egotistical bitch" who would not brook the competition. "We were getting too big for her. She couldn't stand it if some women were doing something she couldn't do." Jerri also believes the FLATs offended the egos of the men in the space program by asserting that they could do the job, and that they were fighting against the unified front of the boys' club. She knew what they were up against: it was a long shot that they would ever be allowed to fly a spaceship in an era when she needed her husband's permission to get a loan or buy property.

Like Jerri, Janey Hart knew Lyndon Johnson as a "Southern good ol' boy." And she says James Webb, who was from Louisiana, had a similar mind-set. She was called upon to introduce Webb when he came to speak at the National Democratic Women's Club in Washington a few years after the congressional hearing. "He gave a long speech about the dangers, all the things that could go wrong out there [in space] and at the end he said, 'And don't you all worry—someday we'll take care of you ladies.' And I thought, You asshole."

Many of the other women say they made a mistake by not all going to Washington to testify together. "I think in retrospect it would have meant more to Congress had we all been there," B Steadman says. "Several of the girls had some good political contacts that could have been drawn on. . . . We should have fought harder. We had to hit them more than once. We had to prove to them with the information that was available at that time from the physicals that there was no reason to exclude women. It's not politically good to say don't let women in, so that was our [opening] to get in." They should have fought all through the sixties, B says, for as long as it took. "There was no reason why we shouldn't have—looking back on it Janey and I both feel the same way, we just didn't fight hard enough." She believes they could have changed something: "Fighting city hall, you know, that was an uphill thing, but I don't feel we made a good enough showing. We should have just shook the paper sack until they got some sense in their heads, and then been the first with a woman in space instead of letting Tereshkova do it."

Gene Nora Stumbough argues that the women were less qualified and there was no way anyone was going to overlook that when there were plenty of qualified men around. "I didn't see any way that anybody was going to promote the idea of taking people basically off the street and making astronauts out of them when they had a bunch of men who were already well trained. . . . You've got test pilots who are engineers, so why would you go and grab a bunch of women who are not qualified and train them for seven or eight years?"

Sarah Gorelick summarizes it this way. "My theory is they just were not ready for a woman then. Public opinion at the time was that women should stay home and be protected—'My God, what if we lose one of them?' This was the era of Kennedy and Camelot. And women were to be protected."

They sat in the first row of the bleachers and held their breath while the night sky suddenly turned orange with flames and the ground shook beneath them. On February 3, 1995, eight of the surviving FLATs were finally at Cape Canaveral for the launch of an American rocket. They were there to watch, not to fly—astronaut Eileen Collins invited them as her guests—but thirty-five years on, the women found themselves warmly welcomed by NASA, given the highest level of clearance on their guest passes, fussed over and invited to receptions.

About the time that Collins's shuttle pilot assignment was announced, a Hollywood movie producer named Jim Cross, who knew Gene Nora Stumbough and had heard about the FLATs, decided to put together a documentary about their story. In the spring of 1994, he arranged for the women to meet at the 99s headquarters in Oklahoma City, the first time they had ever been assembled as a group. He also invited Collins. She came, and the women collectively fell in love with her—she is astonishingly likable: friendly, humble, easygoing and beneath all that presumably as hard as nails, as the second woman ever to earn the wings of a test pilot in the United States Air Force. Collins in turn got a kick out of the "Mercury 13," as Cross, the producer, had taken to calling them.

"They had this magnificent thing, it was poetic," he recalls about the Oklahoma City meeting. "They [the surviving FLATs] were fascinated beyond words to meet this woman who would carry their torch, and this was a woman fascinated to meet these women who had done so much to pave the way for her."

The FLATs had also celebrated Sally Ride's historic first trip in 1983. But Ride was an astrophysicist who performed scientific experiments on the shuttle. She was an astronaut, but she was also, to their way of thinking, a passenger. The FLATs did not feel vindicated until Collins rode the gantry elevator up the rocket and climbed into the shuttle's pilot seat.

Collins was intrigued by the FLATs, NASA was finally interested, and the news media were fascinated: this was an irresistible story, these women of another era denied an opportunity. And it was a propitious time for just such a tale. There was a swell in interest in women's history in the 1990s, for one thing. A wave of anniversaries from World War II brought new attention to the WASPs, and the Mercury women were seen as their successors. The aviation industry was hurting for pilots (because with no major conflict since the Vietnam War there were far fewer coming out of the military) and, with the economic downturn, for business. A large effort to recruit women began, and that led inevitably to a revisiting of aviation history, and the launch of several new publications devoted solely to female fliers. Eileen Collins's attention to the FLATs was the catalyst, and there was now a wide audience eager to hear all about these women of another generation.

But that audience wanted a particular version of the story. Consistently, the press reports of the past decade say that the thirteen women were formally recruited by NASA; that they were tested and trained in secret, by order of the politically sensitive space agency; and that they were abandoned at the eleventh hour, just days from embarking on a space mission. None of this, of course, is accurate.

Why does the erroneous story endure, despite all the evidence to the contrary? "There are several things at play causing this enshrined narrative to be what it is," says NASA's Roger Launius, who has been obliged to consider this issue as the queries about the FLATs pour into the NASA history office. "There is a long-standing tradition in America of rooting for the underdog." It's a tidy, good guy–bad guy narrative, and it is easier to tell with a single, clearly delineated bad guy—NASA. In addition, the FLATs were victims of discrimination of the kind people now like to believe has been eliminated; the shocking story of their rejection allows for self-congratulatory comparison to the society that quashed them in the 1960s.

There is another little puzzle to this process of public myth-making. The story of the FLATs was not new in the 1990s. They were all in *Life* in 1963. Janey Hart attended Sally Ride's first launch in 1983 and was quoted as one of the women denied the chance in 1960. ("It is not true that we've 'come a long way, baby,'" she told reporters. "We've been there all the time—it's NASA that's come a long way.") A cover story in *Ms.* magazine in 1973 proclaimed, "Yes, We Do Have Women Astronauts"— that story was a response to frustration that women were still not being included in the civilian scientist astronaut recruitment, and it presented the dropped-by-NASA version of the story as a shocking exposé. All of this preceded the wave of attention when Eileen Collins singled them out. After that, the FLATs became the subject of two fictionalized plays, a photo exhibit, innumerable newspaper and magazine articles. A major Hollywood production company paid almost half a million dollars for the rights to tell their story (though never made the movie). Their story was discovered over and over again.

In the end, the question is not why nobody knows this story. The question is why no one can remember this story. It seems to vanish from the collective national memory each time it is told, and every time it is retold it is a revelation. "That's societal sexism," says aviation historian Debbie Douglas. "It's precisely our inability to recognize these women in these positions—we can't see them, even when we know they're there."

EPILOGUE

Seven of the surviving FLATs at the launch of the space shuttle
Discovery *with Lt. Col. Eileen Collins in the pilot's seat, Cape
Canaveral, 1995. From left, Gene Nora Jessen, Jerri Truhill,
Jerrie Cobb, B Steadman, Sarah Ratley, Wally Funk, K Cagle.*

Courtesy of Jerri Truhill

The telegram brought the news that the women-in-space
program was canceled. There was no explanation, and there was
no apology. Just the slim piece of yellow paper that canceled their
ambitions. It left the women bitterly disappointed. "The
program is over, the program is canceled, goodbye, go home and
forget you ever did it." That is how Jerri recalls it, her voice acid
with the memory. "The finality of that short telegram, with no

explanation, not a by-your-leave, not even a thank-you, like a slap of cold water right across the face. We were so enthused, we were all so into it, we were ready to go and gung ho, and you get a telegram that just says, Program's been canceled, forget it. The way it was done affected all of us and I don't think we've ever gotten over it."

Of course most of them, including Jerri herself, did get over it. The testing episode became an unusual little story told to their children when they watched the Apollo launches on television. They packed away their dreams of space with the telegram and the letters from Randy Lovelace.

Gene Nora Stumbough was left without a job that September weekend, but she sent off a barrage of letters and soon landed a gig flying for Beechcraft, where an astute marketing executive saw the public relations dividends in female pilots. In 1962, Gene Nora and two other pilots flew a forty-thousand-mile, three-month-long cross-country tour, when Beechcraft introduced its new Musketeer. "It was the best job ever, anywhere," she says. "The kind of flying girls just didn't get to do then." In 1964 she married a fellow Beech pilot, Bob Jessen, and a few years later they moved to Boise, Idaho, to start a Beech dealership of their own. They had two children, and Gene Nora regularly flew to 99s meetings—in 1980 she was elected president of the organization. She and Bob started an FBO (fixed base operation), and soon the astronaut tests were, for her, just "a footnote in history." Today she works with Bob at their Boise Air Service, and has begun a new career writing books about the early history of women in aviation. She flies the Bonanza to their cottage in Oregon most weekends.

Not long after the Pensacola telegram came, Rhea Hurrle quit flying altogether. In 1962, she got married to a fellow in the oil business. They opened an aircraft brokerage together. But in 1966, he died of cancer. "We were still newlyweds," Rhea says. Her husband was an only child, and so after his death Rhea (still the farm girl with the strong sense of duty) moved to Colorado Springs to care for his elderly widowed mother. She did a little teaching at the Air Force Academy in Colorado Springs, and towed glider students high up into the mountains, but it was hard to make a living in a town awash in ex-military pilots. In 1972, she married again, this time to a real estate developer named Len Woltman. He asked her to quit flying, and she did. "I loved flying, but I loved him more," Rhea says with a shrug. "I missed it at first, but I made a deal, and he was worth it." She trained instead as a professional parliamentarian, a job she still does today, running corporate and community meetings according to Robert's Rules of Order.

In 1961, K Cagle went back to teaching flying and, a few years later, became a licensed aircraft and engine mechanic—the only woman anybody had ever heard of doing the job. She went to work as a mechanic at Robbins Air Force Base, where she used to instruct. She made the acquaintance of a general while writing an aviation column for the Raleigh newspaper, and he invited her to Eglin Air Force Base to do a little jet flying. "It was like being in a submarine," she says of her first trip at the controls of a jet-powered plane. "The air was fluid, and the clouds were like little bubbles. I could roll it left, roll it right, like through water." She sighs happily at the memory. "That was one of the highlights of my life." Today she lives in Lizella, Georgia, and still flies out at Robbins whenever she gets the yen.

Sarah Gorelick, who was also suddenly without a job in September 1961, went to work in her father's store. She always had a plane of her own, and in the late sixties she took helicopter lessons. When the tight bunch of guys in the helicopter gang at the airfield gave her a hard time, she simply bought the helicopter. She married briefly in the 1970s and had a daughter, Paula (Sarah flew until the day before she went into labor). She became a chartered accountant and works today for the IRS; she still flies on weekends. People often think she is just a flaky old lady, she confides, and then gives a wicked little grin: "I just let 'em think it."

In 1961, B Steadman went back to running her aviation business, and to racing—she won the International Women's Air Race in 1963, and the AWTAR in 1966. In 1968, she was elected president of the 99s, and went on to help build the International Women's Air and Space Museum in Dayton, Ohio. She and Bob adopted two boys. She had to give up flying after a brain injury in the 1970s, but she remains avidly interested in aviation. She lives today in Traverse City, Michigan; she and Bob bought a taxi company to occupy them in their retirement, and B does regular shifts driving. She also speaks about her career in aviation; she likes the grade-school groups the best. She encourages them to take an interest in the space program, and she tells them anything is possible.

After the astronaut episode, Jean Hixson went back to teaching math to fifth graders, and spending her summer vacations working with the air force reserves. She worked on space navigation research at zero gravity, and at the time of the Apollo moon program she headed projects looking at movement in lunar gravity. Later, she studied life support equipment and aeromedical requirements for female military pilots. In 1984, by then a colonel, she was presented with the Meritorious Service Medal for her work with the Aerospace Medical Research Laboratory at Wright-Patterson. Jean dated a bit and left the neighborhood kids agog when a gentleman came to pick her up by landing his helicopter at the end of her street. But she stayed single: "Although if I found someone who had his own Learjet, I might consider him . . ." she joked to friends. She died of ovarian cancer in 1984. The first line of her obituary in the Akron newspaper read, "Jean F. Hixson never realized her dream of becoming the country's first female astronaut."

Irene Leverton, too, had quit a job to go to Pensacola and found herself stuck that September. The news that the women

weren't going into space training didn't really surprise her: "I was
so used to that kind of thing." She got work instructing in
California but quickly found herself in the same dissatisfying
cycle of landing flying jobs she liked and running into bosses
who, she says, didn't want to give a woman decent work. She
taught at Japan Airlines' flight school, flew into the mountains
for the forest service and even flew government scientists to
secret mountain satellite stations listening to space. She waged a
bitter but eventually victorious fight to have women admitted to
the national pylon racing competitions, and in 1969 got the
dozen women in the country with the top pilot rating together
in the Women Airline Transport Pilots Association. Today she
flies occasionally with the Civil Air Patrol and runs a small aviation consulting business in Prescott, Arizona. She is still fighting
the perception of men who believe a woman—an old woman,
now—shouldn't be flying.

In 1964, the makers of a stunning innovation called Lycra
deemed Jerri Sloan the country's most active woman and sent her
across the United States as an ambassador for their miracle fabric.
Dupont made her a fancy pink flying suit, and her business
partner Joe Truhill painted one of their P-51s a matching shade;
in pink suit and pink plane, Jerri made a national tour. On New
Year's Eve in 1964, she married Joe. He had four kids of his own,
so the Truhill household was suddenly "crowded," Jerri says
dryly. She welcomed the political changes of the sixties, and
embraced the nascent women's movement—not, she hastens to
say, that she went around "with breasts all sagging, burning
bras." Her sense of outrage, ignited by the astronaut fiasco, was
inflamed when she married Joe and suddenly found that as
someone's wife, she had no rights of her own any more. She had
been a single mother, owner of a house and co-owner of a business, but suddenly she had to have Joe's signature on everything.
The same week that she did risky flying, testing an automatic
navigation system out over the ocean for the military, a company

refused to sell her new carpet without her husband's permission. "You think I wasn't for the Equal Rights Amendment?" Jerri asks, still boiling at the memory. She lives today in Dallas, overseeing her brood of children, stepchildren and grandchildren. She is, she acknowledges acerbically, a little less tolerant of sexism with every passing year.

The astronaut episode propelled Janey Hart into a new type of political activity. In 1963, she had just finished reading a copy of Betty Friedan's shocking new book, *The Feminine Mystique*, when the phone rang—it was Friedan herself, whom Janey had never met. "And she said, I've heard about [the congressional hearing] and I think this might be a good time for us to start an organization to make life more fair for women. And I wondered if you could come to New York for a meeting." Janey flew to New York, and joined nine other women at a meeting at Friedan's Upper West Side apartment. The National Organization for Women was born that evening. Janey was part of the founding board when NOW was formalized in 1966 and started chapters in both Michigan and Washington.

She had eight growing children to contend with, and she went back to school herself, earning a degree in anthropology from George Washington University (and zipping around campus on a little yellow Honda motorcycle). She gradually became more and more opposed to the Vietnam War; in 1968 she went to see firsthand what the Americans were doing there, and the experience soon had her out protesting with her children (including her three draft-age sons). Janey was arrested with 185 other protesters at an ecumenical antiwar service held at the Pentagon in November 1969. It was an election year, but Phil just shrugged off the inevitable barrage—"Senator's wife arrested in protest." She made headlines again when she helped set up a shelter for excommunicated priests who refused to follow the Vatican line on birth control. As the criticism poured in, members of Phil's campaign staff asked Janey to "tone it down."

That didn't go over well: "I expect to tell the truth as I see it. The truth, as close as humans can come to it, is not a political disadvantage," she later told a writer who asked about the tension. Janey resented the demands that politics put on her husband and resented the loss of her own privacy, but at the same time she clearly appreciated the platform it gave her. "You can be a Senate wife and do all those nice little social tea–type things or you can stand for something and use it and not just sit there. So I took every advantage I could of it."

Phil died of cancer in 1976. Janey put her energy into sailing (including a transatlantic trip). She now spends her summers on Mackinac Island and her winters sailing her yacht, the *Loon Feather,* in the Caribbean. She gave up flying a while back. "It's too expensive," she says. But she, like all the others, is still a member of the 99s.

And Jackie Cochran? In 1971, she became the first living woman to be enshrined in the Aviation Hall of Fame. That same year, she and legendary French pilot Jacqueline Auriol were both made "honorary members" of the Society of Experimental Test Pilots; they were the first women allowed into the club, although the society would not give them full membership. In 1975, Jackie told *The Washington Post,* "I have never been discriminated against in my life. I think the women complaining they've been discriminated against are the ones who can't do anything anyway. Baloney." Jackie had a heart attack in the early 1970s and her health deteriorated; she had to stop flying and sold her Lodestar. Her husband, Floyd Odlum, died at the age of eighty in 1977. Jackie stayed on the ranch, but Floyd's son Bruce took over management of the estate. He did not have his father's business sense, however, and was eventually so overwhelmed by the scope of the losses that he killed himself in the backyard. Jackie herself died, of another heart attack, in 1980—her obituaries in the major newspapers, which repeated the orphan story, said vaguely that she was living on or near the ranch, but her unacknowledged family says that she had lost the property and had moved to a small condominium. She died without having made a space-flight. It was just about the only time Jackie Cochran didn't do something that she said she would.

Valentina Tereshkova, the first woman in space, was appointed a representative for the soviet of Yaroslavl in 1967 and served on the council of the Supreme Soviet for the next seven years. She was named president of the Soviet Women's Committee and was the Soviet representative to the UN conference for International Women's Year in Mexico City in 1975. She was a hero of the international women's movement. But she was never again a cosmonaut. In 1964 she told reporters in Cuba that Yuri Gagarin was planning to lead the next moon mission and that she would be part of it. She enrolled in the Zhukovsky Military Air Academy and graduated in 1969. For the next decade, she continued to say publicly that she hoped to soon make another flight in space—but her tone was increasingly wistful. In truth, while the Soviets heralded her flight as the propaganda victory that it was, they had no intention of flying another woman. Those who trained with her were dismissed, and no more women were recruited until the late 1970s.

The change at NASA took just as long. From the initial group of six female candidates in 1978, women were slowly incorporated into the astronaut corps. By 2000, 25 percent of NASA's astronauts were women; one-third of the agency's workforce was female, which included 16 percent of the scientists and engineers. Some of the old debates continue, however: in 2002, NASA scrapped plans to develop a smaller space suit, more suitable for female astronauts, saying it could not justify the $16 million expenditure when only 20 percent of the astronaut corps would use it (some women can comfortably wear the larger suits). Yvonne Brill, a retired engineer and former member of

NASA's Aerospace Safety Advisory Panel, was among many
critics who noted that the decision could keep more women out
of the astronaut corps, since smaller astronaut candidates could
not maneuver as well in the bulky suit in their qualifying tests.
(In 2001, NASA spent millions on an extra-large suit, to fit
bigger men.)

Eileen Collins set another milestone when she became the first
woman to command a United States space mission in 1998. She
is slated to do it again in late 2003 as commander of the Space
Shuttle *Endeavor,* flying it to the International Space Station.
Familiar arguments have been raised again in recent years, as
scientists point out that smaller astronauts would use fewer
resources living on the space station. However, in plans laid out
to 2005, only one female astronaut is scheduled to live and work
on the ISS.

For everyone else, life went on. But for four of the Lovelace
women, the idea that they might still get into space did not die
with the telegram about Pensacola.

Like Jerrie, Jan and Marion Dietrich kept up their campaign.
Their surviving correspondence suggests that the twins were
working with Jackie and that they believed for the next several
years that they might still be made part of the space program. On
January 10, 1964, a breathless Marion came in from an aviation
writers' conference where she had met a friend of Jackie
Cochran's and typed out a letter to her sister, who was then flying
in Los Angeles.

> Dear Jan,
>   Repeat this information to NO ONE.
>   We may know this month. We might stay at our
> present locations for a while but possibly after salary.
>   Advise you to get the [airline] captain's rating soonest, just

in case. . . . I talked with Captain Walton who had seen
Jackie Cochran quite a bit in Alaska. Jackie told him she
talked to a congressional committee last summer and they
"promised" her a woman (pilot type rather than scientist, I
gather) would go into space in two to three years. She is
very anxious to have a woman astronaut and has gone to
doctor after doctor and is finally convinced she cannot go
because G-loads would cause great stress on body parts
already weakened by surgery. He said she is very opposed
to Jerrie Cobb and very much for us—that she liked us
and spoke well of us. He said since she could not go he
felt she would like to sponsor someone so that she feels
part of it or that she might back someone just to keep
[Jerrie] from going.

Walton, a public relations officer in the air force, advised
Marion to get their names in the paper—especially to make it
public that Jan was then piloting the forty-passenger Convair
240. "You and I have avoided publicity," Marion wrote
(although in fact, she had been part of two of the three major
pieces of publicity about the program),

. . . but I think it is very important to getting a woman's
program going, not just for us but a discreet and factual
story about a woman flying a Convair be released in the
next 10 days. They kept telling Jackie the women did not
have the jet test piloting experience or any jet experience—
it would be apparent if they could fly the Convair they
could fly a jet. Your experience is the only answer we now
have to this jet thing. At dinner I talked with Ralph
Deighton, aviation and science writer for AP in LA and
"happened" to mention what you were doing. An AP
reporter should contact you very soon. Be sure to see him
as quickly as possible and get this thing in. . . . If you

aren't contacted soon, be sure to let me know. I can diplo-
matically write John Madigan, LA chief of UPI, saying
there is some new consideration of a woman in space
program, there is some question about experience, a short
factual story would bring out experience and abilities.
Even a picture and caption would do it. The LA aviation
and space writers' association will have a program dealing
with various types of aircraft. You will be invited as a
special guest of Tom Self of the LA chapter, president.
Wear your prettiest dress and smile and meet as many
people as you can.

Marion was a gifted publicist. The next year the twins ferried
a Beech Queen Air to Bremen, Germany, and articles about their
transatlantic journey—with irresistible pictures of the pretty
twins clambering out of their plane in matching Jackie O–style
suits—made newspapers across the country. But it made no
difference to their campaign with NASA, and Jackie, NASA's
new consultant, was given the message to drop this issue of
female astronauts.

While they waited, the twins had, of course, to work. Jan was
the first woman in the country to receive an airline transport
rating in a four-engine jet and she went to work as a first officer
on a charter jet. But she could not break that last barrier and get
an airline pilot's job. In 1968 she filed a lawsuit against World
Airways Inc. in a federal court in San Francisco, charging
discrimination under the 1964 Equal Rights Act. She earned a
grade of 98 percent in the company's DC-6 training course but
they turned down her job application. "It's not that I was lacking
ability, but I was told that the image of an airline captain was a
tall, gray-haired man," Jan said. The suit dragged through court
and was costly; she eventually abandoned it. She never did get an
airline job, but she flew a four-engine jet with the commuter
carrier Golden Pacific Airlines. Marion kept writing. And as

years went by but no further word came from Jackie, the twins gradually gave up the idea that together they, or at least one of them, would be the country's first woman in space.

Marion Dietrich died of cancer in 1974. Neither she nor Jan had children; they lived much of their adult lives within a few doors of each other. Jan scattered Marion's ashes from her plane, flying over the bay above the Golden Gate Bridge. Today Jan lives in a nursing home, deaf and blind and suffering from dementia. She told a visitor in the late 1990s, though, before the last of her hearing went, "I was the best damn pilot there ever was."

As Wally Funk tells the story, she read the telegram about the cancelation of the Pensacola testing, and she shrugged. "I wasn't discouraged. I was young and I was happy. I just believed it would come. If not today then in a couple of months." It seemed absurd that someone as eminently qualified, as enthusiastic as she was, would not get this opportunity.

She applied again to NASA's second round of recruitment in 1962, for the Gemini missions, and was told, she says, that the same qualifications were still required—she had to be a jet test pilot and an engineer. She tried again in 1966, but still no women made that cut. Then she decided NASA was not going to be her ticket off the planet, and she would look elsewhere.

Wally had gone out to California in 1962 and eventually rose from instructing to a chief pilot's position at an FBO. In 1971, she became the first female inspector for the Federal Aviation Authority—she gave check rides, inspected schools, investigated complaints. Four years later she was made one of the first female accident investigators for the National Transportation Safety Board. She loved that job: she drove and flew and hiked and once even rode a burro up to an accident site, she had a big office right on the runway at the Los Angeles airport, and even though the work was grim (body parts and personal effects scattered around the charred wreckage of a plane), she relished the authority. She retired from the organization in the early 1980s under circumstances that are not clear, but she parlayed her knowledge of safety into the "Wally Funk Safety Slide Presentation," a monologue of accidents and what could have prevented them, and travels around the country speaking to student and amateur pilot groups. And always, she kept a roof overhead with instructing. By the early 1990s, she estimated that she had soloed more than seven hundred students.

Wally also pursued her space ambitions on her own. For one thing, she was determined to "finish" the astronaut tests. In 1963, she talked her way into taking three additional tests similar to those she would have done at Pensacola. She used connections through a student to take the high-altitude chamber test and the Martin-Baker Seat Ejection test (for which she was strapped in a chair, shot upward and summarily dropped) at El Toro Marine Base. It was the first time that the scientists there had ever done the tests on a woman, she says. At the University of Southern California, Wally rode a human centrifuge to measure her tolerance of increased gravitational pull. Military personnel who took the test were equipped with pressure suits. Wally, a civilian, didn't get one—and so, she says, she borrowed her mother's tightest Merry Widow. When she felt "the gray curtain" of unconsciousness starting, she clenched up and the girdle helped to keep her functioning; she never told the doctors her secret. In 1991, she flew a trainer like the MASTIF Jerrie had spun on so many years earlier as part of her second phase of testing.

Wally also continued her hunt for some other route into space. "When I wasn't selected to go with NASA, I was disappointed but I was never bitter," she says firmly. "I was brought up that when things don't work out, you go to your alternative." In the mid-1990s she made a large investment, a down payment with a company called Space Adventures in Arlington, Virginia—a commercial venture that says it will take paying passengers on suborbital flights within a couple of years. Their craft, not yet built, will take passengers sixty-two miles above earth, where the curvature is clearly visible, and they will be briefly weightless. The flight is currently proposed to cost about $100,000.

In 2000, she made a six-day trip to "space camp" near Moscow. Wally refers to this as having "trained with the cosmonauts," although in fact it is simply an extension of the space tourism policy with which the Russians are funding their ailing space program. The typical cost for the trip is $15,000; Wally says she paid for some of it, she declines to say how much, but "they paid the rest because they wanted my name and publicity from having me." She was with five men—four Americans and one Saudi—and one British woman. They were given medical tests, rode the centrifuge to 5 G's, tried to "dock" a mock-up of a Soyuz capsule with a model space station, and those who were trained as scuba divers (Wally isn't, although she plans to be) splashed around in the 1.3-million-gallon "neutral buoyancy facility." The trip highlight came when an Ilyushin 76 took them up to 35,000 feet and into a parabolic dive that produced thirty seconds of weightlessness. "Zero G's at last!" Wally caroled. Untroubled by even a moment of nausea, she sailed the length of the plane, arms and legs out, "like Superman!"

In March 2002, Wally made headlines all over the world with an announcement that she was going to pay $2 million (raised by sponsors whose identity she would not reveal) for a flight with a California company called InterOrbital Systems, launched from the tiny South Pacific island nation of Tonga. The $2 million will pay for sixty days of training and a first flight of five hours—although InterOrbital says eventually its passengers will stay in space for a week for the same price. Four crew members and two astronaut-pilots will make these trips. InterOrbital said it hoped to train Wally to serve as a pilot for its flights. But officials with the Space Transportation Association immediately dismissed the company's plans, saying that, for one thing, $8 million would never pay for a week in space.

Wally has a book, *The First of Them All,* a collection of brief descriptions of the first women to achieve a whole variety of things—the first woman to be a playwright, the first to appear on television. When she gets the book out to show a visitor, Wally turns quickly to the aviation section. She knows the entries almost by heart. The first woman to fly coast to coast, the first woman to fly commercial, the first woman to deliver airmail. By the time Wally started flying, other women had all these "firsts." The Atlantic was flown, the world had been circumnavigated, the sound barrier had been shattered, all by women. But at twenty-one, Wally had a first of epic proportions dangled in front of her. She could be the first female astronaut. "I just fell in love with the idea of being the first woman into space, or perhaps even to the moon," she told a reporter in 1963.

Wally, of course, has plenty of firsts of her own. Her name appears in the book—as one of the United States' first female astronaut candidates. But not, of course, as an astronaut. And that's the title she wants.

Since 1961, Wally has defined herself by her plan to get into space on her own. The role of astronaut is now a crucial part of her identity. While she once hoped to travel as a pilot or an engineer, she says she will now settle for the role of passenger; all that matters is to cross that new frontier. Finishing the Mercury tests brought her one step closer; the visit to the Russian space camp was another step. The passenger trip, with InterOrbital or one of the other space tourism ventures, will finally end the quest. "Don't forget I'm going," she corrects quickly, if anyone speaks of the women's space bid in the past tense.

Wally is much in demand as a speaker, to aviation groups, women's organizations, colleges, any audience requiring an inspiring and motivational guest, and she is adept at generating media coverage. In every speech and interview, she delivers the same points in her winning, toothy manner. But many of the stories she tells are in fact a wistfully reshaped version of the truth.

Wally says, for example, that she was the only woman other than Jerrie to complete all three phases of the astronaut tests. She has, privately, managed to do many of those that Jerrie did at Pensacola—but she has done them piecemeal over thirty years and never under any sort of organized program, a detail she typically omits. She frequently makes presentations wearing the distinctive navy blue uniform of an airline captain, with four gold bars on the sleeves, although she has never held this job. (And this rankles many female pilots, for the handful of women who fly for major airlines are the most respected in the world of women fliers.) Sometimes, Wally poses in an astronaut's training jumpsuit—the kind that can be purchased in the gift shop at Cape Canaveral. She talks about "training with the cosmonauts," although in fact she bought her way into the vacation romp at the Russian space center. "I did it in one week's time but it was so crammed in, it was really three years' time for a regular astronaut or cosmonaut," she said on-screen in a documentary produced about her called *Wally Funk, Astronaut Candidate*. In articles about the Russian trip, she has said that she was "invited" (which she was, after the $15,000 fee was paid), that no one but cosmonauts or officials had been allowed in before her group (in fact, a dozen space tourists had visited on similar programs previously). "I beat John Glenn on the stress test, bicycle analysis tests and lung power tests. I beat Wally Schirra on vertigo and set a record in the bicycle endurance and isolation tests," Wally has told numerous reporters including *Final Frontier* magazine in 1990. But none of the women other than Jerrie was ever given competitive rankings, and the Mercury men never made theirs public; asked how she knows she beat them, Wally says vaguely that she was "told at the time" by medical staff. She tells interviewers that thirteen of twenty-five women passed the Mercury tests, but only seven of the thirty men. In truth, of course, thirty of the thirty-one men passed—NASA simply chose the best seven. Wally remains competitive with Jerrie Cobb, the only other one of the group who still has active ambitions to get into space. Wally points out, for example, that she reads aerospace magazines, including European editions. "These are the little things that put me just kind of an edge over—I don't think Jerrie Cobb would pick up something like this or even know it existed."

Her exaggerations and competitive statements exasperate the other women. They say she is an embarrassment (especially when she does public engagements in her jumpsuit). She says they are simply jealous because she is finally going to make the trip they all wanted, because she persevered when they gave up. Wally's audiences, be they college classes, reporters or young filmmakers, eat up her stories, and she works the image with undeniable savvy. The crowds love her go-to-your-alternative, nobody-owes-me-a-ride attitude and they don't question the details.

Wally's relentless promotion of herself as one-time astronaut candidate and future astronaut is in truth quite moving. "I felt as though I was in space and I belonged there," she says about her zero-gravity plane trip in Russia. She still lectures on safety and teaches flying today, but how she will get to space—and how she will present and publicize the accomplishment—are her chief preoccupations. Once Wally was almost too young to take the astronaut tests; today she fights against the clock to get that trip to space any way she can. She cannot rewrite the pages in her book that give the first spaceflight to Valentina Tereshkova, the title of first American woman to Sally Ride. But she can get into space, and make it true: "Wally Funk, astronaut."

And what became of the self-appointed leader of this band of women? When Jerrie Cobb ran away in 1965, she fled to the jungle—to the area known as Amazonas, which encompasses parts of Brazil, Colombia, Ecuador, Venezuela, Bolivia and Peru. Most of it is dense rain forest; it was then almost entirely unserviced by roads, and a small plane was the only way to cover it. The region Jerrie adopted as her home is as big as the United States. "I chose the Amazon because it's the most isolated," she explained. "You can fly for hundreds and thousands of miles and not see a mission or road. It's the largest isolated place in the world, except maybe Antarctica. But in Antarctica, there are no people needing services as in the Amazon."

Her father helped her get a loan and she bought a 1962 Aero Commander 500A that the indigenous people she worked with soon christened *la parajita, The Bird.* The consulting that first drew her to Latin America quickly turned into more missionary work, and friends at home began to send Jerrie old tennis shoes (protection from snakebites) and blankets for the indigenous people. Members of the 99s collected seeds and shoes and money at their regional meetings. Jerrie was a project. Gene Nora Jessen's parish raised the Lenten collection for her; Jerri Truhill and B Steadman's kids told their school classes about her work. Her supporters formed a charitable organization, the Jerrie Cobb Foundation, to channel donations to her. The 99s featured ads and photo essays on her work in the jungle in their newsletter and organized national fundraising efforts.

Soon Jerrie defined her life there as that of nondenominational jungle missionary, flying food and medicine and doctors for anyone who needed it; she said she did aerial surveys or aviation consulting only when she and *The Bird* ran out of money. Once shy about talking of her faith, Jerrie became more and more comfortable discussing the hand of God she felt in everything she did. She was, she wrote home, "His co-pilot."

In her letters, she sounded devout, cheerful ("what joy there is in this work," she wrote again and again) and stirred by an immense need. She told of fighting epidemics of yellow fever, flying Indians almost dead from malnutrition to clinics and introducing a nutritious new "winged bean" to tribes who survived on subsistence agriculture. It was rough work—she wrote that she slept in her hammock in the Indian longhouses and ate roasted ants, that she and her plane had become a kidnapping target for leftist guerrillas—but her letters brimmed with her earnest desire to help. "Every penny, dime and dollar contributed to our work here goes directly for the Amazonas Indians," she wrote in May 1974. "In fact I would feel very guilty using any for myself, after seeing how desperately they need this help." Six years later an Oklahoma congressman nominated her for the Nobel Peace Prize.

In 1983, when she heard that NASA had finally launched Sally Ride, Jerrie wrote, "Sure, I wish it were me—but I really wouldn't change the last 20 years for anything—or trade places with anyone. Being God's servant here in Amazonas helping these primitive peoples is the most exciting, fulfilling, worthwhile, useful life I can imagine."

Through it all, she never sounded lonely; every letter spoke of "we." She had friends among the Indians and, most important, her plane, to which she was fiercely devoted. In January 1976, the Commander had to be replaced with a smaller, cheaper plane requiring less maintenance. She wrote, "I would rather cut off my right arm, or sell my own child, but there is no other way. I have talked it over with *The Bird,* and although she hates to leave, she understands." Jerrie bought and rebuilt a twin-engine Islander, the new *Bird.*

Yet her letters home from those years also raise questions. Except for a couple of colorful passages in which she described how a young chief died of a "white man's disease" in her arms, and one in which she detailed a long day of nursing the sick and ferrying supplies, the letters said very little about the culture or customs of the tribes she ostensibly lived with. Her accomplishments seem almost unreal: she discovered not just one but many previously unknown tribes. She introduced rice, a difficult crop to grow, into the Amazon environment. She persuaded a tribe to abandon a historic practice of female infanticide. While disarmingly full of her faith, devoting half of each letter to "rejoicing" and thanking God, Jerrie seemed to be waging a rather extraordinary one-woman campaign.

Very few aspects of her activities in the jungle can be substantiated. In 1983, a reporter for *The Miami Herald* who was intrigued by the astronaut-turned-missionary story went to see Jerrie in the jungle. Meg Laughlin spent weeks there, but never saw Jerrie working with the Indians; instead she saw *The Bird* used to deliver crates of Coke and lumber. There were no winged beans, no starving Indians; Jerrie didn't speak any Indian dialects (let alone the dozens she claimed), and Laughlin learned from an anthropologist that Jerrie had never actually spoken to the tribe whose female infanticide she allegedly stopped. Laughlin also found that contrary to the descriptions of a shoestring operation, several companies and individuals gave Jerrie large financial donations. Dan Doyle, a linguist and missionary who had worked with Jerrie for years in the jungle, told the reporter, "I pity Jerrie Cobb more than anyone else in the world." She has plenty to be proud of in what she does do, Doyle said, but she can't stop exaggerating. "She can make a tremendous story out of nothing."

When Laughlin went back to Jerrie for answers, the missionary pilot insisted she had saved the female babies, that she did not get any donations larger than $1,500, that she had brought winged beans to the Amazon. Laughlin, in the end, was apologetic. Jerrie, she said, was dealing with a public "which looks for superheroes in ordinary humans, as I did in my search for a jungle queen. I demanded one, and Jerrie did her best to oblige."

Gene Nora Jessen, like many of the 99s who raised money for Jerrie, was troubled by the allegations, by the idea that Jerrie had made up her jungle life, and she puzzled for years over her motives. Like everyone Laughlin talked to who once knew Jerrie,

Gene Nora came back to the same point. "She just never got over it. Over not getting that chance."

And indeed, Jerrie has kept her failed bid for spaceflight as an integral part of her identity—a picture of her wired to testing equipment at Lovelace adorned the brochure for her charitable foundation, while another of her holding a flight helmet appeared on many of her letters from the jungle. She was a popular cause for the 99s, the injustice of the opportunity she was denied always a part of the story.

Then in 1998, NASA administrator Daniel Goldin announced that the space agency would have a new mission specialist on a space shuttle trip: John Glenn. It was an open secret that the senator had campaigned heavily in Washington to make another spaceflight, and had enlisted the support of then president Bill Clinton in the effort. Goldin said Glenn, seventy-seven, would fly to provide information on the aging process (which, in the loss of bone density, is mimicked in many ways by spaceflight) and on how the elderly function in space.

The news shocked Jerrie—and immediately gave her new hope. Her dream of space travel, painfully relinquished as she got older and older, was not dead after all. If Glenn could be an astronaut at seventy-seven, so, surely, could she at sixty-seven. After all, she was still flying, while the senator hadn't been at the controls in decades. If NASA was interested in research in geriatrics, who better than she to test? (She assumed this was a serious research effort. After all, in 1962 NASA said thirteen women were not enough, so surely now one man would not count as a test sample.) Friends started a grassroots campaign— Jerrie says that she initially found out about it on a trip home from the jungle to collect supplies—and she embraced the effort. A feminist pilot group produced "Send Jerrie" T-shirts, with a picture of a dimpled Jerrie in a 1962 flight suit superimposed on an American flag. The National Organization of Women circulated a petition demanding that NASA fly her. "Sexism was the only thing that kept Jerrie Cobb out of space in the '60s, and it cannot be allowed to stand in her way now," said Patricia Ireland, then president of the organization. Friends of Jerrie's with political connections apprised First Lady Hillary Clinton about her dream. NASA received thousands of letters. There was considerable optimism in the Fly Jerrie camp, because a few years earlier NASA had been moved by a huge write-in campaign to restore civilian Barbara Morgan to the astronaut corps after dropping her following the 1987 *Challenger* disaster (Morgan was the backup to teacher-in-space Christa McAuliffe).

But once again, NASA was not interested in the services of Jerrie Cobb. Goldin agreed to meet with her. "My hopes soared on that news," Jerrie said. "I spent days and nights making notes." At the time, she told reporters, "It feels so right. There's some way to get this to come together. I'm going to get to go." But after a brief conversation in his office in the gleaming glass Washington headquarters of NASA, Jerrie said the meeting was pointless, that Goldin gave no indication she would get the trip or how she could work for it. Through a spokesperson, Goldin praised Jerrie's achievements but said the agency had no plans at that time to fly another geriatric mission specialist. And Margaret Weitekamp, the historian who was then working from NASA's history office in the headquarters, reports that the fly-Jerrie-Cobb issue was handled entirely on the level of public relations and never seriously considered at the administrative level. "It would be nice to be able to fly Jerrie Cobb as a consolation, but that's not going to happen," NASA spokesperson Jennifer McCarter said. The implication in her comment angered Jerrie. "I don't want a joyride," she said. "I have fifty-five years' experience flying. I would be perfectly capable of handling any one of a number of jobs."

The campaign came to nothing. Jerrie eventually realized that NASA had no more intention of allowing her to make this flight than it had in the 1960s.

Jerrie, more than any of the others, wanted to hear the promise implicit in Randy Lovelace's invitation. She believed as she excelled through his tests that she could achieve this as she had all the rest of her goals. But this time, she could not change the rules. She could not be first, or best. And it has cost her dearly.

Eileen Collins knows, as few other people can, what Jerrie missed. "Anyone who would do what these women did believed in the cause. They wanted to be a part of the mission." But her voice grows a bit soft when she talks about Jerrie's ongoing struggle to "go up."

"I wish I could speak to her," Collins says. "It's probably not worth being desperate about. It's great to fly in space but I wouldn't want anyone to fall on their sword, to cause themselves grief and anxiety over it."

When two men from earth stepped onto the moon on July 12, 1969, Jerri Truhill was watching her television in Dallas, her husband, Joe, and the children all gathered around. She thought it was "fantabulous," she confides, sitting at her kitchen table thirty years later and leafing through the yellowed press clippings she cut out the next day.

But as with every space mission, Jerri watched the moon landing with mixed feelings—just like the rest of the nation, she says, she was pulling for the men, and praying for them, hoping their mission would be safe and successful. And she was bitter.

Why?

She grows a little pensive at the question and leans back in her chair. Her pilot's eyes, a little milky now, look off in the middle distance. She felt, Jerri says, as if she was the victim of something immensely unfair.

"I think all of us did," she says. "If we had been given a chance and had failed, we could have accepted that. And I think that's the reason that Jerrie has—that we all have a resentment and a hurt and a bewilderment that we were not given the chance to compete on a level playing field. That's all we asked for. We didn't ask them to cut us any slack on anything. We didn't ask them, because we were women, to grant us special privileges or grant us special favors—because we had children or were married or weren't married. All we asked was a chance to prove we could compete on a level playing ground, in which case a lot of us would have made it. Some of us wouldn't. But a lot of us would. I think that is the deep-seated root of the bitterness. That we weren't given the chance to compete."

These were strong, courageous women with enormous dedication to their country. They had a rare set of skills, and at the moment their country needed those skills (in small, tough bodies), they all stepped forward with an unhesitating willingness to serve. There is no way to know what they might have brought to the Mercury program or subsequent space exploration—no way to calculate what the United States lost by not including them.

Sooner or later, over cups of tea in their kitchens, in Michigan and Kansas and Arizona, the FLATs all come around to one point. Some of them are wry, and some still speak the words with rancor.

We were too good, they say. We were too good, too soon.

BIBLIOGRAPHY

Books

Aldrin, Buzz, and Malcolm McConnell. *Men from Earth*. New York: Bantam Books, 1989.

Atkinson, Joseph, and Jay Shafritz. *The Real Stuff: A History of NASA's Astronaut Recruitment Program*. New York: Praeger Publishers, 1985.

Bilstein, Roger. *Orders of Magnitude: A History of the NACA and NASA, 1915–1990*. Washington: National Aeronautics and Space Administration, 1989.

Brooks-Pazmany, Kathleen. *United States Women in Aviation, 1919–1929*. Washington: Smithsonian Institution Press, 1991.

Burrows, William. *This New Ocean: The Story of the First Space Age*. New York: Random House, 1998.

Butler, Susan. *East to the Dawn: The Life of Amelia Earhart*. Reading: Addison-Wesley, 1997.

Carl, Ann B. *A WASP Among Eagles: A Woman Military Test Pilot in World War II*. Washington: Smithsonian Institution Press, 1999.

Catchpole, John. *Project Mercury, NASA's First Manned Space Programme*. Chichester: Praxis Publishing, 2001.

Cobb, Jerrie. *Solo Pilot*. Sun City Center: Jerrie Cobb Foundation Inc., 1997.

Cochran, Jacqueline, and Maryann Bucknum Brinley. *Jackie Cochran: The Autobiography of the Greatest Woman Pilot in Aviation History*. New York: Bantam Books, 1987.

Collins, Martin J., and the Division of Space History, the National Air and Space Museum, The Smithsonian Institution. *Space Race:*

The U.S.–U.S.S.R. Competition to Reach the Moon. San Francisco: Pomegranate Communications Inc., 1999.

Cunningham, Walter, with Mickey Herskowitz. *The All-American Boys.* New York: Macmillan Publishing Co., 1977.

Davis, Madeline D., and Elizabeth Lapovsky Kennedy. *Boots of Leather, Slippers of Gold: The History of a Lesbian Community.* New York: Penguin Books, 1993.

Dean, Robert D. *Imperial Brotherhood: Gender and the Making of Cold War Foreign Policy.* Amherst: University of Massachusetts Press, 2001.

Douglas, Deborah. *United States Women in Aviation, 1940–1985.* Washington: Smithsonian Institution Press, 1990.

Friedan, Betty. *The Feminine Mystique.* New York: W. W. Norton and Company, 1997.

Glenn, John, with Nick Taylor. *John Glenn, A Memoir.* New York: Bantam Books, 1999.

Goldsmith, Donald. *Voyage to the Milky Way: The Future of Space Exploration.* [n.c.]: TV Books, 1999.

Goodwin, Richard N. *Remembering America: A Voice from the Sixties.* Boston: Little, Brown and Company, 1988.

Haynsworth, Leslie, and David Toomey. *Amelia Earhart's Daughters: The Wild and Glorious Story of American Women Aviators from World War II to the Dawn of the Space Age.* New York: Perennial, 1998.

Hodgman, Ann, and Rudy Djabbaroff. *Skystars: The History of Women in Aviation.* New York: Atheneum, 1981.

Jessen, Gene Nora. *The Powder Puff Derby of 1929.* Naperville, Illinois: Sourcebooks, Inc., 2002.

Kennedy, Gregory P., editor. *Apollo to the Moon.* New York: Chelsea House Publishers, 1992.

Kraft, Chris. *Flight: My Life in Mission Control.* New York: Dutton, 2001.

Markham, Beryl. *West with the Night.* Berkley: North Point Press, 1942.

May, Elaine Tyler. *Homeward Bound: American Families in the Cold War Era.* New York: Basic Books, Inc., 1988.

Merryman, Molly. *Clipped Wings: The Rise and Fall of the Women Airforce Service Pilots (WASPs) of World War II.* New York: New York University Press, 1998.

Oakes, Claudia M. *United States Women in Aviation, 1930–1939.* Washington: Smithsonian Institution Press, 1991.

O'Brien, Michael. *Philip Hart: The Conscience of the Senate.* East Lansing: Michigan State University Press, 1995.

Oldenziel, Ruth. *Making Technology Masculine: Men, Women and Modern Machines in America, 1870–1945.* Amsterdam: Amsterdam University Press, 1999.

Rendall, Ivan. *Reaching for the Skies.* London: BBC Books, 1988.

Scott, Joan Wallach. *Gender and the Politics of History.* New York: Columbia University Press, 1988.

Sharpe, Mitchell R. *It Is I, Seagull: Valentina Tereshkova, First Woman in Space.* New York: Thomas Y. Crowell Company, 1975.

Shepard, Alan, and Deke Slayton, with Jay Barbaree and Howard Benedict. *Moon Shot: The Inside Story of America's Race to the Moon.* Atlanta: Turner Publishing Inc., 1994.

Siddiqi, Asif A. *Challenge to Apollo: The Soviet Union and the Space Race, 1945–1974.* Washington: National Aeronautics and Space Administration, NASA History Division, 2000.

Spidle, Jake W. *The Lovelace Medical Center, Pioneer in American Health Care.* Albuquerque: University of New Mexico Press, 1987.

Stott, Carole. *Into the Unknown.* New York: Hampstead Press, 1989.

Unger, Debi, and Irwin Unger. *LBJ: A Life.* New York: John Wiley and Sons, 1999.

Weaver Francisco, Patricia. *Lunacy.* Woodstock, Illinois: The Dramatic Publishing Company, 1984.

Wolfe, Tom. *The Right Stuff.* New York: Bantam Books, 1989.

Yeager, Chuck, with Leo Janos. *Yeager: An Autobiography.* New York: Bantam Books, 1985.

Articles

"2 Astronauts 'Scrub' Bid of Women Pilots." *Chicago Tribune.* July 19, 1962.

"2 Would-Be 'Astronettes' Plead: Let Us Beat Reds." United Press International. July 18, 1962.

"22 years ago, the right stuff wasn't enough for NASA." Karen Klinger. *San Jose Mercury News.* June 12, 1983.

"A Lady Proves She's Fit For Space Flight." *Life.* August 29, 1960.

"A Probe of Discrimination Against Women in Space: House Group: 9 Out of 11 Men." *New York Times.* June 15, 1962.

"A Woman Passes Tests Given to 7 Astronauts." *New York Times.* August 19, 1960.

"Adventurer In Sky and Schoolroom." Lloyd Stoyer. *Akron Beacon Journal.* 1957.

"Air Race Won Again by Mrs. Steadman." *Detroit Free Press.* May 29, 1963.

"American Advertising and Soviet Reality: We have different wings, Jerrie!" Valentin Goltsev. *Izvestia.* July 6, 1963.

"Another Giant Leap." Francis French and Wally Funk. *Spaceflight* Vol. 41., December 1999: 517.

"Apollo Project Engineer Is a Pretty Grandmother." Daniel J. McKenna. Philadelphia *Evening Bulletin.* November 6, 1964.

"'Astronaut Test' Passed By Jean." Helen Waterhouse. *Akron Beacon Journal.* July 18, 1962.

"'Astronautess' Tells Clubwomen: Pre-Space Tests Show Gals Can Take It As Well As Men." Helen Waterhouse. *Akron Beacon Journal.* January 11, 1962.

"Astronette in Town." Peggy Powell. *Los Angeles Herald-Examiner.* October 2, 1964.

"Aviator Serves Amazon People's Needs." James Johnson. *Sunday Oklahoman.* November 8, 1987.

"Brainy gals help push America's race-into-space." Eloise Engle. *Dodge News Magazine.* April 1962.

"But Some People Simply Never Get the Message." Clare Booth Luce. *Life.* June 28, 1963.

"Bykovksy Nears a Flight Record." Henry Tanner. *New York Times.* June 18, 1962.

"Dad Flew a Jenny; Daughter a Jet." Marion Dietrich. *San Francisco News.* October 8, 1957.

"Damp Prelude to Space." *Life.* October 24, 1960.

"Doctor's Job to Pick First Space Man." Associated Press. March 8, 1959.

"Dr. Donald D. Flickinger, 89, A Pioneer in Space Medicine." Henry Fountain. *New York Times.* March 3, 1997.

"Duckings, Probings, Checks That Proved Fliers' Fitness." Randy Lovelace. *Life*. April 20, 1959.

"First Woman into Space." Marion Dietrich. *McCall's*. September 1961.

"'Flying Schoolteacher' comes home to Hoopeston." *Commercial News*, Illinois. August 22, 1974.

"From Aviatrix to Astronautrix." *Time*. August 29, 1960.

"Gerry Sloan: Potential Astronaut." Paula Breibart. *Miami News*. September 29, 1964.

"Girl 'in Space' Six Days without a Hallucination." United Press International. *Chicago Daily Tribune*. November 6, 1959.

"Glenn Sees Place for Girls in Space." Yvette Cardozo. *Miami Herald*. May 22, 1965.

"Glenn Would Yield Space in Space." William McPherson. *Washington Post*. July 19, 1962.

"Her Goal: to Be 1st Woman 'Spaceman.'" *Herald-Examiner*, California. January 17, 1963.

"Her Turn in Space." Claudia Feldman. *Texas* magazine, *Houston Chronicle*. June 12, 1994.

"Hermosa Woman Breaks Precedent, Joins All-Male Realm of Safety Investigators." Mary Ann Lee. *Los Angeles Times*. July 13, 1975.

"Hero Dodges Women's Ire." *Associated Press*. July 19, 1962.

"High Flying Cowgirl." Susan Laws. *Women and Guns*. May–June 2001.

"Hoopeston Girl, 24, Is Veteran of the Airways." *Chronicle-Herald*, Illinois. December 30, 1946.

"Hoopeston Native Describes Tour of NATO Bases, Berlin." Jean Hixson as told to Tim Schelhardt. *Commercial News*, Illinois. August 29, 1965.

"House to Probe Bias Against 'Spacewomen.'" United Press International. June 15, 1962.

"I reached stars the hard way." Jacqueline Cochran. *Life*. August 16, 1954.

"In Terms of Three Dimensions." Marion Dietrich. *Bee Lines*, California. December 1950.

"Is Space a Place for the Ladies?" Erik Bergaust. *This Week*. September 2, 1996.

"Jackie: Stork Stops Space Girls." Tom Tiede. *Idaho Statesman.* September 7, 1969.

"Jackie Cochran: Famed Pilot Says Women Shouldn't Fight." Richard C. Barnard. *Times Magazine, New York Times.* January 23, 1978.

"Jacqueline Cochran." *Current Biography.* New York: H. W. Wilson and Company, 1941.

"Jean Hixson, pilot, ex-teacher, dies." *Akron Beacon Journal.* September 23, 1984.

"Jerrie Cobb." Joe Werne. *Miami Herald.* April 18, 1965.

"Jerrie Cobb Thinks Cooper Wrong on Women in Space." Jim Maloney. *Houston Post.* July 1, 1963.

"Jerrie May Be First Spacewoman." Dorothy McCurdle. *Washington Post.* August 22, 1960.

"Lady Fliers Ask to Be Astronauts, Too; Plead for Co-Eds in Space." *Wall Street Journal.* July 18, 1962.

"Legion of Angry Women." Jack Anderson. *Parade.* November 16, 1967.

"NASA Decision Not Suited for Women." Andrew Lawler. *Science* Vol. 295, No. 5,560. March 1, 2002.

"NASA Lagged in Hiring Women." Associated Press. June 22, 1983.

"NASA Pioneer Asks for Her Shot at Space." Marcia Dunn. *Washington Post.* July 13, 1998.

"NASA Refutes Space Girl Story." *New York World Telegraph.* September 29, 1960.

"NASA's secret women." *Atlanta Journal.* October 25, 1998.

"NASA to Use Women in Space." Marie Smith. *Washington Post.* October 22, 1963.

"No Liftoff." Earl Lane. *Newsday,* New York. October 27, 1998.

"No Skirts in Space?" Marion Dietrich. *Oakland Tribune.* October 29, 1966.

"Of Sex & Spaceniks: Cochran Briefs Congress." United Press International. July 18, 1962.

"Ohio Teacher Crashes Sound Barrier in Jet." Helen Waterhouse. *Christian Science Monitor.* March 21, 1957.

"Oklahoma State Alumnus Awaits Her Debut in Space." Greg Bond. *Oklahoma State Alumnus Magazine.* September 1961.

"'On a Comet, Always': A Biography of Dr. W. Randolph Lovelace II." Richard G. Elliott. *New Mexico Quarterly.* Vol. 36, No. 4. 1966–67.

"Only Males Need Apply: The Lovelace Women and the Not-So-Right Stuff." *Space Flight,* Vol. 41. January 1999.

"Our almost-astronauts." Guy Wright. *San Francisco Examiner.* February 8, 1978.

"Pioneer flier shoots for stars, bids for spaceflight." Francis Donnelly. *Florida Today.* June 21, 1998.

"Prospective Women Astronauts Selection Program: Rationale and Comments." Betson, Johnnie R. Jr., and Robert R. Secrest. *American Journal of Obstetrics and Gynecology.* February 1, 1964.

"Red Space Girl Irks U.S. Woman Flier." Joy Miller. *News Messenger,* Texas. July 7, 1963.

"Rocket Grrrls!" Susan Carpenter. *George.* September 1997.

"Russian Blonde Spins Around Earth Toward Possible Rendezvous." *Dallas Morning News.* June 17, 1963.

"Senate Wife Could Be First Woman in Space." Isabelle Shelton. *Sunday Star,* Washington, D.C. March 11, 1962.

"Sexism Charge Unfair—Glenn." Richard Sisk. *New York Daily News.* October 16, 1998.

"She Orbits Over the Sex Barrier." *Life.* June 28, 1963.

"She's no fan of John Glenn—TC woman trained as astronaut, but never got to fly." Mike Norton. *Record-Eagle,* Michigan. October 28, 1998.

"Should a Girl be First in Space?" *Look.* February 2, 1960.

"Space Cowgirl." Sharon Krum. *Guardian,* London. April 22, 2002.

"Space Doctor." Shirley Thomas. *Space World,* Vol. 2, No. 4. March 1962.

"Space Girl Ready for Countdown, Wants to Be 1st Person to Go." *New York World-Telegram and Sun.* January 20, 1960.

"Spacelady." Jerrie Cobb as told to Ivy Coffey. *American Weekly.* October 23, 1960.

"Spacewoman Ready for Flights with Men." *Washington Star.* August 24, 1960.

"'Spacewoman' Would Let Man Come Along On Trip." *Sun,* Baltimore, August 24, 1960.

"Spacewoman's Hopes Crushed By Tragedy." Ann Marshall. *East African Standard,* Nairobi. June 1967.

"Stargazer." Patrick Rogers *et al. People.* October 19, 1998.

"Supersonic Schoolmarm." Jean Hixson. *NEA Journal.* September 1957.

"Tar Heel Sets Sights on Moon." Edith Hills Coogler. *Observer,* Charlotte, N.C. July 14, 1963.

"The 13 Astronauts Who Were Left Behind." Joan McCullough. *Ms.* September 1973.

"The Airess." *Women's Wear Daily.* October 21, 1964.

"The Discarded Astronaut." Meg Laughlin. *Tropic* magazine, *Miami Herald.* June 12, 1983.

"The First Women Astronauts." Kelly Patricia O'Meara. *Insight,* Washington. April 25, 2001.

"The Jerrie Cobb 99 Fund Drive." Barbara Jenison and Mary Waters. *99 News.* December 1978.

"The Mercury 13." Nicky Humphries. *Sleazenation,* London, Vol. 2, No. 18. July 1999.

"The 'Mercury 13': Were they the first ladies of space?" Amy Laboda. *AOPA Pilot,* February 1997.

"The Reasons Why Soviets Sent a Woman into Space." Sue Solet. *International Herald Tribune.* June 18, 1963.

"The U.S. Team is Still Warming Up the Bench." *Life,* Vol. 54, No. 26. June 28, 1963.

"The Wrong Stuff." *Final Frontier.* May–June 1990.

"They were prepared to go into space." *Woman Pilot.* July–August 1996.

"To Fly—To Live—Irene Leverton." Barbara Forton. *Out 'N About,* Arizona. March 1998.

"Twelve Women Test for Space." Associated Press. January 27, 1961.

"Up and Up Goes Jerrie Cobb." Jane Rieker. *Sports Illustrated.* August 29, 1960.

"Vive la difference!" *Popular Mechanics.* October 1963.

"Wally Funk Trains with the Cosmonauts." Wally Funk with Francis French. *Aviation for Women*. January–February 2001.

"Was Spacewoman's Flight Necessary?" New York Times News Service. *Richmond Times Dispatch*. June 18, 1963.

"Why Valentina And Not Our Gal?" Louise Sweeney. *Berkshire Eagle*, Massachusetts. June 21, 1963.

"Woman 'astronaut' details flying history." Rebecca Frank. *Glenwood Post*, Colorado. August 11, 1976.

"Woman 'Astronaut' Scared of Traffic." Marilyn Arvidson. *Miami Herald*. September 29, 1964.

"Woman Flier Claims She Won't 'Give Up.'" *Los Angeles Times*. July 19, 1962.

"Woman Qualifies for Space Training." *Washington Post*. August 19, 1960.

"Woman says Glenn's sexist remarks in '60s still sting." Associated Press. October 29, 1998.

"Women, Affirmative Action, and the US Space Program." Brigid O'Farrell. *AWIS Magazine*, Vol. 27, No. 4. Fall 1998.

"Women Astronauts." Donald Cox. *Space World*, Vol. 1, No. 10. September 1961.

"Women Astronauts Needed." *Times Herald*, Newport, Virginia. June 17, 1963.

"Women Find Place in Space, Too." Judith Vorst. *New York World-Telegram and Sun*. September 1964.

"Women Fliers Try to Crack Barriers on Space Travel." William McPherson. *Washington Post*. July 18, 1962.

"Women in Orbit." Jane Briggs Hart. *Town and Country*. November 1962.

"Women in Space." Jacqueline Cochran. *Parade*. April 30, 1961.

"Women Pilots Angry at Webb." Drew Pearson. *Washington Post*. June 20, 1963.

Collections, Dissertations, Oral Histories, Papers and Reports

Aeronautics archives. National Air and Space Museum. Smithsonian Institution, Washington, D.C.

Congressional Record—Senate. June 27, 1962. Pg. 11228–11230.

Flickinger, General Donald. Interviewed by John Pitts for NASA, October 18, 1979. NASA Historical Collection, NASA Headquarters History Office, Washington, D.C.

Jacqueline Cochran Collection. Dwight D. Eisenhower Presidential Library. Abilene, Kansas.

Jerrie Cobb Papers. Ninety-Nines International Organization of Women Pilots Headquarters. Will Rogers Airport, Oklahoma City, Oklahoma.

"The Job to Be Done." Speech by Jacqueline Cochran, Zonta Club of Cleveland, November 28, 1962. Reprinted in the Appendix to the Congressional Record, April 4, 1963. Pg. A2057.

John Fitzgerald Kennedy Presidential Library. Presidential collection. Boston, Massachusetts.

Lyndon Baines Johnson Presidential Library. Presidential and Vice Presidential collections. Austin, Texas.

NASA Historical Reference Collection. National Aeronautics and Space Administration. History Office, NASA Headquarters, Washington D.C.

"Project WISE." Speech by Jerrie Cobb to the Air Force Association Sixteenth National Convention. September 21, 1962.

"Qualifications for Astronauts." Published Hearing, House Committee on Science and Astronautics (Subcommittee on the Selection of Astronauts). 87th Congress, 2nd Session, July 17–18, 1962.

"The Reminiscenes of Ruth Nichols." Interview by Kenneth Leish, June 1960. New York Times Oral History Program, Columbia University Oral History Collection, Part IV (1–219), Columbia University, New York.

"The Right Stuff, the Wrong Sex: The Science, Culture and Politics of the Lovelace Woman in Space Program, 1959–1963." Dissertation to the Graduate School of Cornell University. Margaret Weitekamp, May 2001.

Skelton, Betty. Oral History Interview Transcript, Interview by Carol Butler. July 19, 1999. NASA Oral History Project, NASA Headquarters History Office, Washington, D.C.

"Space for Women." Presented by Jerrie Cobb, First Women's Space Symposium, February 22, 1962.

"Woman's Participation in Space Flight." Presented by Jerrie Cobb, Aviation/Space Writers Association 23rd Annual Meeting, May 1, 1961.

ACKNOWLEDGMENTS

My first and most heartfelt thanks to the women who were the Fellow Lady Astronaut Trainees. They were unfailingly generous with their time, their scrapbooks and their stories. I count myself lucky for knowing them.

I am grateful to Patricia Weaver Francisco, who first told me about the forgotten lady astronauts and was generous with what she knew, and to Margaret Weitekamp, who shared her considerable knowledge and research. Reporter Meg Laughlin at *The Miami Herald* provided valuable information, while historian Debbie Douglas at the Massachusetts Institute of Technology helped me to better understand it. Insight came as well from NASA historian Roger Launius; the NASA History Office has preserved the slim official record of this story and helped me find it. Pat Daly and Pauline Vincent kindly shared memories of their sisters. I also thank those who shared their memories and personal archives with me, but who did not wish to be cited by name. Many people helped me to better understand flying, space and 1950s America; all mistakes are of course my own.

My parents, Jim and Barbara Nolen, taught me early that books are the best thing in the world, after family; they provided great encouragement for this one.

Many people pitched in, in myriad kind ways, and helped get this story told: Anita Davies with research; Alper Ozdemir with soup; Jan Wong and Stephen Kimber with sound advice; Kathleen Gallivan with piercing analysis; Christina Hasley with shelter and encouragement; Brad Nolen with crucial explanations about aircraft and Amy Nolen with uncomplicated faith that I could pull this off; Louise Dennys, Rick Archbold and Knopf Canada with tolerance for my distraction over that *other* book; Chris Gainor with an encyclopedic knowledge of space; Scotty Rice with faith; Celia Donnelly with ace librarian skills.

My heartfelt thanks to the friends who believed in *Promised the Moon* from the first, and who listened to me talk about it long past the point where it was interesting. Many of them also typed, researched and encouraged in the bleak hours: Joanna Chen; Kathryn Morris; Ben Davies, Mona Thayagajarah and Miss Maya; Jennifer Amy; Monica Noy; Lucy Matthew; Roberta Best and Jen McDonald.

Stephanie Chambers and Andy Pedersen provided valuable comments on an evolving manuscript and constant enthusiasm. Andrea Clegg was gracious, supportive and eminently helpful. And I am eternally grateful to Marney McDiarmid, for this and for everything.

Finally to Andrea Clegg, who was gracious and supportive from the first, who made meals and did "favors" while rockets began to creep into her own dreams, who stood by uncomplaining while I disappeared for eighteen months. This is not a debt I can repay.

Stephanie Nolen
Toronto, May 2002

INDEX